Maravilla

By Laura del Fuego

La Mujer Latina Series • Floricanto Press, 1989
Giselle K. Cabello, Series Editor

Maravilla

by

Laura del Fuego

Floricanto Press

Maravilla

Copyright © 1989 by Laura del Fuego.

ISBN 0-915745-15-1
Cover illustration by Phyllis Martinez.

Floricanto Press
16161 Ventura Blvd., Suite 830
Encino, CA 91436

Chapter 1

It was the evening before I came into this world, stunned and mortified, that my mother saw the *Virgen de Guadalupe*. It happened while she paced up and down Calle Fisher, lumbering past Black Virginia's, the *vieja negra*, who lived on the corner, and was later to pierce Maria's and my ears, and steep yerba hediondia for us when we got poison ivy. She walked past Simon Limon's, the old Russian Jew who screamed *Stu-pie-da-moi!* whenever we ran into his back yard chasing balls. She passed Aunt Cora's house still lit up at three a.m., enviously, wishing that she too could sit complacently, as she imagined Aunt Cora doing, reading or playing solitaire, listening to music, or best of all sleeping peacefully all night long.

Afterwards, more than once, I overheard her talking about how she had spent the two days preceding my birth cursing, with intermittent praying. *"Hijo de la chingada! Madre! Please, dear God, help get this over! Cabron!"* she whispered, exhausted and anxious from the constant pressure building inexorably against her vital organs, taxing her heart, constricting her breath. Three weeks past her due date, overwhelmed by nausea and claustrophobia, wretchedly sick from having to pee every hour, or feeling as if she had to, she began to see a vision of *La Virgen Guadalupe*. The Virgin had first come to her out of the dark corner of her desperate, befuddled mind. She saw her shrouded in opaque, dim light, draped in her Indian reboso, surrounded by circles of muted pastels, cactus green, dusty rose, indigo, ochre, black.

"This circle of light fanned out around *La Virgen*, pulsing and throbbing, like she had been plugged into a powerful

1

electrical socket," my mother said, leaving her, if not relieved, at least calmed, prepared to face her ordeal with hope, restoring her tattered sense of dignity.

But then, when she turned the corner and saw the lovers, holding hands, young and slender, walking first towards her, then crossing to the other side of the street, she felt a crushing sense of betrayal. An agonizing loneliness consumed her. She clenched her fists, wanting to strike out, digging her nails into her palms. Why me? Why did I let this horrible thing happen to me! she thought. And once more, she began to feel her clumsiness, her incoherence, her lumbersome body, this *thing* that had taken over her entire life. Something monstrous was pressing in on her. She felt its ominous presence in every fiber of her being. She began weeping uncontrollably. "Oh, God!" she cried for what seemed like the millionth time. "To just be able to sleep through the night. That's all I want. To be slender, normal. Not like this!" She held her rotund belly, big as a watermelon feeling trapped, possessed, insane. Tears swam down her contorted face.

But then, she felt the kicking and prodding inside of her. My poor darling, she thought, contritely, struggling to regain her composure, my sweet little baby. So that now she began to persistently hold the vision of the Virgin in her mind until it had crystallized into a clear and beautiful jewel held ruby-like in the center of her being. The colors surrounding the Virgin were now sharp and bright as precious stones, filling her mind with a stillness, then her body, then the whole world with wondrous light.

Just before the remaining dim stars had begun to fade into the morning sky she felt a hot flush surge up her legs through her abdomen, searing her spine. Water trickled down her swollen thighs.

"I hope it's a girl," she said to my father as they drove down Olympic Boulevard. Behind them the first light of dawn rose a hush of burnt orange above the smokey gray San Gabriel mountains.

I was born in L.A., city of the angels, at the county hospital three hours later, to the whirring sound of ceiling fans on the hottest day of the year in August, the summer of 1947.

"I named you Consuelo," my mother said, "because you

2

didn't stop screaming for hours when you were born. I figured you needed hope." Actually, I was named Consuelo Concepción, after my grandmother, Conchi, whose father, Pablo Rosales, was half Yaqui.

We lived with my grandparents, Nana Conchi and Tata Cabezon, on Fisher Street, for two years after I was born when my father lost his job. My father, Sam, was a paratrooper in WWII. He came home from the war with a bad leg, a permanent limp, after being wounded in Lieg, Belgium. In '49, out of work, partially due to his disabilities, my father moved my mother, Terry, and my sister, Maria Hortensia, and me (my younger brothers, Tony and Eddie, weren't born yet) to Maravilla in the Belvedere projects where hundreds of barracks left over from the war had been moved and dropped down like gigantic concrete beasts on the outskirts of the East Los Angeles barrio. They stood, flat and square, in long straight lines, with outdoor toilets and showers in the back, surrounded by asphalt except for those in front that had a tiny patch of lawn bordering the street.

On one side of us, Brooklyn Avenue ran all the way to the train station in downtown L.A. On the other side, Belvedere Park spread out in a blanket of grassy, rolling slopes with picnic tables and a playground for the elementary school. Across Brooklyn Avenue and up the corner were the *new* projects, bigger and better housing, where we were to move later, with two and three bedrooms, indoor toilets and showers, front and back yards, and a view from Floral Drive of the soft, brown hills, undeveloped in the 50s, which looked to me then like huge sleeping bears curled up against the blue-gray sky.

The summer my brother Tony was born, my father, Maria and I would often walk to the Ford Boulevard drug store on Sunday evenings while my mother rocked my baby brother to sleep. Out in the balmy night air, we'd stroll up Brooklyn, past the projects and the older wood-framed houses, past the *panadería* with its wafting odors of freshly baked bread and *pan dulce*, past Mendoza's Shoe Repair, over to Ford Boulevard, passing Carmen's Taqueria with its blinking red and green neon sign, crossing ourselves as we walked by Our Lady of Soledad, with its bell tower sticking up in the dusky sky. We'd wander through the stalls, past the counters of El Mercado, loaded with

3

its stacks of blue jeans, cotton goods, fruit stands, racks of leather belts, bags, and jackets, over to the drug store.

We'd sit at the counter, Sam ordering beer, and Maria and I, double decker ice cream cones, listening to the clear, high sound of Lola Beltran belting out over the juke box, "*Aqui vine porque vine a la feria de las flores,*" and the tolling bells of Our Lady of Soledad, announcing the evening mass over the noise and traffic of the street.

Maria Hortensia, my mother's first child, was born two years before me in downtown L.A. in the back seat of a Yellow Taxicab on the way to the hospital. As soon as she popped out, slimy and wrinkled, waving her tiny fists, my mother ordered the cab driver to turn around and take them home.

"This may or may not," says my father, "have something to do with the fact that Maria Hortensia, having had her own way since the beginning, is the most bull-headed and smart-ass person in the family since Viejo Cabezon."

Grandfather Contreres, a union organizer for the IWW who died in 1955, said he was nicknamed Viejo Cabezon after spending three years at Fort Leavenworth, the federal penitentiary, for the possession of a cache of illegal military weapons. Viejo Cabezon swore till he died that he had been framed by the Feds. Years later, grandmother Contreres said that the weapons had been hijacked from a train coming from Guadalajara on its way to the U.S. border by Joaquin Murietta, the phantom Mexican bandit, who then delivered them to Viejo Cabezon. But when I asked her about it, my mother said Nana Conchi was batty and that grandfather Cabezon was a big liar, having never been out of the state of California in his life, much less to Fort Leavenworth.

When I was eleven years old, my sister Maria held up a picture from a book she had been reading. "Look, Cece, if you were fatter and had a feather in your hair, you'd look just like Chief Sitting Bull," she said, blocking my way with her chunky body.

"You're crazy, Maria!" I said, pushing her aside.

4

"Don't," she said, grabbing my wrist, twisting it.

I yanked her hair.

"Let go, Cece!"

"You let go."

"Stop fighting, *traviesas!*" my mother yelled.

"It's her fault," I said.

"Make her let go," Maria cried. She was older, bigger and supposedly smarter, but I always managed to make her cry in a showdown.

"*Andale, Maria, llorona, vayase pa su cuarto!*" my mother said, separating us. "*Y tu*, Consuelo, go to the back and stay there till I tell you to come out. *Desgraciadas.*"

I slunk into the laundry room and sank into the corner next to the wringer washer and flipped them the finger, just like cousin Vera did when she was pissed. "I hate her!" I muttered. I didn't want my mother to hear me. There were certain words you couldn't use in our house. Like *hate*. We were forbidden to say, "I hate you." And the word *dead*. You could never say, "I wish you were dead!" or you'd be practically killed yourself. Sitting there thinking about all the restrictions I had to live with made me furious. I started to cry. That's when I heard the noise. I remember it distinctly.

"*Que usted tiene, mujercita?*" Her voice sounded raspy and sing-song. At first I thought I had imagined it.

I glanced around the tiny room filled with old, dusty cardboard boxes, piled high with wrinkled, musty clothes. Some overgrown ivy from the porch had broken through a crack in the window screen and was winding its way to the floor. A black widow spider crept down a leaf. I pulled my legs in closer.

"*Mujercita?*" There it was again.

Then I noticed that propped up on a dilapidated box a few feet away was a gold-framed picture of Saint Teresa. The light turned fuzzy and a strange sound buzzed in my ear as I stared at it.

"*Porque usted llore?*" she said.

"Who are you?" I asked, even though I knew.

"Do you es-speak es-Spanish?" She sounded just like my great-aunt Rebecca.

"A little," I said. "I mean, *un poquito.*"

5

"*Soy Teresa de Avila.*"

"That's what I thought," I mumbled.

"*Que año es?*" she asked.

"What?"

"Time, what time eet ess?"

"I don't know," I sniffled, "maybe about one. *Uno,*" I said, holding up one finger.

"No, no," she said. "*En donde estamos?*"

"Oh, that. We're in my mother's laundry room."

"Who-air?"

"The *laundry room,*" I mouthed, pointing to the dirty clothes piled up on the floor.

"*Ay, Dios.*" She sounded disappointed.

"My father probably stashed you back here just like my mother did me. It wasn't always like that. Before you came here, Nana Contreres had you on her dresser next to a statue of the Virgin Mary holding the baby Jesus."

"Ah, *si,*" she said approvingly.

"But then nana gave you to my father when he got sick. You know, after he came home from the army. Anyway, he stuck you in this old box. I know because I heard him telling my mom that the whole thing was silly, just an old wives' tale."

"You maum?"

I realized that she hadn't understood, so I said, "*Mi madre.*"

"*Ah si, su madre,*" she said reverently.

"I hate her! She's a witch."

"*Ay, Dios, Santito!*" she gasped.

"What's wrong?"

"Ess thees Sail-em, seventeen cent-oory?"

"What are you talking about?"

"*Su madre, es una bruja?*"

"*Bruja?*"

"A weetch?"

"Yeah," I shrugged. "She forced me into this dump when I had a fight with my sister, even though she started it. She said I looked like this dumb old Indian."

"*Ay, pobrecita,*" she sang.

"That's the way they treat me here," I sobbed. Just having her interested made me let go and cry. I began to weep wildly.

"Leesten, what year et ess?" she broke in, probably trying to get me to stop.

"1958," I sniffled.

"*Ay, que bueno!*"

"Why?"

"You mothair ess not rr-eally a weetch, no?"

"That's what you think."

"Your seestair ess right, I think. You look like Indian. He is very, *como dice? Simpático. Un hombre muy valiente.*"

"You really think so?"

"Jes. *Oye, Senorita, como se llama usted?*"

"Consuelo, but everyone calls me Cece."

"*Su nombre es muy hermosa.*"

"Thanks, I mean, *gracias.*"

"*De nada.*"

"Where did you come from?"

"Sixteen cent-oory *España.*"

"Uh-huh." At this point my eyes were starting to close. All the crying had made me sleepy. I began to drift off.

The last thing I remember her saying was, "Cece, I wan you take me out of thees bad place. Take me to jor altar. Anothair thing you must love jor mothair and seestair. Love ess the only way. You must think of," she pointed to her heart, "Love."

The next day I dusted off the picture of St. Teresa and hung it on the wall next to the upper bunk where I slept.

Then, after carefully studying my profile in the bathroom mirror, I decided that, except for my kinky hair, Maria was right about my resemblance to the old Indian chief. So I started wearing my hair in two thick braids, entwining gray seagull feathers that I'd found at the beach around the ends.

Whenever I was alone, I would talk to Saint Teresa. One afternoon Maria came home unexpectedly and caught me.

"Who are you talking to, Cece?"

"St. Teresa."

"Oh, sure."

At the dinner table that evening Maria said to my mother, "Cece talks to herself and says she's talking to St. Teresa."

"I am."

"Don't you dare tell anyone at school," Maria sneered.

"Why?"

"It's embarrassing. You're so weird."

My father looked up and winked, signaling that he'd defend me. "She's not weird. She probably inherited it from your mother. Didn't you see something religious, Vieja? Remember when you had Cece? You said you saw God. At least, that's what you claimed, honey," he said, scooping beans and salsa in a wad of tortilla and stuffing it into his mouth.

"It was Guadalupe, la Virgin, I already told you hundreds of times. Not God. I saw her. I swear it," my mother said, glancing at Nana Conchi, who was having dinner with us. "She was as close as you are, Conchi. In the most incredible colors--yellow, pink, red. *Muy claro, te digo.* It was right before Cece was born. Remember when I was having such a hard time? Wishing I was dea--well, I didn't really want to die," she said, eyeing my father, "*pero que horible.* We had no money, nothing. Not even a pot to piss in. Sammy was out of work."

"Your mother didn't talk to me for months," my father interjected, "even though I used to bring her flowers and her favorite candy almost every day."

"He used to pick flowers out of Aunt Fila's garden. Half-wilted geraniums and petunias. Boy, was she mad," my mother laughed. "And candy? *Enbustero*--what candy? Tootsie rolls! He'd steal Tootsie Rolls from Hector's Five and Dime. Anyway," my mother said, "I only saw *la Virgen.* I mean, seeing is one thing. Hearing is another."

"*Como la Becky,*" nana said, gesturing at me like I was wacko. "She used to hear voices, *como ella.*"

"Yeah, we know what happened to Aunt Becky," Maria said, pointing at her temple and making circles with her finger. "Norwalk State Hospital."

"Aunt Becky's sick. Don't make fun of her," my father said. "There's nothing wrong with you, *mija.* You just have a wild imagination like your mother."

Maria kicked me under the table. I kicked her back.

"Don't," she cried.

"You started it."

"Be quiet!" my mother said. "You'll wake up the baby."

"OK, that's enough. How many times have I told you, no arguing at the table," my father grumbled.

8

"Shock treatment," Nana muttered, clicking her false teeth. "They gave her shock treatment. She didn't even know who I was when I went to see her. *Fijate no mas.*"

"Eat your vegetables, you kids," my mother said.

Maria chomped on a carrot stick. "Maybe that's what Cece needs," she snorted. "Shock treatment."

"That's enough!" my father said. "There's nothing wrong with Cece. It's her own business if St. Ann talks to her."

"St. Teresa," I said.

"Gaah," Maria whined.

"Oh, don't worry, Cece," my mother said, "as long as she doesn't tell you to jump off the roof like Aunt Becky's voices did."

"Did she do it?"

"She tried to, but your father caught her in time."

"I don't have to worry about you two girls," my mother said. "Maria is the smartest girl in her class, Conchi. And you, Cece," she paused. "Well, you're the most, uh, talented one."

"I am?"

"Sure. You got the part in *Snow White*, didn't you?"

"As a dwarf," I said.

"Dopey," Maria snickered.

"*Pero no se creen que su mierda no pesta,*" Nana cackled.

My mother ignored her. "It's your turn to do the dishes, Cece," she said. "Maybe you should ask St. Teresa to help you. Last time you left food stains all over the forks and spoons."

Maria tittered.

I glared at her. I was thinking about what St. Teresa had said about love. It wasn't going to be easy. After that, I decided not to tell anyone. I would just pretend that I was talking to myself. It was better to be lonely, I decided, than ridiculed.

At any rate, I didn't see St. Teresa again until after Chuck Valdez was shot down in Montebello and I almost died of the Asian flu.

In 1960 my Mother's prayers were answered and we moved into the new projects. But by then, she was praying for our own house with three bedrooms and a two-car garage.

9

Maravilla

"Give me a few years, *vieja*," said my father, who was working with Johnnie Loo, the Chinaman whose father owned the Golden Lantern restaurant on Fourth Street, doing gardening and landscaping in West L.A. and Orange county.

After we moved into the new projects, I discovered that my mother had misplaced my St. Teresa picture. But then, I was more interested in Elvis, Diana Ross and the Supremes, and masturbation, and couldn't have cared less.

It was right after I met Rainbow and the chicks from the club that I stopped wearing braids and feathers and locked myself in the bathroom to dye my hair Miss-Clairol-fire-engine-red.

"*Ay, que horible*," my mother said when she saw what I had done.

Chapter 2

It was in '63, the year President Kennedy was shot down, that I met Rainbow Rochin and joined Las Belltones. Rainbow was a tall, slender mulatta with an elegant, Egyptian looking head. She reminded me of a voodoo queen. She wore bright colors--purple, orange and green combinations, multi-colored scarves in her kinky, unruly hair that was dyed and faded to a rusty red. We met at Belvedere Park where I was on a softball team with her younger brother, Chuy. I played catcher. Chuy pitched.

Rainbow used to stand behind the backstop and yell at the other team, "Strike out!" or "Hit that ball, *cabron!*" Whenever she was around, there were lots of laughs and a kind of electrical tension in the air.

After a game one day she said, "Hey, Cece, I like you, *esa.*" I'd been laughing crazy at her jokes. "How'd you like to come to a club meeting?"

"Alright," I said. I'd heard about the Belltones and I was impressed.

I met the other members at the park the following week and joined.

The initiation rites: no make-up for a month; no talking to guys for a week; wearing blouses and sweaters backwards for one week; doing chores and running errands at the club meetings and social events until someone new had been initiated. Our club jackets were mint green, with a black bell and a musical note emblazoned on the back under *Belltones E.L.A.* The reverse side was of shiny black nylon with a mint green trim.

We met at each other's houses, at the park, or at lunch behind the bleachers. We'd plan record hops, slumber parties, or talk about guys, comb our hair, stuff like that. Sometimes we'd just cruise.

Like the day Esther Sandoval drove up to my house with some of the chicks from the club, in her brother's customized, metallic blue '49 Plymouth, and honked the horn. It was only eight o'clock in the morning but already a penetrating heat beat down making the sidewalk sizzle.

I ran out to the car as she was taking a big, juicy bite of an apple. She looked at me, munched, swallowed, and said, "Wanna ditch?" Carmen and Corky were in the back seat.

"Yeah, Cece, come on, *esa*, we can spend the day cruising or going downtown or somethin'," Lorraine McKenzie said, half hanging out the window, waving a wine bottle from which I could tell she'd already taken a few drinks.

"Sure, why not?" I said, sliding into the front seat next to her.

"We got food, Cokes, and yessca, Cece." Esther had packed five apples, four burritos, three minced ham sandwiches, a six pack of Coke, and a couple of reefers in a brown grocery bag. We took off, cruising slowly down the street, heading for the Santa Ana freeway.

"Where's Rainbow?" I asked.

"She couldn't make it. She had to take her mother to the doctor," Esther said.

"Too bad."

"Yeah, man," Lorraine said.

"So, how'd you talk your brother into lettin' you have the car, girl?"

"By promising I'd clean his room for two weeks and not telling my mother that he's been spending the night with his girlfriend," Esther said.

"Bitcheen!"

Corky Cruz leaned forward. "Where we gonna go?"

"Let's cruise the park," Esther said.

"OK," chimed Lorraine and I, at the same time.

"Jinx! You owe me a Coke," Lorraine said, punching my leg.

"Ow! Hey, not so hard!"

"Sorry, Cece," she said smiling, revealing her braces.

We were rubbing shoulders and I could smell her chewing gum.

"Got any more gum?"

"Yeah." She rifled through her purse, cracking her gum, and handed me a stick. I could smell the wine on her breath.

"Ga! Are you high already?"

She looked at me and giggled. Her braces gleamed.

"Where'd you get the wine?"

"I snuck it outa the house. I also got a pack of Camels."

"Yuk! I hate Camels."

"So? You don't have to smoke 'em, ya know."

"You gonna tell her, Esther?" said Carmen.

"Look," said Esther, holding up her right hand.

"Wow," I said. She had a small diamond on her finger.

"Where'd you get that--At Woolworth's?" Lorraine smirked.

"She's engaged to Louie Martinez," said Corky, sticking up for Esther. They were cousins. "Esther's getting married."

"Oh, no," Lorraine hissed. Ever since Louie started calling her Gorgeous George, saying that if she had blond hair instead of red, she'd be a perfect imitation of the flamboyant wrestler, she'd begun to bad-mouth him.

"You are? When?" I said.

"In five years," said Esther.

"Groovie!"

The asphalt smouldered. The heat rose in waves from the ground. The skyline was a dull gray in the smog as we drove through the projects, passing blocks and blocks of identical square houses, symmetrically stark and pale yellow, with army-green trim and a tiny patch of brown lawn in front. At the playground little kids romped on the monkey bars. Graffiti glared from a concrete wall, in black spray paint, *"VIVA LA RAZA--con safos"*, *"Jesus y Gloria por vida '59."*

We cruised around the park, pulled over, and walked to the pond. I sank down on the grass, shading my eyes from the blazing sun. Corky sat next to me cross-legged. One of her large, brown knees touched my shoulder. Esther stretched out on her side and pulled her skirt down discreetly below her knee. She was wearing a starched white blouse under her navy blue cardigan. She smelled like soap and her hair was brushed neatly off her face.

Carmen had taken pieces of bread and was tossing them into the pond.

"Quack, quack, quack," she clucked, as the ducks floated around. Her slip crept down from under her skirt, exposing a ragged hemline. Her elbows stuck out from her sides like spikes. She had long spindly legs, and you could almost see the hinges on her joints as she moved, not the least bit self-conscious.

Lorraine McKenzie sat facing the sun, her millions of freckles bright orange against her milky white skin. Her hair was messy and matted with spray and stuck out like an electrical current in kinky, little waves. She was frowning and chewing at her nubbly nails, already bitten to the quick of her fleshy fingers. Her black, wrinkled sweater looked like she slept in it. Gold, spangly earrings, the kind you get in Mexico, hung from her pierced ears. She smelled stale and covered her mouth whenever she laughed, in order to hide her braces.

"Hey, look at those cuties," she squealed, waving to some guys that were going by in a lowered, candy-apple red Chevy.

"Shad up, man!" Corky said.

"Oh, gawd, here they come," Carmen said. "They look like T.J. rejects."

The guys slowed down, whistling and shouting, "Hey, mama, wanna cruise?"

One of them stuck his tongue out, licking his lips.

"Shit!" Corky spat, standing up.

The rest of us got up, brushing off our clothes, and got back in the car.

"Listen, *esa*, you better cool it," Corky said. "You wanna get us in trouble with those punks?"

"Hey, *esa*," said Lorraine, affecting a Chicano accent, "I wuz only fool-lean around, maan."

"Gimme that bottle!" Carmen grabbed the wine bottle out of her hand. "From now on, you get permission from me."

"Yeah," said Esther. "I'm not gonna be the one to carry you in your house again and have your *jefe* blame me for getting you drunk."

"Me either!" Carmen said.

"Awright, awright," grunted Lorraine.

Maravilla

The Chevy was following us.

"Speed up, Esther, so we can ditch 'em," Corky said.

Esther shifted into second, went around the block, swung a U-turn and sped away.

On the freeway, the engine hummed in tune as Lorraine, Carmen, and I joined Diana Ross singing, "*Baby love, oh, baby love, oh, how I miss you so.*"

"Where we going?" Corky asked.

"I have an idea," Esther said. "Why don't we go try on wedding dresses?"

"That sounds dumb," Corky said.

"I'd rather hang out in the sun," Lorraine said, reaching for the wine.

Carmen handed her the bottle. "Just one drink, *esa.*"

Lorraine took a long slug.

"I think I wanna try on wedding dresses anyway," Esther said.

"Oh, no," Corky hissed.

"It's her brother's car, so she gets to call the shots," Lorraine said.

"OK, let's do it," I said.

"Alright," Carmen said.

"You guys are weird," Corky moaned.

We got off the freeway and cruised through the L.A. traffic, past the business district, into the garment district, and found a place and parked, then walked the couple of blocks to "Ida's Wedding Parties and Accessories."

"OK," Carmen said, "you guys gotta act like you got some class."

"Look who's talking!" Lorraine snorted.

"Take a picture, it'll last longer," Carmen said, glaring at Lorraine.

"Ay, *cayate*," Corky shrilled.

"I'm gonna tell you somethin'," Carmen said with her hand on her hip. "We're gonna have to be cool. We'll say that Esther here is getting married and we're gonna be her bridesmaids." Esther smiled wanly.

Carmen led us in, adjusting her winged rhinestone glasses.

15

A saleslady, dressed in a discreet black dress and smelling of Estee Lauder, glided over.

"May I help you?"

"Yes," Carmen said. "We'd like to see some wedding and bridesmaids' dresses."

"Which one of you girls is the bride?"

"She is," Carmen said, pointing to Esther.

"Come over here. I'll show you what we have."

We followed her to a rack of fancy looking dresses.

"Would you like something lacy, full, with a train?"

"I'd like something with a lotta lace," Esther said.

The saleslady pulled out a stiff lacy dress. In unison we chanted, "Wow! Ooh, ahh!"

"Would you like to try it on?"

"I guess so." Esther blushed.

The saleslady unhooked the dress and led Esther to the dressing room, calling back over her shoulder, "Stella, can you help these young ladies? They're looking for bridesmaids' dresses."

Stella, in a discreet beige suit and a waft of Tabu trailing behind her, guided us to a rack of different colors and brusquely pulled out several long gowns. Another chorus of "oohs" and ahhs" followed.

"Why don't you girls pick out one you like?"

"I'll take this one," I picked out the coral taffeta with matching bow and elbow length gloves. Carmen selected the smallest since she was the skinniest. It was lime green with a matching pillbox hat and short gloves. Corky grabbed the bright yellow with matching beanie and long gloves, leaving the large, hot pink one for Lorraine.

"Hey, man, I don't think I'm gonna be in the wedding after all," Lorraine said, sulking.

"Aw, go on," I prodded her.

"Anyways, it ain't gonna be for five..."

"Shh!" Carmen hissed.

"I'll show you girls to the dressing room," Stella said.

As we were departing, Esther glided out, smiling like a toothpaste ad, decked out in a white, lacy dress with a high neckline and long tight sleeves. The skirt hung in a bowl around her feet, and a train with layers of stiff material

16

trailed behind her. A veil topped with a crown of little, plastic white flowers sat on her head.

"Wow! Groovie, Esther!" We all flocked around her hooped skirt, except for Lorraine who hung back scowling.

"You look fabulous, girl," Corky said. Lorraine snorted. Carmen glared at her.

"Since you're not gonna be in the wedding, why don't you go wait in the car?"

Lorraine snapped her gum. "Louie's a jerk. I hope she doesn't marry the creep."

"We better try these on," I said, shoving past Lorraine to follow the saleslady.

I took the dress and hung it on a hook on the wall. Stripping off my sweater, being careful not to mess my hair, I peeled down my half-slip and pantyhose, unhooked my bra, removed my shoes. I unzipped the stiff, shiny dress and pulled it over my head.

Halfway up my back, the zipper stuck. I felt hot and sticky perspiration roll down my sides and under my arms. Then, presto, unruffled in the hundred-degree heat and smelling as if she had bathed in a quart of perfume, Stella appeared. With an air of efficiency, she zipped me up and began assisting me with the bow.

"Thank you," I said as she led me out to a full length mirror. I knew immediately that there had been a mistake. My head looked lopsided and coral was definitely not my color. Maybe it was the lighting, but I appeared to have a layer of gray powder on my skin.

Carmen loped out of the dressing room, frowning and looking like a scarecrow with her pillbox hat askew. She pointed at me rudely and began giggling. Next Corky marched out with her chin set like concrete. Carmen and I looked at each other, then quickly glanced away. I could see Carmen's back heaving up and down as the saleslady tried to adjust Corky's yellow beanie and pull the gloves neatly up to her elbows. The three of us stood looking at ourselves in the mirror.

"You look like a guy in a dress," Corky said to Carmen.

"You look like my fat *tia*, Dora," Carmen said.

Lorraine stood behind us, biting her fingernails and staring sullenly.

17

Meanwhile, Esther had tried on another wedding dress. We all stood around looking at each other, giggling and trying to be tactful, then flocked over to the display case and asked to try on different hats and veils, exchanging bows and gloves, helping Esther adjust her lacy dress and rhinestone tiara.

After trying on most of the accessories, I went back to the dressing room and changed.

We filed out of the shop with Carmen waving at the door. "Thank you. We'll be back soon."

Stella sailed over, offering her card.

"If you come back, ask for me."

"OK," Carmen said, adjusting her glasses.

"You guys are too much," Lorraine chortled on the way out.

"Let's hit another store," I said. "This time, I'll be the bride."

"No way," Lorraine grunted.

"Let's flip a coin," I said.

"OK," said Esther. "Tails."

"Heads," I said, flipping it. I won.

"Come on," I said, leading them down the street to the Bride Shoppe.

This time I coaxed Lorraine into trying on a yellow bridesmaid's dress. I selected a full-length, lacey white dress, white gloves, and shiny, white, pointy high heels. A saleslady helped me to dress. With the long train gathered in my arms, I teetered out of the dressing room, over to the display case, and picked out a tiara with a full-face veil. As I was adjusting my crown, Lorraine lumbered over with a panicked look.

"Help, Cece." Her zipper was stuck, of course. I tried forcing it down and the seam began to tear.

"Quick, go back and take it off."

"I can't!" she said, glaring at me and tugging at the bodice.

"OK, be quiet." I shielded her as we both slunk back to the dressing room. "Take a big breath and hold in your stomach," I whispered, trying to force the zipper up and down in a seesaw motion. My scalp felt sweaty and itchy, and the crown was beginning to fell like little needles stuck in my head.

The zipper wouldn't budge, so we forced it down over her gargantuan hips, ripping out the seams, and she kicked it away.

She dressed and I handed it to her.

"Sneak it back and don't let anyone see you," I said, thrusting my head out to see if the coast was clear. "OK, go on!"

On my way back to my dressing room I noticed that a saleslady was going through the rack where Lorraine had stashed the torn dress.

I motioned to Carmen. "Help me outa this thing!" She began unbuttoning the forty or fifty tiny buttons that trailed down my back.

"Hurry up!" I groaned. It felt like bugs were crawling up my spine. She finally unbuttoned me and we tried pulling it down over my hips, but the waist was too narrow. So we tried pulling it up over my head. I was bent over, my arms dangling with the dress pinning them straight up against my temples.

"Shit, get this thing off before I tear it off!"

"OK, OK, calm down. Don't get twittered out. It was your idea, wasn't it?" Carmen said, tugging at the thing as the saleslady entered. The three of us pushed and pulled this way and that until it came off, making my hair stand on end. Carmen put her hand over her mouth, stifling a giggle as the grim-faced saleslady stiffly draped the dress over her arm and left.

"Ga, girl you look fried."

"I know. Let's cut out."

The girls were back in their street clothes, standing around looking bored.

"It's about time," Lorraine said as we scurried out.

Outside, the light was a flat gray, and carbon monoxide fumes permeated the air. We walked back to the car through the crowds and traffic and ate our lunch.

Afterwards, we went to a movie at the Old Broadway, a theatre built in Hollywood's heyday. The plush, red carpets were faded and dirty. Tiny dim lights glittered from the art deco ceiling.

We bought popcorn, Cokes, and Mister Goodbars, then walked up a long, narrow corridor, past the lounge and bathrooms to a rickety staircase on which the antique, gold paint was chipped and peeling, then wound our way up into the balcony. As we entered the theatre, Shirley Maclaine, her hair

19

dyed bright orange, her mouth painted fire-engine red, lit up the screen. She blubbered to Frank Sinatra, who acted cool and unconcerned in his army fatigues.

"I'm nothing but a dumb broad. I wish I was as smart as you are."

Corky snorted.

"Boo," Lorraine hissed.

Some guy in front of us turned around and shushed them.

"Be quiet," Carmen whispered.

"Don't look at me!" Lorraine said, putting her feet up on the back of the seat.

I munched popcorn, took a bite of chocolate, and washed it down with Coke.

At the end of the movie, Shirley threw herself in front of Frank, caught the bullet meant for him, and died. I cried.

"Ga, Cece, why are you crying? It was jest a stoopid ol' movie," Carmen said.

"Yeah, that chick was dumb. Man, she should've let the cat die. Anybody that stoopid deserves to die," Lorraine said.

"Oh, shad up," I said, wiping my tears.

She reached into my popcorn box. "You OK?"

Before I could answer her the next movie, Godzilla, had started.

Chapter 3

I started to hang out with Rainbow. I used to walk over to her house after school, cutting across our neighbor's, old lady Anderson's, back yard. She was usually out there, white hair sticking straight up, watering her tiny lawn and talking to her fat dachsund. Then I'd pass by the Hernandez' house, where all the neighborhood kids played.

Mr. and Mrs. Hernandez lived three doors down from us and had twelve kids.

"*No tiene verguenza, esa mujer,*" my mother would say of Mrs. Hernandez. Not because she had twelve kids, but because she was a Jehovah's Witness and tried to sell my Father the *Watch Tower* at least once a week.

When Maria and I came down with head lice, my mother said, "Don't play with the Hernandez brats, *tienen piojos.*" When Maria told my mother that we had probably gotten the bugs from cousin Vera (who had them) by using her brush, my mother ignored her.

"I've seen the *piojos* crawling down their dirty, little necks!" she said.

"That's crazy," Maria countered. "They're too small to see from far away, and you never get that close. Besides you're just prejudiced because they're not Catholics, and Mrs. Hernandez is a *gabacha.*"

"Don't talk back, Maria."

"It's true," Maria said.

"*Digame, Dios,* what have I done to deserve a crazy, old *gabacha* who talks to dogs, and a Jehovah's Witness with twelve brats *que tienen piojos* for neighbors, and a daughter *con boca de pura mierda?*"

After crossing the Hernandez' yard, heading towards Rainbow's, I'd turn up Brooklyn, go past the Kress and the butcher shop, past the *raspada* man, clanging his bell, pushing his little cart filled with shaved ice and flavored syrup, past the empty lot where the *vatos* hung out, rain or shine, drinking wine, shouting and whistling at girls, "Ay, *guerita*, or *negrita, como stas buenota!*"

Of course, you could always see cops patrolling the streets, any time of the day or night, pulling over lowriders or stopping pedestrians.

Rainbow's place was small and crowded and smelled musky. She lived with her mother and six kids, including her older sister, her husband and their baby.

In her bedroom, which she shared with her two sisters, metallic green, red, and gold Christmas tree ornaments hung from the ceiling. A plastic, Hawaiian lei was draped over the bureau mirror. Starched doilies, lipstick tubes, powders, jars of bobby pins, combs, and rubber bands sat on the dresser, along with costume jewelry from the five-and-ten and a photo of Rainbow posing with a beach towel draped over the front of her bathing suit. There were bunk beds in one corner and a double mattress in another, next to a 1930's nightstand with colored plastic flowers in a soda bottle and a plaster statue of St. Christopher holding the Baby Jesus.

Rainbow shared the mattress, which was covered with a pink chenille bedspread and an old, faded teddy bear, with her younger sister. On the wall above the bed was a poster of Little Richard bent over playing the keyboard and one of Marlon Brando as Zapata. On the opposite wall was a picture of the Virgin Mary with her hand over her heart. The other walls were bare except for a stark, wooden crucifix with a small well intended for holy water. Rainbow kept it filled to wet the spit curls that she glued to her cheeks with clear fingernail polish.

We'd lie on the bed smoking Salems and drinking Cokes, listening to Chuck Berry wailing *Johnny B.Goode*, Fats Domino singing *Blue Monday*, Ray Charles, Little Eva, and Leslie Gore on Rainbow's scratchy forty-five record player.

Maravilla

Occasionally, I would pass out on top of the bed or on the floor on top of a pillow and wake up in the middle of the night to find Rainbow still smoking and playing records so low just static would be coming through. She'd be trying on clothes or doing her hair or painting her toenails, humming along with the static. Sometimes I'd wake at dawn and she'd be gone. Once or twice when I woke, Rainbow was lying next to me with her arm draped around my waist.

At the time, it seemed to me that she had some kind of awesome power. She could go for days without sleep. Booze didn't seem to affect her. The first time I got drunk it was on a bottle of white port that we had shared. I got sick and threw up, then lay on the pink bedspread with the room spinning around until Rainbow shoved me fully clothed into a cold shower.

Regardless of how much Rainbow insisted that she loved me, she always kept a wall or distance between us. She'd invite me over, then ignore or criticize me. We'd be in her bedroom and she'd say to her sister, "Lookit Cece's *cheechees*. They look like mosquito bites," and they'd giggle. At a club meeting once, she said in front of everyone, "I bet Cece is faking being Chicana, *es gavacha que no*, Cece?" I was embarrassed but I didn't say anything. I watched her carefully, copying the way she walked, thrusting her hips out, and the way she held a cigarette in her hand, letting the ash grow long and flicking it, or drinking wine and beer straight out of the bottle. I began wearing lots of make-up and loud colors like she did.

Right before Easter vacation, we ditched school one morning to visit Chuy, who was being detained at juvenile hall for being out after curfew and loitering. The youth authorities wouldn't release him to his mother because she couldn't speak English and wasn't able to find either of their birth certificates. She was going to have to go to the county courthouse to get copies.

When we got there, we were told that it was too early for visitors. Standing in the hallway, we could see Chuy peering through a barred window. Rainbow shouted and waved, "Hey, Chuy!" He waved back. She started down the hall towards him and a guard blocked her way.

"You can't go over there," he told her.

Maravilla

"You can't stop me," she said, zigzagging to get through. "I have a right to talk to my brother." He stood in front of her, pushing her back. She darted around him. Another guard came over, grabbing her arm.

"Get your goddamn hands off me!" she yelled.

I went over to her, saying, "Come on, girl, let's get outa here," whispering in her ear, "or else they'll put you away too," pulling her out by the elbow.

"*Pinchi cabrones!*" she screamed as we went out the door.

The next day we were called into the principal's office. The truant officer said that they knew we had ditched and, if it happened again, we'd be expelled.

"I don't give a damn," said Rainbow. "I'm not learning shit here. It's stupid and boring and I hate it!"

"What about you, Consuelo?" he asked, tapping a pencil on his desk.

I didn't answer.

"Do you want to continue to go to school here?" he demanded.

"Yes, I guess so," I said, looking out the window. Rainbow glared at me. I could hear shouts from the P.E. field and see the acacias blooming outside. A fly buzzed around the room.

"I'm going to let you go, Consuelo. If you promise not to get into trouble again, I'll keep this off your record."

"OK," I whispered.

"You can leave now."

I got up and quietly walked out. After I shut the door, I heard a scuffle and he yelled, "Goddamn you, pick it up right now or I'll beat your black ass!"

The next day I found out that Rainbow had been expelled for a month.

I was in the bathroom at school just before she came back, combing my hair when Julia Cooper walked in with a couple of *bad* looking chicks. She stood next to me, cracking her gum and ratting her hair. Julia Cooper liked to act tough and was always trying to pick fights with Chicanas. She looked into the mirror, picking at her peroxided bouffant, and deliberately poked me with her elbow. A black chick was on the other side of us, leaning against the wall. I could feel her eyes on my back. I looked in my purse for my eyeliner. Out of the corner of my eye, I could see Julia's ugly face with its thick slash of coral lipstick on her hard little mouth. Ignoring her, I began drawing a black circle around my eyelids.

"I hate beaners!" she snarled, looking at the other chick's reflection in the mirror. The other one twittered. I could feel a fire rising in me. I glared at Julia. Tiny, black balls of mascara clung to her stubby eyelashes. The other girl banged out of the bathroom stall and bumped me from behind, knocking me into the sink.

"Hey, watch out!" I said.

"Sorr-rree," she giggled.

Gathering my stuff off the counter, I put it into my purse. I could feel them watching me in the mirror, waiting to see what I'd do. Someone came in and said, "Hi, Cece." It was Paula O'Brien.

"Hi," I mumbled. She looked around the room apprehensively.

I opened the door to go out and Julia slurred, "I'm gonna get you, greezer!"

I knew that Julia was crazy, but what I didn't know was why she was after me. What had I done?

During P.E., I was restless and unable to concentrate. While I was dressing, a chick came over and said, "Julia Cooper said to tell you to meet her after school by the parking lot."

"Why should I?"

Another girl stood behind her, staring at me sullenly.

"Julia said yer chicken and that she'd come get you if you didn't show."

I looked at her evenly. "She knows where she can find me," I said, shaking with rage.

I asked Carmen Estrada, whose brother was going with Julia, if she knew what was going on. She said that she had heard that Rainbow told Julia I called her a whore and a dirty-scuz-bag. It was true. But I never dreamed Rainbow would tell her.

"There's something else," said Carmen.

"What's that?"

25

"There's a rumor going around that you snitched on Rainbow."

I felt dizzy, like I was going to faint.

"That's not true," I mumbled.

Carmen said something, and I turned away shaking and stumbled home in a daze.

I stayed home for a week, straggling around the house in my bathrobe. When my mother tried to get me out of bed, I stood up reluctantly, then swayed and fell back.

"I can't!"

"Ay, *Dios*," she said. "OK, get back in bed. But you're going to have to see a doctor!"

The next day, Rainbow called while I was sleeping and told my sister to tell me that she hoped I was doing better and that my friends missed me. I began to feel better immediately. At this point, my mother was threatening to have me hospitalized if I didn't get out of bed and go back to school.

I went back feeling shaky and out of control, remembering that my cousin Vera told me to give her a call if I was ever in trouble. Vera lived in another part of L.A. and had her own gang. She was known as "Amazon Woman". She had a flat, dark, moon-shaped face. Her coarse, black Indian hair fell to her waist and hung full and frizzy around her face. She liked to arm wrestle boys and she could box like a man. There was only one thing in the world I knew of that scared her and that was snakes. The tinsiest baby snake could send her into hysterics.

Big Sara was Vera's best friend and constant companion. She had tangled, bright orange hair and white, Irish skin and was built like a Russian wrestler. She was totally dedicated to Vera. Big Sara had a reputation for being mean and fearless, but I happened to know that she was mild mannered, shy, and terrified of mice and spiders.

Vera and Big Sara hung out with Chano Cada de Platano, who had a long narrow face and jaundiced looking skin. They'd cruise around town in his lowered, black '39 Chevy coupe. The girls sat in the back and Bennie Rodriguez, a fence, who professed to be able to get you anything from black beauties, blue meanies and white crosses to color TV's, fur coats and fine china, rode shotgun.

I had never mentioned Vera to Rainbow. I was torn. I knew that Vera had an insane temper and was always looking for an excuse to fight. But I felt trapped, so I called her and she told me to come over.

As soon as I saw her, I blurted out, "Rainbow Rochin and Julia Cooper are gonna get me."

"What?" she hissed.

"Julia and Rainbow are after me."

"You scared of her?" she asked, glaring at me.

"Yeah," I said, holding up two fingers. "Two against one."

"Hey, I can count, _pendeha_," she said. "That bitch, that _wesa flaka_. I know her. I know her whole, goddamn family, fucking cholos. She ain't shit, not _mierda_! So, who's this Julia bitch?"

"A white chick at school who's always picking fights with Chicanas."

"Alright, point her out to me."

"OK," I whimpered.

Vera's eyes blazed. "Stop it, Cece!" she screamed. "Gawd, you make me sick!"

As fast as it came in, the storm died down, and she put her arm around my shoulder.

"You gonna help me?"

"Don't worry, _chiquita_. I'll take care of it, man."

That was Friday. I went back to school the following Monday and ran into Julia. She had a black eye and there was a splint on her finger. She acted like she hadn't seen me. Later, Ray Lopez told me he saw the whole thing. Vera accosted Julia at Mel's Drive-In. As Ray watched from a car, Julia tried to get away and Vera snapped her palm back and socked her. One of the car-hops rolled over on skates, bumping into them. Vera hurled insults at her, and the manager came out threatening to call the cops. Everyone scattered.

About a week later, I saw Rainbow at the Tastee Freeze. She looked scared.

"How you doin'?" she said.

"OK."

"You look bitchin'."

"Thanks."

"Hey, *esa*, I didn't know that Vera, the 'Amazon Woman' from Evergreen, was your *prima*. Why didn't you tell me?"

"I don't know," I said, shrugging.

"Cece, man, I don't know what she wants from me. She pulled my hair at my cousin's party in front of everyone and she's been calling me on the phone and threatening me. If it's something I did to you, I'm sorry."

I couldn't look at her.

"Would you please tell her to back off? Please."

I had never seen this side of her. It made me nervous.

"Ah, I'll try talking to her," I said.

"Thanks, Cece," she said, smiling moonily. As I turned to leave, she said, "You wanna come over and spend the night? I've got the new Richie Valens' 45."

"No, thanks. I have a lot of homework to do."

I had a hard time making sense out of what happened. I really cared for Rainbow and I was sure that she felt the same way about me. I felt guilty about calling Vera. I went back and forth in my mind, feeling vindictive, then remorseful, then angry, then sorry. I finally decided to forget the whole thing.

A few weeks later, Rainbow got caught smoking weed in the bathroom at school, and her locker was searched. Found among other things was a pint of Johnny Walker, a hunting knife and a couple of reefers.

While she was sitting in the office waiting for the youth authority to come and get her, she asked to use the toilet. Mrs. Toomey, the middle-aged secretary, escorted her outside. When they reached the bathroom door, Rainbow pulled away from Toomey and took off in a sprint across the campus before anyone could stop her.

The next day, I saw Chuy and he said, "Rainbow said to tell you she'd be in touch--and that she left something for you at the house."

That night I went over there. Her mother came to the door.

"Sheece gone," she said, wiping tears from the corners of her eyes with a ragged dishcloth.

"*Sabes donde?*" I said.

"*No se. La policia vine ayer--pero mi hija no estaba aqui. Ya se fue, y yo no se a donde.*"

"OK," I said, turning to leave.

"*Esperece*, Consuelo," she said. Looking over her shoulder she shouted, "*Oye, Bertha, tra la jacqueta!*"

Little Bertha trotted over with Rainbow's club jacket.

"*Tenga, mija*, Chata (Chata is what her mother called her) *queria que le di a usted. Andale lleve lo,*" she said, handing me the jacket.

I took it home and tried it on. It was too big so I hung it in the back of my closet. Later, I heard that Rainbow was living in New Mexico with relatives.

When Rainbow and I had our hassle, I stopped going to the club meetings. After she left I decided to go back. Corky Cruz was the new Prez. She said she'd like me to come back and asked me if I wanted to cruise with them that afternoon.

Esther Sandoval had her brother's Plymouth. Paula O'Brien, Lorraine McKenzie and Corky were in the back seat. I sat in the front next to Esther.

We cruised through town over to the 7-11 and got some guy to buy us a six-pac and a bottle of sloe gin. Then, we headed for the freeway.

Each of us had a beer, except for Esther who didn't drink. Corky opened the gin and passed it around.

"I don't think you should have any," she told Paula. "You get too drunk and loca."

"I can too," said Paula, intercepting the bottle and taking a long slug.

"Hey, cool it, girl," grunted Lorraine, taking the bottle from her.

Paula had this dumb look on her face like she was already drunk. She never could hold her booze. But she seemed to be in a wild mood and wouldn't pay attention to us when we asked her not to drink anymore. She just kept guzzling it down.

By the time we'd gotten downtown, she was out of it, acting stupid, babbling and slurring her words.

Maravilla

"Esther, pull over," she groaned. It was too late. She lurched forward trying to stick her head out of the window, didn't make it, and barfed all over Esther's head and shoulders.

Esther, always the perfect lady, hissed, "Darn it!"

"Get away from me!" groaned Lorraine, who was sitting next to her.

"Here, Paula," I said, handing her a paper napkin.

Esther pulled off the freeway.

"My cousin lives around here," she said. "I'm gonna have to go and clean up."

Paula hung her head out the window, groaning.

"Hey, *esa*, just keep yer head out there, OK?" Lorraine said.

Hauling Paula by the armpits, we dragged her into the house with her head bobbing back and forth like a rag doll.

Esther's cousin took one look at her and said, "Better get that girl some black coffee."

"I'm gonna take a shower and do my hair. You guys can take the car, but be careful," Esther said, handing the keys to Corky.

We went downtown, cruising through the porno section. Neon signs glared out from gaudy marquees. Showcase windows, plastered with pictures of naked women with huge breasts, lined the street.

"Have you ever seen one of those?" Lorraine asked.

"No," I said.

"You've got to be kidding," Corky said.

"Wanna see one?" Lorraine said.

There was a long pause, and I said, "OK, why not?"

"Oh, no, you're crazy," Corky wailed.

"Aw, come on, don't be square," Lorraine said.

"Aren't you curious, Corky?" I said.

"Well, OK. But if I don't like it, I'm walking right out, with or without you guys."

Lorraine, who looked the oldest, flashed her phony I.D. at the fat, pimply-faced guy in the box office. He never bothered to look up as we paid our fifty cents and went in, stopping at the snack bar for Cokes and candy bars. The place smelled dank and musty and was almost empty except for a handful of men.

"Beach Blanket Bango," the flick that was playing, had already started. We sat down in the back of the theatre, and a couple of men in front of us got up and moved. The movie was a take-off on an old Annette Funicello-Frankie Avalon flick. Instead of teenagers, the actors, if you could call them that, were around thirty or forty years old.

Some guy who looked like a conservative businessman was doing it to a woman who looked like a tired-out housewife. Other naked men and women were doing the same thing in different positions.

Lorraine twittered. Corky stared ahead, expressionless. Except for the dirty pictures that circulated around school, I'd never seen anything like it. In the beginning, it was interesting in a clinical kind of way. But they kept doing the same thing over and over.

"Is that it?" I whispered, nudging Lorraine.

"How should I know?" she snorted.

After about a half hour had passed, Corky said, "Let's go."

Back at the car, Lorraine said, "Wow, that one guy had a big *pilingi*."

"I don't know how that chick ever got it into her mouth," I said.

"Yuk," squealed, Corky, "I'd never do that in a million years."

"That ain't nothin'. I've done it before," Lorraine said.

There was a silence.

"*Mentira*," spat Corky. "Man, you lie like a rug."

"It was no big deal," Lorraine said.

"Was it just a little one?" I asked.

"Well, it wasn't that big," Lorraine said. "You just pretend that it's an ice cream cone and lick it."

Corky and I were speechless, but only for a minute.

"I'd prefer Rocky Road," Corky said.

"I'll take a hot fudge sundae," I said.

"You guys don't know anything about that stuff," Lorraine said. I could tell she was getting pissed.

"I don't want to," said Corky.

"Me either, if it's anything like that. That one dark haired guy reminded me of gross Mr. Polanski from the science department. Yuk."

31

"You mean Polanski the Pervert," Corky said.

"Hey, too bad Esther didn't get to see it," said Lorraine.

"Why?" said Corky.

"So's she'd know what to do when she and Louie get married."

"Esther and Louie would never do anything like that, man," Corky said.

"Heck no, they both go to Holy Communion every single Sunday," I said.

"Esther probably thinks that Louie's doing it when he sticks his tongue in her mouth," Lorraine guffawed.

"OK, you guys stop talking about my *prima* behind her back," Corky said.

On the drive back to pick up Esther and Paula, I started thinking about Liz Delaney. Liz was one of the prettiest and smartest girls I'd ever known. I met her when I was in the seventh grade. She had a knack for telling stories and cracking jokes. And she acted like she knew all about sex. One day, as we walked from school, I asked her what the word "cunt" meant.

"It's the place between your legs, you know, where a guy puts his thing when you fuck," she said.

"What do you mean?" I asked.

"You know, when a guy gets a hard on."

"Oh, yeah," I said, not knowing.

Mary Lou Anderson was walking with us and said, "I've seen dogs doing it. They get stuck together from behind."

"That's different," said Liz.

"Why?" I said.

"Because, stoop, dogs are different from people."

"I know all about it," said Mary Lou, smugly. "My mother explained the whole thing to me."

"Then, you should know that dogs do it different," said Liz.

I could tell that Mary Lou was getting upset. She hated to be wrong, you could tell that.

"Well, I've seen pictures in a book," she said.

"What book?" I asked.

"Oh, never mind, I don't want to talk about it." With that, she turned up the street.

Maravilla

After a few minutes, I got up the nerve to ask, "Where's the hole?"

"It's the one in front," said Liz.

I had tried probing for it with my fingers and I found a place in front that sent off delicious little explosions and felt wonderful but I couldn't find the hole. I secretly worried that there was something wrong with me.

"But where is it?" I said.

"It's between your legs," she said, looking at me like I was a complete dodo.

"I know it!" I said, trying to conceal my embarrassment.

"Want me to show you?" she said.

My heart was racing.

"OK," I said.

When we reached my house, we went into the bathroom and locked the door. She pulled her panties down and sat on the toilet seat, lifted her skirt, arching he legs open. I could see the tiny opening covered with fuzz above her ass. I'd never seen it quite like that.

"That's it," she said.

I felt dizzy and my stomach was queasy.

"Do you want to touch it?" she asked.

My hand jerked back. She took hold of it, pressing it against the throbbing spot, helping me push in the tip of my finger. It was soft and mushy. For a minute, I couldn't tell if I was the one sitting on the toilet or standing up. The room pitched and I fell to my knees in front of her. Someone was rattling at the door.

"I gotta pee."

"Ok, just a minute," I mumbled deliriously. We both were giggling as she pulled down her skirt and wiggled into her panties.

Going into the bedroom, I turned my back to her and began changing my clothes. My cheeks were on fire. She combed her hair and, without looking at me, said, "I have to go." I felt awkward and stupid. Everything had changed. I was tense and my stomach was upset.

Back to school, she acted as if nothing had happened. Neither of us mentioned it again.

33

When we arrived at the house to pick up Esther and Paula, Esther's hair was perfectly coiffed with every strand ratted and sprayed into place. Paula was still messed up but walking on her own.

"We went to the Peeka-Boo and saw a dirty movie."

Corky blanched. "It was dumb."

"Oh, really," Esther said, looking in the rear view mirror. "How stupid."

The fall of my sophomore year, I went out for basketball. Corky Cruz and Carmen Estrada were on the same team, playing guards. I played front position. Carmen, all elbows and knees and fuzzy brown hair, ran like a deer. She was smooth and agile. When she had the ball, she would start off with slow, calculating moves, then pick up speed, pacing herself. She'd come leaping across the court, bouncing the ball, and throw it at me. First chance I had, I would shoot for the basket. It was a thrill every time I sank one. We'd stay after school, practicing three and four nights a week. I loved the competition, the excitement of playing, of winning. The first year we played together, our team won the Best Girl Basketball Team award. Of course, we could have never done it without Corky. She was mean as hell and cheated like crazy. When the referee wasn't watching, she would use her body and arms, pushing and shoving to block or grab the ball out of the opponent's hands. Built thick and square, Corky seemed to possess a sheer physical force and strength, as well as a bluntness that belied emotions and feelings. Her dark face was always cool and aloof as the moon.

Corky and Carmen, considered homely by most of the boys, never seemed to care one way or the other. Where Corky was closed-mouthed, Carmen was talkative and witty, cynical to the bone, a perfect complement to Corky.

Corky and I always walked home together after practice. One night she said, "I'd do anything for you, Cece. You're my best friend, besides Carmen. I like you a whole lot, *esa*," she said.

"Bye," I said, going into the house. It was getting so that she would do anything I asked her to. It made me feel weird. I liked her a lot, but she wasn't as much fun as Rainbow had been. Another thing, she didn't understand certain things, so I had a hard time discussing stuff, like "Was ratting your hair really good for it?", or say, "What was the best way to translate a certain sentence from English into Spanish?", or "Did Paul Wagamoshi really have the smallest penis in the whole school, even through he had an I.Q. of a hundred and sixty?" The only other chick besides Carmen Estrada I could talk to was Paula O'Brien, and she had absolutely no sense of humor.

Then I met Gerry Rodriguez.

Chapter 4

The first time I saw her, I noticed how she kept her small hands neatly folded in her navy-blue lap and the way her calf curved above thick white socks and freshly polished saddle oxfords, how her long, plain brown hair was coarse and stubborn as a horse's tail, and her skin pale and sallow from lack of sunlight. The tiny freckles across her nose seemed to save her face from a total solemnity.

She was reading with her head bent, and her glasses slid down on the bridge of her nose, giving her an austere, studious look. It was her first day in the class.

I wore an orange mini skirt that day, my hair ratted into a French twist, pink matte lipstick, and false eyelashes. I craned my neck to see *Geraldine Rodriguez* written at the top of the paper on her desk.

I cracked my gum and smiled. Mr. Riley, the social studies teacher, said, "Ok, Consuelo, get rid of it."

"Of what?"

"That ridiculous gum."

I stared at him without moving.

"Now!" he demanded.

I giggled, then, watching for her reaction, slowly removed the gum from my mouth and pasted it on the back of my hand. When Mr. Riley turned back to the blackboard, I popped it back into my mouth. I was wondering if she was Chicana.

After a few minutes, I reached over and tapped her on the shoulder, whispering, "Geraldine, did you come from Sacred Heart?"

She ignored me. I thought she hadn't heard me.

36

"Hey, girl, did you come from the Catholic school?"

She turned around and deliberately looked in my eyes without speaking. What a bitch, I thought.

A few months passed and Gerry had rid herself of that Catholic school pallor. Her hair, peroxided with gold streaks, was ratted and sprayed, her lips caked with pale, pink matte lipstick, her eyebrows painted like wings, and her skin tanned to a dark brown. There was a quick, sarcastic ring to her voice, and she had the greatest tits in the world, which she accented whenever she had the chance. But the reason I fell in love with Gerry wasn't because of her tits but because of her laugh. I loved her laugh, raucous and daring. I recognized it in a group even when I couldn't see her. I was familiar with little things about her like the way she lifted a soda bottle to her lips with her pinkie extended and the sexy way she swung down the street, languidly swaying her hips, holding her books close to her breasts. After school, I'd watch her walking home with Carmen Estrada, hear them laughing and singing Supremes and Mary Wells songs. I saw Gerry everywhere, in passing cars, walking towards me in the supermarket, cruising the boulevard on Saturday nights, and in my dreams. Gerry remained aloof, merely nodding in the hallways at school, hardly noticing me.

I knew that Gerry didn't have a boyfriend and Carmen Estrada had told me that she wanted one. So, I called my cousin Rio.

"Hi, Rio?"

"Yeah?"

"This is Cece."

"Yah?"

"Rio, I know this chick who I happen to think would be perfect for you."

"Yeah?"

"Yeah. Her name is Gerry Rodriguez. She's got gold hair and you know how you like blondes and she also has a fabulous bod, Rio."

Rio had never mentioned to me that he liked blondes. His vocabulary usually consisted of two words, "yeah" and "wow."

"Yeah."

"Yeah, she's really bitchin'."

"Wow."

"Yeah, so why don't you make it up here to meet her and we can go cruising or something like that?"

"Yeah, awright."

"I'll call her and set it up, then get back to you."

"Yeah," he grunted.

With that done, it was only a matter of getting Gerry to come.

"Hello, Gerry Rodriguez?"

"Yes?"

"This is Cece Contreres."

Pause.

"You know, from the Belltones, ha, ha." My heart was pounding.

"Yeah, whatya want?"

"Oh, I wanted to know if you could, ah, make it up to my house tonight?"

Silence.

"I've got a couple of my friends coming by--some guys from 'White Fence,' one of them is my cousin Rio."

"Wait a minute. I'll ask my mother."

She came back saying, "My mom said I could go, but only until eleven o'clock."

"OK, I'll meet you halfway, say on the corner, by the Market Basket."

I watched her moving towards me from a couple of blocks away. She was wearing a short, pleated skirt and a matching orlon sweater. Her hair was ratted and sprayed into a huge, shellacked bonnet. Her knees were a soft beautiful brown.

"You hair looks tuff," I said.

"Yeah," she said, patting it. "I just did it."

We started down the street.

"You smell good. Are you wearing perfume?"

"No, that's my hair spray, 'Just Wonderful.'"

"Ga, I'm gonna get some of that. It smells bitchin'."

After a few minutes, I said, "I've been wanting to be your friend for a long time, Geraldine. I think you're beautiful."

"My name is Gerry," she said. "I hate Geraldine."

"Yeah, I know what you mean. I hate to be called Consuelo."

We walked down the sidewalk, with me in beer can rollers

and faded Levi's, smiling at her, and her staring straight ahead, cool and acting controlled.

"Gerry, my dad left some beer in the refeer, maybe we could share a bottle. I'm sure he wouldn't miss it."

"I hate beer," she said.

"Oh, yeah, well, I'll drink it myself then," I said quietly. I didn't want to say the wrong thing.

The guys were waiting when we arrived at my house.

"Oh, shit! Man, I'm gonna go around the back and comb my hair and put some make-up on. You talk to them," I said.

"Me?"

"Yeah, go ahead--don't be scared."

"I'm not scared," she said, regaining her fake composure.

I ran around to the back door and into my bedroom where I began to rat my hair. When I'd gotten it ratted into fan-like tufts, I sprayed it. Then, I tilted my head close to the mirror and began applying a coat of beige pancake make-up to my face. With liquid eyeliner, I drew two, thin, black lines over the edges of my upper lids and one under the lower lids. Over the natural line of my brows, I drew wing-like arcs. Then, I took a lipstick brush and painted a pale, pink matte line following the contours of my lips, except the corners which I overlapped. With a matte, white tube, I filled in the space of my mouth and dabbed mocha rouge onto my cheeks. When I completed my face, I took a double pronged pick and lightly, so as not to flatten it, raked it over the top of my hair, which stood out about four inches all over my head. I used a hand mirror to make sure there were no odd places in the back. I worked with it, blending and spraying until it was smooth and varnished as a piece of polished mahogany. Unbuttoning my blouse, I threw it on the floor and selected a button-down sweater so as not to ruin my perfect hair-do, went into the bathroom, and stuffed a small piece of toilet paper into each cup of my 32AA bra, put a dab of Evening in Paris behind each ear and on my wrists and bolted out the front door.

Both the guys were wearing khakis and plaid shirts. Their pants were ironed with a center crease that came to the middle of their shiny, black shoes.

"Eh," grunted Rio.

"Hi, man, how's it goin'?" I said, cracking my gum. I turned to the other guy. I didn't want to waste time talking to Rio. I was positive that he wouldn't respond. Sure enough, he grunted and shook his head back and forth like one of those plastic Chinese dolls. The other guy was around eighteen but looked older. Burned out, but handsome in a desperate sort of way. There was something secretive and dark about him.

"How'd you guys get here?" I said.

"Art," grunted Rio.

"You got wheels?" I said.

"Yeah, I show do, lady," said Art.

"You have a car?" chimed Gerry.

"Thas' right, man--but it ain't mine."

"Hey, I'm not getting into a stolen car!" she said, looking at me. "My cousin just got busted for being in a stolen car that he didn't know about and ended up in juvie."

"Is that a stolen car?" I asked.

"*Orale!* You don't trust me. Don't worry, it belongs to a friend of mine, swear to God," said Art, raising his hand in testimony. "We gonna cruise, or what?"

Rio, true to form, never said a word as we walked down the street to a green, '55 Chevy convertible with the top down. Rio got in the back and Gerry slid in next to him. Art got in the driver's seat and I sat next to him. As soon as Art switched on the ignition, I reached over and flicked on the radio to Martha and the Vandellas singing "Doo-Run-Run." I began to snap my fingers and sing, "Met him on a Sunday, a doo-run-run, oh, a doo-run-run."

I glanced back at Gerry and smiled. I could feel the wind catch my hair and move it back and forth in one, solid piece. Art passed me a brown paper bag with a bottle of white port. I took a hit and handed it to Gerry, watching as she took ladylike sips while the wind blew across her face, not even denting her beautifully sculpted hair. We cruised slowly past the projects, heading for the boulevard while the southern California sun slipped beneath the horizon, golden orange in the smoggy, brown sky.

Gerry fell in love with Rio. At least, that's what she said. But I knew that she cared for me more than she did him.

After all, it was with me that she spent most of her time. Another thing, whenever they were together, I was with them, because he never cared about being with her unless I came along too. I could never understand what she saw in him. He was cold and strange, almost mulish. But it didn't seem to bother her. I guess she wanted a boyfriend no matter what. I'd call Rio and ask him to drop by, and he and Art would come over in the convertible, bringing wine and a couple of reefers. We never talked much, just cruised in the Chevy with the top down. Once in awhile Gerry and Rio made out in the back seat. Art never seemed attracted to me which was fine. I was more interested in having the guys pick us up after school, so our friends could see us climb into the flashy, green convertible. Art's mirror sunglasses, reflecting glints of light, Rio, in his shiny, black, Japanese baseball jacket, a fedora pulled low on his forehead. "Peel out," I'd say to Art, and he'd rev the pipes and take off with the radio blaring, tires spinning out, laying rubber.

After a while, Art disappeared from the scene, and Rio stopped coming by. But by then, Gerry and I were best friends.

"Why don't you ask Gerry if she wants to join the club?" Corky Cruz said one afternoon at basketball practice.

"I did," I said, dribbling the ball to her, "and she said she wasn't interested."

She shot it back hard, hitting me on the chin.

"Sorry," she mumbled. "You ought to give back your jacket if you're not coming to the meetings anymore."

"OK," I said. After I met Gerry, I lost interest in the Belltones and hadn't been going to the club meetings. When I gave my jacket back, Corky stopped talking to me. She ignored me, acted as if I were invisible.

Then, something strange happened. Gerry had been getting a ride home after school from Mousie Figueroa, and his girl-friend, Rosie, found out. Ester Sandoval told Gerry that Rosie was pissed.

Gerry brushed it off. "Who cares?" she said.

On Friday, Corky invited Gerry and me to a party. When we got there, Gerry danced with Mousie. They were fooling around, nothing serious, just joking and flirting, more or less. He brought us a couple of wine coolers, and we sat sipping them.

When Gerry went into the bathroom with the glass of wine, Negra, one of the toughest *pachucas* around, knocked it out of her hand. It splattered against the wall, clattered to the floor and broke. Gerry, not knowing at the time that it had been deliberate, bent over to pick it up and Loca, another *pachuca*, jumped her from behind, yanking her hair and twisting her head back. Then, Negra grabbed her glasses, threw them on the floor, and stepped on them.

Gerry screamed. I heard her and went over to the bathroom, banging on the door.

"What's going on?" I shouted.

The door swung open, and someone yanked me in. Before I knew it, I was on the ground, wrestling with a big, brown, fleshy body. Loca, her eyes wild with rage, was trying to pin my arms back. I started to kick and scratch. She grabbed hold of my hair. I raked my fingernails down her arms. Somehow I managed to get on top of her, pinning her back. When Negra saw I was getting the best of Loca, she let go of Gerry and came after me. I saw Gerry run out the door just as Negra pulled my hair and yanked me down. The three of us, all arms, legs, hair and sweat, rolled around the floor, grunting and flailing. I was fighting with everything I had. It was no use. They had me down. Things started blurring. I must have lost consciousness.

Then, it was quiet. I looked up to see the vague outline of someone.

"*Que paso? Que paso?*" An old woman, with a tiny shriveled-up face in a loose black dress, was standing over me. "*Hay vienen la policia. Andale, vayase, apurase!*" she cried, shoving me out the door. I darted through the empty house, dashing over to the couch to get my purse, which was miraculously still there, and ran out the door, sprinting past the front yard just in time to see the cops cruising by.

From behind a hedge, I could hear the static from their radio, see the glow of red and blue lights. The cool night air soothed the pitch of fever that was rising in me. I was frantically worrying about Gerry. I knew she couldn't see without her glasses. A few minutes later I spotted Donny Johnston's black Ford. As it drew closer, he stuck his head out the window.

"Is that you, Cece?"

"Yeah." I ran over to the car and got in.

Gerry was crying. "They broke my glasses!" she sobbed.

"Oh, no," I said.

"Too much," Donny mumbled.

"Guess what?" I said.

"What?"

"I wet my pants."

"How gross," Gerry said. "Cece, what am I gonna tell my father? I just got those glasses last week."

"I don't know," I said. "Why don't you tell him that you lost them?"

"Yeah, man," Donny drawled. "Tell him that they just fell off, or something like that."

"Oh, sure. Like he'll never believe it. He'll say, 'What do you mean, THEY JUST FELL OFF!'"

"Hey, man, they just fell off, that's how," he said.

I couldn't help giggling.

"How can you laugh?" Gerry cried. "It's so humiliating. Promise you'll never tell anyone."

"Everyone already knows, man," Donny said.

Gerry started crying again.

"Hey, you chicks gotta be careful. You can't fool around with Negra and her gang," Donny said.

"I don't even know her," I said.

"Yeah," Gerry said. "We didn't do anything, anyway."

"That's not what I heard," Donny said.

"What do you mean?" Gerry asked.

"You guys were set up."

"Why?"

"Because, this is what I heard," he said, lighting a cigarette. "Gerry was seen cruising with Mousie Figueroa, and Negra and Loca are friends of Rosie's."

"Who was it?" Gerry asked.

"I don't know," Donny said, shaking his head.

"Come on, Donny. You know," she said.

"Well, it might've been, now I ain't sayin' for sure, man, but it might've been Corky Cruz."

"That's a lie!" I said.

"It is?" Gerry said, glaring at me. "She's the one that invited us to the party."

"I don't believe it," I said. "She wouldn't do that."

"Hey, man," Donny said, "it ain't gonna do you chicks any good to hassle over it, man." He turned on the radio and we drove the rest of the way in silence.

I woke up the next morning stiff and aching all over with bruises, scratches and a black eye.

"*Ay, Dios!*" my mother winced when she saw me. "What in the world happened to you?"

"Nothing."

"*Valgame Dios!* What do you mean, nothing! You have a black eye! Tell me what happened or you're not leaving this house."

"On the way home from the party last night, we stopped at the liquor store for some Cokes and these white chicks jumped us and beat us up."

"Who's us?"

"Gerry and me."

"But, why?"

"I don't know. We weren't doing anything."

"*Fijate no mas.* I don't want you going out at night then! Get ready. You're going to church with me today. Hurry up."

"Alright," I said, limping over to the phone to call Gerry.

When I talked to Gerry, she said that Carmen Estrada had called to say that she had heard about what happened at the party. And she wanted us to know that Corky had nothing to do with the fight. She said that Negra had asked Corky to invite us to the party because she wanted to tell Gerry that Rosie, Mousie's chick, was pregnant and to ask Gerry to stay away from him. "But later, when she saw them dancing and flirting and stuff, and her probably being high on Red Mountain and bennies," Gerry said, "she lost her temper."

"Rosie is pregnant?"

"That's what Carmen said."

"What is she going to do?"

"I don't know, but that's the last time I ever talk to Mousie Figueroa. I mean he's so weird. He acts like nothing at all is going on with him and Rosie."

"Cece, get ready, hurry up. I don't want to be late," my mother yelled.

"Listen, Gerry I have to go to Mass. I'll call you as soon as I get back."

"OK, bye."

Chapter 5

Every Sunday my family went to Mass at Our Lady of Soledad. The church was elaborately decorated with purple and white lace trimmed linens, tiers of lighted candelabras, tall vases of pink and purple gladiolas, dark red roses and yellow daffodils. In the center of the altar sat the opulent golden chalice, containing the blood of Christ, transformed from wine by the ritual of the Mass. The tabernacle was a miniature Gothic castle painted a glittery gold color, with fancy turrets and columns.

When I was a kid, I actually believed that Jesus lived in the little cubicle that housed the Eucharist and half expected Him to burst out of it with the Sacred Heart pulsing and His right hand extended in a reverent and holy version of "V" for victory sign. Surrounded by resounding soprano voices and the pungent odor of incense and burning candles, I used to daydream during the long Latin Mass that the little Jesus would come straight out and whisk me up to heaven, with its ethereal angels, beautiful Madonnas, and soft music.

I'd lie with my head on my mother's lap and gaze up at the mural of fat, white clouds floating against a dark blue background, rosy-cheeked cherubs, and old men with flowing beards and dramatic eyes that was painted on the high domed ceiling. In the middle of all of it, the Virgin Mary ascended into the sky wearing a blue gown, surrounded by a circle of gold stars. All around the altar were statues of St. Francis of Assisi, St. Theresa, St. Ann, and St. Joseph holding the Christ child, the Virgin Mary in powder blue again, with her arms

46

extended. St. Joseph winked at me; the Virgin whispered my name.

During Lent, I'd follow my mother, copying her as she genuflected and crossed herself, whispering, "In the name of the Father, the Son and the Holy Ghost." We prayed in front of the Stations of the Cross, which began with a large picture of Jesus and his temptation in the desert. Then one of Him being crowned with thorns, and another carrying the cross on the long road to Calvary (I saw His dark red blood spill to the polished floor of the church) and so on until he was at last crucified. After saying a silent prayer at the end, my mother would cross herself and go over and light a dime candle at the altar. I'd kneel down next to her, staring at the tiny, dancing flames.

Way in the back of the church was a large crucifix of Jesus as a black man. (Were there two Jesuses, I wondered, one black and one white?) Below that was a statue of St. Christopher carrying the Baby Jesus piggyback.

St. Chris was my favorite Saint. I had been praying to him all my life for protection. I felt cheated when he was decanonized. I hoped for my mother's sake the Church wouldn't decree St. Anthony a fraud and have him decanonized too. He was her patron saint, the one she prayed to for finding things that she'd lost or misplaced, like her keys, reading glasses, and stuff.

Once, after she had prayed on her knees in front of St. Anthony's statue, asking him to help her to win the church lottery of twenty dollars, she came triumphantly into my room, waving the bill in my face, saying, "See, he won it for me!"

"Come on," I said.

"You don't believe me, do you?" she said huffily.

"Sure, Mom. How about a car for me? Would you ask him?"

"Go ahead and make fun of me. But you'll be sorry when God punishes you, *ingraciada!*"

Catechism, which I had to go to every Saturday, was full of exciting stories of the saints' lives. There was Joan of Arc burned at the stake as a witch (which always thrilled and terrified me) for leading the troops into righteous and holy rebellion, cavorting and riding off to war like a man. I guess they showed her.

Then there was Mary Magdalene. The illustrious Lady of the Night. I often wondered what happened to her after the crucifixion. Did she go back into the business? Or was she too old by then?

"Maybe she got a job taking dictation from a Roman businessman, or worked as a waitress, slinging hash," said my sister, Maria, in that smart-alecky way of hers when I asked her what she thought about it.

Once, when Maria wanted to shock and provoke my mother's rage, which she did a lot, she told her that she'd had a dream about the Virgin Mary and Mary Magdalene.

"They met over wine, after work one night. Magdalene complimented Mary the Virgin on her beautiful and perennially youthful appearance. Mary said that it was probably the lighting, but that, possibly, eating fresh vegetables and fruit and washing her face three times a day with Clearasil soap helped." (This is what Mother recommended for Maria and me, along with praying the Rosary.)

"But more importantly," added Maria, "being *in* with God was a big plus."

Mother pshawed. *"Como eres mentirosa, Maria!"*

"That's not all," Maria said. "After they'd had a few more drinks, Magdalene loosened up and asked the Virgin, 'Er, Mary, what about the Immaculate Conception?'"

Mother clucked.

"'You know, dear, you can tell me and it will be in the strictest of confidence,' said Magdalene, flashing Mary that dazzling smile that had won over Jesus and the Apostles."

"Get out of here, Maria!" Mother wailed.

"So what did Mary say?" I wanted to know.

"Nothing," Maria said. "She just got a funny look on her face and right then and there she turned into a statue. Then I woke up."

"Ay, no tienes verguenza, Maria. I hope God doesn't hear you talking like that because you'll be sorry, girl, I swear," Mother said. "You have a dirty mouth. I don't know where you get it from!".

"No, I don't. It's clean. I just brushed my teeth," Maria said sarcastically. "Anyway," she continued, "at least I don't play with myself while watching T.V. like Cece does."

Maravilla

"What! You liar!" I said.

"I saw you with your hand in you pants last night while we were watching 'I Love Lucy,'" said Maria.

"You're crazy, Maria," I screamed.

"Oh, leave her alone," my mother said as I slammed out of the room.

According to the Catholic church, there are two categories of sin--venial and mortal. Venial being less serious of the two, sort of like a misdemeanor, with mortal sin being more like a felony.

I used to lie in bed wondering what category the sin of masturbation fell into ... especially after having brought myself to orgasm, with my hand rigid from applying constant friction to my clitoris. I began to think that, if I only played with myself and stopped before reaching that little, gratifying explosion, it might be classified as a venial instead of the deadly mortal.

After going backwards and forwards about it in my mind, I decided to shoot for the sky and get to confession as soon as possible.

My favorite place for doing it was the bathroom. I'd lie in the bathtub for hours with my eyes closed, imagining that I was being forced into all kinds of sexual positions by a bunch of different characters. If I was forced, then it wouldn't be my fault. Would it? If I wasn't totally responsible, I could plead innocent and have the charges dropped or at least reduced. Then, if I happened to die without making it to confession beforehand, I might end up in purgatory instead of burning in hell.

I imagined purgatory to be like an honor farm. If enough friends and relatives prayed devoutly and lit dime candles in church for you, in time, perhaps centuries, you would be sent to heaven. Of course, only Catholics were allowed onto the celestial turf. So you'd be certain to be with your own kind.

I was always nice and considerate to my younger brothers and sister in case I died first, hoping they would remember me with prayers. But the older I got the more I realized how dumb this was, since most of my relatives never bothered to pray except in church on Sundays and even then I'd seen them only mouthing words and staring out through vacant eyes. I knew for certain that no one in the family ever prayed for, much less remembered, my uncle Ray, who died of cirrhosis of the liver after spending every day of the last ten years of his life dead drunk. I knew that my mother never prayed for him, as she often accused my father, whenever he drank too much, of being another sonovabitching Ray Contreres.

I doubt that my mother prayed for anyone. Except to St. Anthony to find her lost keys and what-nots. Of course she prayed directly to God for more money. It was to the Virgin she prayed for patience and perseverance.

One Saturday, Maria, my two brothers, and I were in the living room watching the tube, arguing over who was going to watch what next. Mother came in acting holier-than-thou, which she usually did once a month, especially after a big drunk or a family squabble, and announced in a phony reverent tone, "I have just appealed to the Virgin to help me not to lose my temper," she said with her lips pursed together, "and I'd appreciate it if you kids cooperate with me so that I may go to communion tomorrow with a clear conscience."

"Watch out," Maria whispered. "She's got the Virgin on her side."

"*Que dices?*" Mother replied.

"Nothing, Mother."

"But I want to watch 'The Lone Ranger'!" my little brother Eddie whined.

Tony, my older brother, pushed him, knocking him down.

Eddie let out a howl. My mother, with her eyes blazing, marched over, grabbing him by the ear.

"*Hijos de la chingada!*" she shrieked, dragging him away. "And you, *cabron*, get in there and do your homework right now!" she yelled at Tony.

Then, she began screaming about how it was our fault that she was going to hell.

"And by God," she spat, "I'm going to drag every one of you *pinchi* brats down with me!" Then, she started banging doors and slamming cupboards shut, raving and ranting to God and his saints.

I think these constant threats of damnation were beginning to have an effect on me.

Maravilla

It was right after a masturbating session that I decided that the tiny lumps surrounding my nipples were cancerous.

I lay in bed, shaking and reciting the Act of Contrition, over and over again.

Even though I believed I was close to death because of my sinful behavior, I continued to do *it* every day, afterward making promises to the higher ups. I'd give up drinking cokes and beer. I'd stop stuffing my bra with T.P. (Of course, that meant I'd have to wear a coat to school every day without ever taking it off as it would look strange if I turned up flat chested all of a sudden.) I promised to stop lying and stealing candy bars from Market Basket.

"Please, God," I prayed on bended knees, "have mercy on me. Let me live to be thirty and I'll quit masturbating."

My promises never lasted for more than twenty-four hours.

After a few weeks of thinking about malignant tissues and tumors, I went to my mother, thrust up my T-shirt and bra over one breast, and said, "See these bumps? I have cancer. Do you think you could give me a ride to the hospital?"

She pshawed. "Oh, that's common. Look. I have the same thing." She lifted up her blouse, showing me hers. "Don't worry, Cece. You're normal."

I was embarrassed but relieved. That night to celebrate I masturbated. Afterward, I remembered my promise to quit. I began coughing during the night. The next day I was certain that I had contracted T.B. I had lied to God, broken a solemn vow. I deserved to die an agonizing death.

I hacked hoarsely, my chest racked with pain. I spit up wads of phlegm, checking my spit for blood. After a few days of gagging, spitting and coughing, my mother gave in and took me in for an X-ray. Nothing was wrong. For a spell I worried about radiation exposure.

I began to hate going to confession. I was positive that Father O'Dowd recognized my voice in the confessional, even though I disguised it by putting a pencil between my lips or holding my nose.

Every Sunday, Father O'Dowd railed from the pulpit against the "sins of the flesh," as he called them, with his fist clenched and his fat jowls jiggling in his red face. I could tell that he was looking at me, as he warned the girls in the congregation to remain pure (he pronounced it pee-your) and chaste. With his face seething and bloated, he would add that the boys who took advantage of us were nothing better than pigs.

When I confessed that Chuck Valdez had stuck his tongue in my mouth, I sat there scared to death, expecting his wrath. But he merely asked, "Is he a Cath-o-lic?"

"Yes, Father," I lied, holding my nose. I really didn't know for sure. My mind raced. (Which is worse? To lie in confession or french a non-Catholic?)

"For your penance say ten Hail Marys and ten Our Fathers," he said. "Now repeat after me the Act of Contrition."

"Oh, my God, I'm heartily sorry," I said. I was thinking that maybe I should stop confession for a while, at least until I quit playing with myself and frenching guys. I could see his shadow through the mesh screen, making the sign of the cross, and hear him whispering a Latin incantation before he slammed the little window shut and left me kneeling there, staring into the dark.

Chapter 6

I was in the kitchen doing the dishes the day that Joanna Valdez called. Shouts drifted in from outside where the kids were playing kick-the-can. The transistor was on the shelf above the sink blaring *Fever*. My mother walked in grumbling, "Ay, Cece, how can you stand that racket. It's disgusting. Turn it down!" Oh, shit, I mumbled, turning it lower. *Fever* was one of my favorite songs. At the last school dance Gerry and I had gotten on stage at the gym and belted out:

> *Fever, you give me fever*
> *Fever when you kiss me*
> *Fever when you hold me tight*
> *Fever in the mornin'*
> *Fever all through the night*

Gerry's brother Marcos' band, Los Gatos, was playing and they let us sing with them. Donny Johnston dared us to do it. Afterwards I was totally embarrassed. Marcos said we sounded like we were stuck on the wrong speed. Gerry and I had gotten into an argument about which one of us was out of tune. We hadn't spoken to each other for a couple of days when I saw Ray Lopez after third period and he said that he thought it was Gerry who was off. That made me feel better so I told her that I actually thought she had done alright, adding that maybe we should practice a little bit before the next time we do it. Later I found out that Ray had told her that he thought it was me who was off key. I was thinking about getting

53

together with her to practice for the next sock hop when the phone rang.

"Hello?"

"Hi, Cece."

"Who's this?"

"Joanna... you know, from Las Rienas."

"Oh, hi, Joanna."

"How you doin', girl?"

"Alright, just doing the dishes, listening to *Fever*."

"That's groovy. Hey, Cece, did you know that my brother Chuckie is home?"

"Yeah, that's what I heard. How's he doing?"

"OK. He wanted me to ask you if you'd cruise with us today."

"Er, I don't think so .... I have a lot of stuff to do, for my mother, you know, clean up my room and vacuum and stuff like that."

"Ah, come on. Please, Chuckie really wanted to see you before he goes to Texas."

"Texas?"

"Yeah," she said, "he might have to go and live with my brother Henry to work or something."

"Well, OK, but I can only be out for a little while."

"Oh sure. We'll be by after four."

"OK."

I had first met Joanna when our clubs had a benefit together to raise money for our club jackets. She was the leader of Las Rienas from Pico Rivera. Our jackets were similar. Theirs were red and black with a gold crown on back and Las Rienas inscribed beneath it.

One evening after a sock hop Joanna asked me if I'd like to meet her brother Chuck. He had told her that he thought I was really groovy and wanted to go out with me, but he was too shy to ask me himself. I had seen him cruising the boulevard and hanging out on the corner by the Tastee Freeze with the other guys and he always acted aloof, almost cocky.

So I said, "If he thinks I'm groovy, why doesn't he ever talk to me or anything? I mean, he never even looks at me when I wave to him."

"Ah, you know how guys are, kinda shy, when they don't know you."

"Yeah, I guess."

Chuck was short and I liked short guys. For one thing they were easy to dance with because you didn't have to strain your neck reaching up to them.

He turned out to be a nice guy after all. For one thing he never tried to feel me up like some of the other guys. He had slanted, chestnut-brown eyes and honey colored skin, smooth as a girl's. Besides his being short, I liked to dance with him because his skin was cool and dry. Consequently my hair never got wet and sticky where he pressed his head against it.

Most of the time we met at record shops or at the show and held hands and made out. He could really french. He never jammed his tongue down my throat or barely stuck it in so that I couldn't tell if it was in or not. At the show we often sat through a double feature making out, except during the intermission when we'd hold hands. I liked holding hands with him. His hands were thick and square and reminded me of my grandfather's hands. However, where grandfather Avevez' were rough and callous, Chuck's were soft and smooth.

The year that we met he was sixteen and I was fifteen. Neither one of us had a car so that was kind of a drag, but we had such a good time together I didn't mind too much. After we'd gone out a couple of times he gave me his ring and I wore it on a chain around my neck. Since we went to different high schools, I only wore it when we were together. I knew that he went out with other chicks which was alright as long as he didn't tell me about it or I never saw him doing it.

Things went smoothly between us for a few months until he asked me if it was OK if he took Gloria Escobar to a party that we both had been invited to. No way! I said. It wasn't that I was jealous, but I didn't want my friends to see him scamming on a chick I happened to think was cuter than I was. Besides I hated Gloria Escobar. She had big tits and a curvy ass. Later on she got fat and ended up married to Mousie Figueroa, the biggest Cholo around. They had a shotgun wedding when she was seven months pregnant. But at the time she was the sexiest chick in school. Whenever she walked by all the guys would whistle and groan, "*Ay, que buenota!*" and stuff like that.

The day of the party I put a Nestles Cherry Red rinse on my hair. It turned out shiny and soft but it streaked where I had peroxided it. Bright cherry strips bled through the darker parts. But, once it had dried it was too late to do anything about it. In a way I liked it. I ratted the top to a point and sculpted two large C's on my cheeks using clear nail polish to hold them down. Spraying it a few times seemed to help blend in the color. I used scotch tape to plaster my bangs down below my eyebrows to keep them straight. Then I selected a purple, A-line mini dress with a white stripe around the bell shaped arms and hemline and white fishnet pantyhose with matching white pumps. Hooking two large hoops into my pierced ears and draping my brown and white rabbit fur coat around my shoulders, I went into the bedroom and sat looking out the window in the dark waiting for Gerry. Around nine o'clock I saw the headlights to Marcos' car. I grabbed my white vinyl purse with the gold chain and headed out the door yelling, "I'll be back by midnight!"

My mother peered out the door as we took off yelling, "Cece, stop cracking your gum!"

Gerry looked bitchin', as usual. I felt deflated, thinking that no matter how hard I tried I'd never be as sexy and pretty as she was.

"Wow, you smell good. What is it?" I blurted out.

"Arpege," she said, pressing her wrist to my nose for a whiff. "It's my mother's. She let me use it."

"Ummm," I sighed, glancing at her cleavage and at the gentle slope of her profile. "Do you have any more of it?"

"Naw, my mother wouldn't let me bring it."

"Oh."

"But I have some gum, do you want some?" she said.

"No thanks, I already have some," I said, looking out the window.

We stopped at a 7-11 and Gerry went in to get cigarettes for Marcos.

"I like your socks," he said. "They're sort of weird, but they're so *you*."

"They're not socks, they're pantyhose," I said. "Anyone knows that. Anyone over twelve."

Marcos could be nerdy. Cute but nerdy.

"Do you think my hair looks alright?" I knew he'd tell me the truth.

"Looks OK--if you like two-tone pink," he laughed.

When we arrived at the party, I told Marcos, who was going to a basketball game, not to bother to pick us up because we'd probably get a ride home with Chuck Valdez.

"Is that your new boyfriend?" Marcos said sarcastically.

"None of your business." I said.

"Don't lock the door when you get home, Marcos," Gerry said.

We walked into the dark living room where people were standing around watching couples dance to Little Junior Walker:

> *I'm a road runner baby*
> *And I love the life I live*
> *And I live the life I love...*

When my eyes adjusted to the light I saw them. Their arms were wrapped around each other and he was nuzzling her neck. She was a whole head taller than him. I felt the blood rush to my face and a choking rage as I marched over and threw his ring at him. They stopped dancing, acted startled and stood stupidly staring at me.

"Oh, wow," Gloria smirked.

Chuck stooped over slowly and coolly picked it up. He never said a word, just shook his head back and forth.

"Don't ever speak to me as long as I live, Chuck Valdez! *Cabron!*" I spat.

Someone was tugging at my arm, pulling me away, out the door. It was Gerry. "Ga, girl, you didn't even dig him that much, did you?"

"It doesn't matter," I said. "Why did he bring her here? He knows I hate her!"

"So what," she said as we walked down the street. "Everyone knows she's nothing but a *puta!*" We were headed down the road way away from the sounds of the party.

"Yeah," I sniffled, blowing my nose on a leaf I'd pulled off a tree. "I guess you're right."

"You OK?"

"Yeah, I guess so, but I'm not going back there," I snorted. The evening breeze soothed me. I inhaled a waft of night blooming jasmine and sighed, "What are we gonna do?"

"I don't know," she said. "Barbara D is having a party in Downey, maybe we could go there."

"Right, but how are we gonna get there?"

"Oh, someone will come by we can catch a ride with," she said. I linked my arm through hers. "Wow, Cece, did you see the look on her face when you threw the ring at him? You blew'em away, man!"

"Think so?" I smiled, feeling better.

"Yeah, honey, you really did."

I guffawed, then giggled, "Too much."

"Gawd, Gloria looked like a monster next to little Chuckie."

"You think so?" I squealed.

"Yeah," said Gerry, throwing back her head, encircling the air with her arms as if she were dancing with someone. She made a face mimicking Chuck.

"Stop it!" I roared.

Puffing her cheeks out, she bounced around the sidewalk like a puppet. I giggled, holding my crotch.

"I gotta pee."

"Go ahead, pee in your pants, *mensa!*" She was doubled over, laughing so hard spit dribbled out of her mouth.

"I'm going in the bushes." I headed over behind a hedge that was in front of someone's house. I had barely gotten my pantyhose down when she whispered, "Hurry, Cece, someone's coming."

As Gerry inched toward the sidewalk, I peed, then hurriedly pulled up my hose in time to see Donny Johnston's black '49 Ford.

"What's happening, *esa?*" he said to Gerry, straining his neck to see who was in the bushes.

"Nothin'," Gerry said.

As I sauntered out I felt the crotch of my pantyhose down by my knees. Little pleats hung down around my ankles.

"What chew doin' in the bushes, Con-suelo?" he asked.

"What d'you care?" I snickered. Little drops of pee dripped down my legs into my hose. I giggled in Gerry's ear, "I barely missed my shoe." She roared hysterically.

"Hey, man, those chicks are crazy," Donny said, flicking his cigarette out the window as the car started off.

"Hey, wait!" Gerry said. "Wanna go to a party?"

"Where?" he asked, sticking his head out the window. We were hysterical again.

"Psss, forget it," he mumbled.

"Let go of my arm," she whispered, "maybe we can get a ride with them."

"It's in Downey," she yelled.

"Yeah, so?"

"It's better than that," she said, indicating the house where the fiasco had taken place.

"Yeah?"

"Yeah," she said. "It's nowhere, no chicks except in couples." A lie but it worked. They pulled over and we climbed in. Both the guys were slumped low in the seat. We cruised very slowly down the street. The car was so low it almost scraped the pavement.

"Donny, lower the radio," Gerry said. Huggy Boy was on doing requests at the Mel's Drive In.

"What's up?" Donny glanced at her in the rear view mirror.

"Cece and I are gonna sing *Fever* for you."

"We are?"

"Yeah, come on. We've been practicing, huh, Cece?" she said as she passed me the brown paper bag with the bottle of gin. I swallowed.

"Yuk," I spluttered, spitting it out. "It tastes like medicine."

"Ready," said Gerry, snapping her fingers. "One, two, three!" This time we stayed together and right on cue. We went through the whole song twice. "You chicks can really wail," Donny drawled. We looked at each other, smiling.

The other guy didn't say anything. Gerry scooted up on the seat rapping him on the shoulder.

"Hey, what's your name?"

"This here is Spook," Donny said.

"What d'ja think, Spook?"

Maravilla

"All right man," he grunted. They both shook their heads with Donny adding, "Yeah, hey, Cece, you oughta be on stage." He paused, then said, "You, too, Ger!"

I smiled and cracked my gum. We cruised on in silence. I was still feeling weird about what had happened at the party. I was wishing I hadn't reacted. I should have pretended that I didn't care. Forget it, I said to myself.

I ran into Joanna about a month later and she told me that Chuck had gotten busted as he was coming home from a party when the cops had stopped and searched him. They found a joint in his back pocket. He was going to have to spend six months at boys' reform school. He wrote to me a couple of times. I answered him but didn't hear from him after that until the day Joanna called.

I was watching from the living room window as Beto's green, lowered Chevy pulled up. I ran out of the house and slid into the back seat next to Chuck. I was wearing a short, dark blue mini skirt, a powder blue orlon sweater, and white boots. My white vinyl purse with the gold chain dangled from my wrist. Chuck Berry was on the radio wailing:

> *Nadine, honey is that you?*
> *Oh, Nadine, honey is that you?*
> *Seems like every time I see you*
> *You're up to somethin new*

"Hi," Chuck said. His voice sounded shy and cocky at the same time. He was cuter than ever. I slid over to the opposite end of the seat. He glanced at my knees. I tugged at my hemline.

Beto reached back, handing me a beer.

"*Quieres?*"

"Sure," I said, reaching for it with my hand shaking, hoping he wouldn't notice. We were cruising slowly through the Barrio. A picture of Chuck and me making out flashed through my mind. I glanced at him, then quickly looked away. He reached across the seat for my hand. His palm felt dry and cool. He picked up a bottle of beer that was between his legs and sipped. I sipped mine. He smiled. I smiled back.

Joanna looked back at us as he was taking a drink.

"Chuckie, you shouldn't be drinking," she said. "We're not supposed to have booze. If you get caught, Chuck, you gonna have to go back to that awful place."

"Oh, wow, man, lay off. Nothin's gonna happen, I swear, baby, don't worry so much," Beto said, massaging the back of her neck. "Man, Joanna, you worry all the time, stop worrying so much."

"No I don't, Beto. I'm telling you it's too risky for us to have booze in the car, especially with Chuck."

Chuck brushed it off. "Will you cool it, sis?"

We were driving past the ticky-tack stucco houses lined with the scraggly, barren trees and stunted shrubs in front of faded brown lawns. Everything seemed dry and parched in the bleak atmosphere. Beto slowed down to a crawl. An old, black mongrel was sprawled like a dish rag in the middle of the road. Beto hit the brakes. "*Pinchi perro!* Look at that stupid dawg man! Move it, *cabron!*" he shrilled.

The animal languidly pulled himself up by his scrawny back legs and limped away, scattering flies.

"Did you see that?" Beto chortled.

"Yah, what a dumb dog," Joanna said. "Pobrecito."

"Hey, man," Chuck said, "that's Red's dog."

"Hah, no wonder *ese*, he's so stupid he's jest like Red," said Beto, glancing at Chuck in the rear view mirror.

I looked at Chuck expecting him to respond. He was staring out the window. It wasn't as if he were looking at anything in particular. His eyes were veiled and there was something strange and forlorn about him. I wondered if he had heard Beto at all.

Joanna looked back at Chuck and then turned to Beto.

"So what's wrong with Red?" she asked.

"Hey, man, you know what's wrong with him," Beto barked.

"What?" she said insolently.

"He's queer, man!"

"So what, Beto, I suppose you think you're so perfect."

There was an awkward silence. They seemed to be trying to get a reaction from Chuck more than anything, as Beto kept glancing back in the mirror. Joanna nervously looked around to see if Chuck was listening.

61

"Yeah, man, at least you don't see me actin' like a chick!" He wagged his hand foppishly in the air. "Oww, Joannie and Ceeece, how are you girrrls," he said in falsetto.

"Oh, so what, Beto!" Joanna said, "I like him, I think he's a nice guy." She was looking back at me for what I thought was an agreement, trying to get me in the conversation.

"I like him, too," I said. "He's sweet."

"Yeah, ha ha, *esa*, he looks jes like a fairy dancing. All he needs is wings, man." With that he wildly guffawed. Joanna smirked and I laughed.

Chuck didn't say anything. He hardly moved.

"Oh, shut up, Beto!" Joanna barked. I could see Beto's inscrutable eyes in the rear view mirror looking out through hooded lids. There was something Oriental, almost Mongolian about him. He shook his greasy head back and forth, staring at Joanna as if he could not fathom her. There seemed to be some unbreachable gap between all of us. I felt depressed and lonely. I started thinking of all the things I still had to do at home.

"Hey, Beto," I said, "why don't you take me home."

"*Vez que hisistes!*" Joanna pouted, glaring at Beto. "Now she wants to go home."

"Oh, wow, Cece, don't go yet, we just got started," said Chuck, finally coming out of his reverie.

"I don't know, I told my mother I'd be right back."

"Hey, man," Beto drawled, "it hasn't been that long."

"If she goes, I'm going too," Joanna said.

"Come on, Cece, you're not serious, are you?" Beto said. "Hey, we're jes having a little fun, man." He gave a quasi chuckle. "Don't be so serious. Hey, *esa*, why don't you smile or somethin'?"

Chuck sipped his beer and smiled at me, squeezing my hand. There were some dirty, barefoot kids in a tiny yard, surrounded by a chain link fence. I glanced up at the drooping angle of the roof on the small, wood-framed house and the broken plastic toys scattered in disarray. In front an old, rusted Chevy coupe stripped of its tires, sat on its bent rims. Everything was covered with a thin film of dust.

"I got it!" Beto said, snapping his fingers. "Let's cruise Montebello Park. There's a carnival happening there."

"What d'you say, Cece?" Joanna asked.

"Ah, I guess so, for a while." I was thinking that Beto would be OK if he wasn't so dumb and thick skinned. He wasn't at all like Chuck. Not like Chuckie at all.

Beto slid down in his seat. Joanna moved closer, slipping her arm around his neck. I slid over next to Chuck. But still I couldn't seem to shake the strange feeling of despair and loneliness.

We had barely gotten to the outskirts of the barrio when Beto glanced in the rear view mirror. "Oh-oh, it's the *ley.*"

Turning back I saw the flashing light.

"Oh, no," I groaned, pushing the bottle as far back as I could under the seat.

Joanna said, "Quick, Chuck, hand me your bottle." He ignored her, shoving it back. We pulled over to the side of the road.

"OK, you guys, be cool, they might not do nothin'," Beto said. We sat there waiting for the cop. He sauntered over, thrusting his big, red face up the window. His mouth was a straight, white line.

"Can I see your operator's license?" His aviator sunglasses glinted. He was blank and alien as the Moon.

Beto grunted, "What we doin' wrong, man?" and passed him his license.

"Not observing the speed limit. Going way too slow," he said impassively. Beto sighed, tapping the steering wheel, looked around at us and said, "Hey, man, I didn't see no other cars, did you?"

"No," Joanna said. A stifling tension hung in the air. Another cop came over, small, slender and young. Wiry, black hairs stuck out from the neck of his T-shirt. He was wearing aviator sunglasses too. They exchanged words and the big one said, "We have a report on a stolen car, seems to match this description."

The young cop went back to the squad car. Across the street I could see some kids playing. Cars rolled by slowly. I could hear a radio blaring, felt hostile, curious onlookers sizing up the scene.

"Where you people going?" the cop asked.

"Jest cruisin', you know, taking my chick for a ride," said Beto.

The other one came back. They talked, and the big one said, "We're going to have to ask you to get out so we can search you."

"Psss," Beto snorted. "Oh, wow, hey, man," he said, looking up at him. "You think I'd take my chick cruising in a stolen car? D'jou ever see another *caroucha* like this one man?" he said, looking back at Chuck. Chuck shook his head. Turning slowly, Beto addressed the cop.

"You sure it's bright green with one black fender in front?"

Chuck was sitting very still with both hands on his knees.

"That guy must think we're stupid," Beto chortled to Joanna.

"Come on, get out," ordered the cop.

You couldn't see his eyes, just the reflection of light on his glasses. He seemed to be looking at the dashboard, avoiding our eyes. Maybe he thinks there's a stash in there, I thought. My mind was racing for something to focus on. Anything other than what was happening. I was trying to think of something funny to say to break the mounting tension and fear. But, it was hopeless. I felt as if we were riding the crest of a powerful wave. To go against it was impossible.

We filed out. The sun hung in the sky, vague and obscure behind the smog. The light was a dull, flat grey. He pressed the guys against the car and frisked them. The small one was going through the car. He came around the front holding the two bottles of beer. With his legs planted firmly apart, no expression on his face, he grunted, "Look at this."

I felt a sinking sensation. I stared at his gun. I was thinking about how it would feel to wear a gun on my hip. I tried to stop but I couldn't seem to look away. I could feel it in my hand heavy and cold. I pulled the trigger and it blasted. Somewhere in my head something exploded.

The small one took the bottles over to the squad car and then continued his search. He came back holding a tiny, ancient-looking roach which had been honed down to the nub with the tips of his fingers. His hands were thin, a pale, whitish yellow, his fingernails immaculate.

"Found this on the floor of the back seat," he said tersely.

"Oh, wow, that joint's probably been there for months. We didn't have anything to do with it. My brother is just visiting us. He had nothing to do with it. Why don't you let us go?" Joanna pleaded.

"Yeah, man, tha's true, they didn't have nothin' to do with it. I swear. That's my fault. They din't have nothin' to do with that stuff," Beto croaked. They conferred, ignoring us.

Garbled messages were coming through on the radio of the squad car. Numbers, codes, bleeps. Cars cruised slowly by. A fat lady waddled down the street carrying grocery bags, a couple of kids were skipping behind her. The air felt hot and muggy. Another squad car pulled up and two more cops came over. They asked what was going on. All the time Chuck hadn't said a word. He stood by the car with his hands sunk in his pockets, his neck pushed back stiffly, chin thrust out.

The big cop turned to us. "OK, we're gonna have to take you in," he said.

I glanced at Chuck. His face was a mask.

We were being corralled towards the squad car.

"What's gonna happen to my short?" Beto asked sullenly.

"Your vehicle will be impounded. You can pick it up when you get out, after it's been searched, or you can have someone pick it up for you."

"Oh, shit!" Joanna spat.

"*Chingaau!*" Beto snorted, hesitating, pulling away. The rookie shoved him against the car door by his shirt.

"Come on, move it, Mexican!" His hand rested on the butt of his .45. As we straggled towards the cop car, out of the corner of my eye I saw something moving. It was Chuck starting off in the opposite direction. I was thinking, no, that can't be true. I wanted to look away but something kept me riveted to his moving body. Our attention shifted towards him.

"Hey, come back!" barked the rookie who was closest to him.

He broke into a sprint. Joanna gasped. He was heading for someone's back yard. I figured he'd jump the fence and hide in the alley till dark. My heart was pounding. I felt exhilarated and terrified watching him bolting away.

"Stop or I'll shoot!" the rookie shouted. I turned to look at him, thinking he was bluffing. But he wasn't. He was aiming his .45. I could see his jaw twitching violently.

Then I heard the blast.

The air exploded, turning dark grey. Black spots swarmed in the graininess of it. Chuck was still running. I couldn't tell if he had been hit or not. There was another shot and he slowed down, staggering before he hit the ground. The tension split into jagged fragments ricocheting insanely. I felt a hot surge shoot through me. My mind clamped shut incomprehensibly. Frozen with shock, no one moved. I was hardly breathing. I was standing next to the big cop and I smelled the animal fear mingling with the heavy, sulphurous odor of the grainy air. Blood was seeping out of Chuck's back. He was groaning and writhing. Joanna lurched wildly towards him, thrusting herself at the rookie who was bent over the body. The other cop had gone over to the radio. Joanna was screaming, "You shot my brother, you shot my brother!" Beto's face had turned a dark purple, his eyes were black fire. He whispered repeatedly, "Did you see what he did?" as if he were in a trance. A crowd began to gather around us. People with strained, bewildered faces shook their heads and murmured softly as they stared in disbelief at Chuck's body, that was now laying in a pool of bright blood.

An angry rumble shot through the crowd, distilling waves of fearful rage and hostility. One after another, cop cars screeched up to the scene with more coming every minute, their shrill sirens and flashing red and yellow lights and the noisy static from radios. The last of them came wearing tact helmets, armed with rifles, hand guns, and tear gas. Someone threw a bottle and it splintered against a cop car, cracking the window. Rocks began to fall on the squad cars. I could see children's heads bobbing up and down trying to get a glimpse of what was going on. A voice blasted through a megaphone warning the crowd to disperse with threats of tear gas. Some kid squirted a water gun at me, splashing my arm. I hadn't moved. I was standing rooted to the same spot. Beto was squatted down next to Chuck, whose face had turned a sickly yellow. Joanna frantically begged for someone to get help.

That was the first time I remember looking at myself from somewhere else. It was strange because before that I had thought of myself as rather large and big boned. But now I could plainly see that I was only a miniature of what I thought I was. I looked stupid and pathetic, shrunken and insignificant. I felt a horrible flush of embarrassment. I didn't know what I was supposed to be doing. I stood there like a fool, stupidly twisting the chain on my purse hoping that no one would notice me. I was trying not to look at Chuck's body. I knew he was in bad shape and somehow I felt responsible.

Squad cars backed away as the ambulance arrived. Two men carried a cot over to where he was laying. As they lifted his body off the asphalt, Joanna clutched his arm crying, "You're gonna be OK, Chuckie, you're gonna be OK." There was a trail of blood as they carried him past the cars to the ambulance. All I could see of him was his forehead and curly brown hair sticking out from beneath the grey blanket. Joanna staggered behind, wiping the blood from her hands onto her white and pink plaid skirt. Most of the cars had taken off, and the onlookers had wandered off except for a few men who had clustered around Beto and Joanna. One of them held Joanna to keep her form flailing out. I could hear another one as if from a long way away saying, "Man, he's pretty bad, I don't think he's gonna make it." Beto was crying like a baby, sobbing, "It's my fault, I don't know why he did it, I swear, I don't know why he did it."

I was still standing in the same spot when the ambulance door slammed shut and took off down the street with the siren screaming and the red light spinning, holding that stupid little purse in my hands, watching as it turned the corner and disappear.

Chuck died at the county hospital the following night. He was buried on a smoggy Saturday afternoon during a heat wave.

I attended the funeral with Marcos and Gerry. Chuck's friends from school and the neighborhood gathered around his shocked and grieving family at the cemetary. Beto wasn't there. He was in jail. Joanna, her face a mask of grief and rage, was silent and immobile. A garish, flat light locked into a stifling dense gray skyline surrounded us in a monotonous palpable dread.

Three weeks later, I came home from school feeling hot and dizzy, climbed into bed, and stayed there for the rest of the day.

That evening my Mother took my temperature. "It's a hundred and four. I better call the doctor," she said.

Chapter 7

La Llorona wanders on the banks of the brown river. Her hair wild and knotted, is tangled with spiders and burrs. She whines a low, wailing moan, mourning the hundred of babies she has cast into the raging waters. The wind whips across the river, bending trees to the ground. It is pitch black.

I move carefully through dark caves around jagged cliffs. Below me the ocean rages, white caps crash against rocks.

The cloven-hoofed men gather around a fire. Flames lap up and dance on the black hills, illuminating the night.

Angels with long, white hair float by. Behind them Saints Peter and Paul, the Virgin Mary, and the devil are chanting, "Do-re-mi-fa-so-la-ti-do.

Gliding through clouds, cherubs fly by, shooting red and black arrows into the purple liquid sky.

God the Father speaks in flaming tongues, making crazy sounds.

"Cece, Cece!" Someone is calling me from far away. It is my mother. She hands me a long brass sword with a jeweled handle. I try lifting it but it is too heavy. Liquid warmth seeps across my lap and down my legs.

The cloven-hoofed beast man licks my face, hands and feet. He hands me a cape of bright colors. I drape it around, hugging it to me, moving through yellow and black smoke. It is very peaceful here. I sink down into a cavern of darkness.

"Cece, Cece!" The fools! Why do they call me that? My name is Corona--Little Corona queen of the night. I wear the six colors of rainbowland--yellow, blue, red, orchid, ochre, and gold.

69

Maravilla

We walk through the forest, Nedley the beast-man and I. My hair is raven. My nails painted bright green, my body glowing, silver speckled.

In the forest the trees are tall, wide as a barn. They have arms and legs and wave to me. I understand them. A small patch of blue sky peeks out above their black branches like the jagged spokes of a wheel. Turning, turning, turning. Down here it is dark and moist. Moss grows on the rocks and stumps and gnarled, gray roots.

"Oops!" I trip and fall over the roots. They are so, so big, big as boulders and rippley as a desert dune.

I am falling into the water! Help, help! I am drowning in the filthy river. I am suffocating! I see a dim light through the din of the raging water. It is a shrill flourescent color. It glows like little wax statues at Knotts Berry Farm. I am part of the blue light. It is cool, then cold, ice cold. I am freezing, trembling! Then stone still, rigid. I am warm, warmer, then hot! I arch my body over the gnarled roots grappling at the veins and sinewy muscles of the trees. I am soaking wet. Baptized by fire water. It pours down my ice-hot body, stinging and burning my skin and bones. The light grows whiter, turning violet.

Something is wet and cool on my forehead. A liquid, green and blue. Cool as night.

Dinosaurs, boats, giraffes and Chevies float by. Beto, Joanna, Chuckie in a red plaid bathrobe, my dead Tia Felicia, Viejo Cabezon, Uncle Ray, St. Teresa. They wave to me, calling me to them.

Large, white cranes fly overhead, their gigantic wing span darkening the sky like black feather clouds.

I am falling, falling, falling.

This desert is cold and flat. The sky is midnight blue. It glows like a black diamond spinning on its axis.

Someone is ripping my legs and arms apart.

I watch outside of myself, laughing and laughing at my chopped up pieces. I like to watch myself writhe and thrash. It is so stupid and dumb.

My father's head floats by like a pink neon sign in a long, white bed.

I wake up dry as a desert stone, a dead coyote in a long white bed. Over my head majorettes in red and blue striped

70

Maravilla

tights, white boots, twirling batons and cheerleaders in bloomers, shaking red and pink pompoms, and a band with horns blasting, drums beating, cymbals clashing, all march out the window into the dull, gray light.

Something wet and cool is in my mouth, red raspberry jello, vanilla pudding, chocolate ice cream.

There is a woman in white standing over me. It is St. Teresa!

"Wake up, wake up! she shouts.

"No, no, no."

"Levantate," she screams.

"I can't--no puedo."

"You must--you must--you must!" Her screams crash into my head and fill up my burning body.

I awoke to an eerie silence, soaking wet and shivering. I heard someone moaning and groaning in the next bed. Someone else was gasping desperately, gagging, taking long shallow breaths, whispering prayers. A dim light shone in from the doorway. Footsteps, hushed voices, ringing phones, muffled laughter drifted in. Where was I? I wondered. My mind was in a thick fog. I felt as if I were climbing out of a deep hole. I couldn't even remember my name! My ears were ringing. I felt panicky. I threw off the covers and got up. The night was hot and muggy. A stale, medicinal odor hung in the air. I groped for the glass of water on the night stand and gulped it down.

That's when I noticed a strange light coming in from the window. I went over and glanced out at the deserted parking lot. Beyond the cars I saw a muted, greenish light, moving in from out of the shadows. It seemed to be heading straight for the window where I was standing. All of the sudden I felt dizzy and nauseous and crawled back in bed. But as soon as I got under the covers I felt elated, wonderful, happy as could be! Tiny electrical jolts ran up my spine. I almost laughed out loud. When I closed my eyes I felt like I was spinning on a merry-go-round! Then it came back to me. I remembered. Chuck running, falling, lying in a pool of black blood! The screaming sirens. Joanna's face contorted with grief.

71

Wild images--Jesus pointing to his pulsing, red heart, St. Francis in the middle of the freeway during rush hour, scattering seeds to cars that transformed into white doves, deer, rabbits, chirping and yapping, all converged in my head like a movie reel. All at once everything began moving faster and faster, eclipsing, mushrooming into distortion. My elation turned to terror. An intense surge of grief and pain welled up into my chest. I felt like I was suffocating. I started to cry. *God help me please!* I sobbed. I was terrified that someone would hear me and think I was crazy. *I was crazy!* I knew it! I was shaking, trembling uncontrollably. Then I heard this funny noise, like something rustling or jingling. At first I thought it was the person in the next bed. But when I opened my eyes I saw a pale, yellow light by the window.

She was standing there in mid-air. My violent trembling stopped, and I sat up to get a better look, wondering if I were imagining it. But no, I could see very clearly that she was real. It was St. Teresa. She came closer and I felt as if I could almost reach out and touch her. She was wearing a tattered, threadbare habit. There were places around her head where the cloth had worn so thin you could see where it had been mended. I never realized how small she was, short and stocky. Wispy strands of salt and pepper hair crept out around her temples and forehead. A large, wooden rosary hung from her wrist, jingling softly. (That must have been the noise I had first heard.) She was barefoot, and her hemline like her habit was ragged and mended.

I sat there watching her, stunned, unable to move or speak. She was clutching something to her breast. When I looked closer I saw that it was a rag doll in a woolen habit with a delicate ceramic face and painted rosebud lips, grasping a miniature gold crucifix. Its tiny saffire eyes glowed in the dark. It struck me as strange that they were dressed alike, except that the doll's clothes were in better condition. I had always thought that saints wore long silk dresses or satin robes, being in heaven and everything, not worn-out, torn rags.

All of a sudden the light surrounding her began to grow more intense, glowing like a neon sign, vibrating a gold speckled flourescent green. I saw her face clearly. And there was nothing sad, pious, or sanctimonious about her. She held her head high, and looked powerful without being proud. Strong, but open, vulnerable. The pulsing, beaming light spread out, expanding above and over me until it had flooded the entire space around my bed and I was surrounded, engulfed with the incredible feeling of blissful love and harmony. I was exhilarated and terrifed at the same time, and I found myself smiling stupidly.

She raised her bracelet, but now I could see that it was a tambourine, over her head and shook it, rattling it gently, turning round in a circle. As she turned slowly round and round, the rhythmic jingle of the tambourine mesmerized and relaxed me.

Then, as suddenly as she had begun, she stopped and gazed directly into my eyes. I felt instantly electrified, alive! And at that moment everything became clear, calm, sharply focused, intensely vibrant. A cool, fresh breeze wafted through the room. The air was soothing, almost fragrant. The loud groaning which had been coming from the next bed was now only a light snore. And the woman on the other side of me had stopped gasping for breath.

"*Oye*, are you alright?" she whispered.

"Yes. I'm fine."

"I heard you crying earlier."

"I'm OK, now." I said, "I feel better."

"My name is Bertha. What's yours?"

"Cece," I said. "Cece Contreres."

The next morning I woke up to the buzz of the T.V. There was a woman in white standing over me.

"Drink this," she said. "I'm glad to see you're awake. You've been out for a few days."

I sipped something cool, glancing around the room. The bed next to mine was empty. Then I noticed my old picture of St. Teresa on the table next to my bed.

"You're mother brought that," said the nurse. "You better wash your face and brush your teeth before your parents get here. They should be here any minute." She handed me a damp wash cloth.

"What's wrong with me?"

"You have the Asian flu. There's an epidemic going around. You're better now. You'll be OK."

She came back with a breakfast tray. And I picked at the food until someone took it away.

My father was bending over when I woke up.

"How are you, honey?" He kissed my forehead.

My mother was arranging some pink and red carnations in a water glass.

"Thank God, you're awake Cece. We've been so worried."

Maria was holding some books. "I brought these for you," she said placing them on the table.

"Thanks," I whispered.

"Do you remember coming here?" my mother asked.

"We can talk about that later, *vieja*," my father said cutting her off. "Just rest and get well, *mija*, so you can come home."

"If your temperature stays normal today, you can come home tomorrow," my mother said.

Maria read me a clipping from the school paper about my being sick and how everyone hoped I'd get better.

"Last night the whole family prayed a novena for you, Cece. Look at her," she said to my father. "She looks better, doesn't she? I told you the novena would help."

The nurse came in with a handful of pills.

I must have fallen asleep because the next thing I remembered was the nurse waking me up to take more pills.

"Try to stay awake for awhile so you can sleep tonight. Do you wanna watch T.V.?"

"Ok."

Bonanza was on and I settled into my pillow and watched it.

Back at school Gerry linked her arm through mine as we walked by a group of students.

"I feel like everyone is staring at me," I said.

"Don't pay any attention to them."

That afternoon I went home after lunch and told my mother that I felt hot and weak and wasn't going back to school. I stayed in bed for a week, getting up only to eat and go to the bathroom. I returned to school the following Monday for three days, then stayed home for the rest of the week.

Sunday evening my mother came into the bedroom when I was lying under the covers reading and said, "You have got to go back to school tomorrow. You can't stay home for the rest of your life."

I went back for the week, but came down with a cold and sore throat on Friday and stayed home for another week.

When I went back to school the following Monday, I was sent to see Mrs. Tate, the girl's counselor. She asked me a lot of questions like what was bothering me, was I getting along with the family, what were my brothers and sister like.

When I told her that I didn't feel good and wanted to be excused, she insisted that I come back to see her the following day.

"*Esa gringa entrusa!*" my mother said, when I told her what had happened. "*No le digas nada.* It's none of her goddamn business. What does she know about us anyway? She's never been in a Chicano household in her life! What the hell does she think she's doing!"

"Calm down, *vieja*," my father said.

"Don't tell me to calm down!" my mother said. "They tried to get me to talk to someone when I was in school too. You wanna know why? Because I was talking Spanish and they wanted me to stop!"

"That was the Dark Ages, mother," Maria said. "Besides, Cece can barely say yes and no in Spanish."

"That's not true, Maria! I know *La Cucaracha*."

"Listen, Cece, I'm coming to school with you tomorrow, so we can talk to that Mrs. *Tate*," my mother said.

"Oh, goodie," Maria sang, "Mother's going to terrorize Mrs. Tate. I can hardly wait."

"*Ay, Dios, mira no mas.* I'm not going to do anything of the kind. I just want to talk to her. I don't think there's anything wrong with Cece."

"I don't either," Maria said. "She just wants to quit school. I would too if everyone stared at me and then they sent me to the school shrink."

"See what I mean?" I said to my father, who was grumbling and shaking his head.

75

The next day my mother and I sat in the office of Mr. Roger, the principal.

"Let me tell you something, Mr. Rutgers," my mother said, as soon as he had come in and seated himself.

"Yes, Mrs. Conterros."

"I don't want you sending my daughter to see this Mrs. Tape. Do you understand? She has no right prying into our affairs."

"Mrs. Tate thought it might help Consuelo to talk about some of her, ah, problems."

"So what's wrong with Consuelo?" My mother fixed her glare on him. Not bothering to wait for an answer, she went on. "Nothing." She pronounced it naw-thene. "She had the Asian flu. Some people have even died from it. Or didn't you know that, Mr.Rutgers? Maybe you don't read the newspaper?"

"Yes, I am aware of that, Mrs. Conterros." You could see that he was getting up tight.

"Ok, then, Mr. Rutgers, you agree that there is nothing wrong with my daughter except that she is getting over the flu?"

"That's true, Mrs.----"

"Yes, it *is* true, Mr. Rutgers. And another thing that is true is that Consuelo does not have to see or talk to Mrs. Tape."

"Mrs. *Tate*, Mrs. Conterros, her name is Mrs. Tate."

My mother ignored him. "One more thing, Mr. Ruggers. I want Consuelo excused from P.E. until she is ready to go back."

"I don't know about that. I'll have to talk to Mrs. Miller, the girl's gym teacher, first."

"No, no, no, Mr. Rutgers, you don't understand. My daughter isn't feeling well enough to attend P.E. When she feels she is up to it, then she will attend."

"She'll have to have a written excuse from your doctor then."

"OK, I will get a written excuse from the doctor. And then I will go to the school board and present it to them along with my complaint about you not wanting to cooperate with me and my daughter, who has just endured a terrible, almost fatal illness. And that you, Mr.Ruggers, insisted that she go to her P.E. and get in the cold pool and, that's not all, that you sent her without my consent to see Mrs. Tape!"

"If that's what you choose, Mrs. Conterros."

"And another thing, Mr. Rutgers, I will call the L.A. Times and tell them the whole story."

He stared at her for a minute and said, "All right, all right," waving his hands impatiently, "I'll have Mrs. Toomey write up an excuse exempting Consuelo from P.E. and she will not be asked to see Mrs. Tape, I mean Mrs. Tate. Good afternoon, Mrs. Conterros," he said rising.

"*Buenos dias*," my mother said.

"If you have any further problems that you would like to discuss with me, please feel free to call, Mrs. Conterros," he said patronizingly.

"I certainly will, Mr.Rutgers."

"*Ay, que vivo*", my mother said, on the way home, "*viejo simplon!* He thinks he's so smart the way he sat there like a big cheese. It looked like his wife cut his hair with a pair of gardening clippers. The fool! Did you see that, Cece? The way his hair stuck up like a stupid, little picket fence. If there's one thing that looks ridiculous, it is a big, fat man with an oily crew cut. Did you see that? His head was way too little for his big, fat body. Don't you think so, Cece?"

"Now that you mention it, mother." I giggled.

"And that cheap blue suit, *ayuda me, Dios!*"

That evening Maria and I collapsed in waves of raucous laughter when I told her what had happened at school.

The next day I went back to school and, instead of going to the gym, I went to the library and sat in the darkest corner, pulling out my tattered paperback copy of *Lady Chatterley's Lover* from the secret hiding place in my purse, and began to read.

Chapter 8

"Gerry let's make an agreement," I said as we cruised Whittier Boulevard in my father's station wagon.

"What kind of agreement?"

"Let's agree that you won't go steady or fall in love with anyone until I do."

"Steady? With who?"

"Oh, I don't know, anyone."

"Yeah--alright, I guess."

"Ok, I'll write it up, like a contract, and we'll sign it."

"Girl, you think of the wierdest things. Why do you want to do that?"

"I don't know--I guess so we'll take it seriously."

"Alright. Pass me your prong, I wanna do my hair. Did you bring your hair spray?"

"It's in my purse." I said, watching her pick out her ratted hair and spray it. I felt depressed at the thought of possibly losing her someday.

"Wanna get some beer?" I asked.

"Ok, but who's gonna get it for us?"

"Let's find some older dude to buy it."

"Why don't you drive around?" she said.

I drove through the parking lot of the 7-11 until I spotted someone. Gerry jumped out of the car and went over to a guy. She came back saying, "I gave him three dollars."

"What did you tell him to get?"

"Slo gin."

"I hate slo gin! You shoulda asked for beer."

"And I've told you a thousand times I hate beer!"

"Yeah, but you know slo gin makes me sick."

"That's cause you drink it too fast. You should take your time."

The guy was back. He thrust his head in the window, handing the bottle to Gerry.

"Where you chicks going?" He leered at her, eyeing her cleavage, reeking of stale booze.

"We're not looking for company, man." She said, brushing him off.

He staggered forward, pawing her shoulder.

"Hey, man, watch out!" She flung his hand away.

"Whatsamatta, you bitches think you're too good for me?"

"That's right." Gerry said.

He lurched forward clumsily, his red-rimmed, bloodshot eyes flashing with bleary anger, and grabbed a hank of her hair.

"Hey, let go of her!" I yelled

Gerry squirmed away. He yanked her head around viciously.

Furiously, I gunned the engine and the car jolted forward. Gerry lifted her arm and swung with all her might, grazing his nose. He fell back, clinging to the window, holding onto the door. I grabbed my bag full of school books by the strap and flung it in his face. It struck the side of his head with a thud. He grimaced, rearing backwards in a drunken motion, losing control. I shifted into second and we tore off through the parking lot.

"Putas!" he yelled.

"*Hijo--le!*" Gerry cried, cradling her arms. "What a *loco!*"

"Are you OK?"

"I'm alright. He didn't hurt me. He was just an old wino *loco,*" she said, opening the bottle of gin and taking a long slug.

As we cruised slowly down the boulevard I glanced into the rear view mirror.

"Don't look now but it's Manuel the Mouse sliding up behind us. I think he's with ... He *is*, Gerry!"

Gerry turned around.

"Don't look, dummy! He'll see you. Duck down!"

She slid off the seat, crouching under the dashboard.

"Is he gone?"

"Yeah. Looks like he had another date lined up. Boy, that guy works fast."

"Who was he with?"

"Carmen. At least I think it was her. She was wearing rhinestone glasses."

"Shit!"

"What ja tell him, that you were sick or what?"

"No--I told him my parents wouldn't let me out. I said to call me next week."

"You're kidding."

"I know,I know, he's wierd. But he's the only guy that's asked me out in a month."

"So?"

"Sew your socks. It's none of your business."

"Hey," I said, glancing in the mirror, "there's Angel Green Corvette."

"Where?"

"Behind us."

"Let him catch up to us. I wanna talk to him." Gerry said.

Angel pulled up beside us in his candy apple green Corvette, gunning his engine. Gerry rolled down her window, smiling coyly, coming on to him.

"Wanna drag?" he said, oozing charm.

"Wanna drink?" she mouthed, holding up the bottle of gin.

"No." He lifted a bottle in a brown bag. "Seagrams," he boasted.

We came to a stop signal, revving our engines, side by side. Then he tore off, tires sqealing, laying rubber.

"Oh, wow, how boss!" Gerry shrieked.

"Alright!" I screamed, bearing down on the gas pedal.

"Catch up to him, Cece!"

I sped forward trying to catch sight of him. The city was just coming to life in the razzle dazzle of the evening with neon lights flashing, people bustling up and down the sidewalks, honking horns, cruisers, low-riders showing off their metallic, cherried out paint jobs and rocking front ends, blasting their pipes. There was a tension building, an anticipation of something. A kind of elation. A promise of something wildly exciting yet to come. You could feel it in the air.

Gerry opened the glove compartment, pulling out a film container. She took out a reefer and lit it. We came to another stop. Sounds of a low wailing *ranchera* drifted out from the Boom Boom Club. Angel pulled up next to us.

"You chicks wanna go to a party?"

"Where?"

"Montebello."

"OK."

"Follow me," he said.

I kept my eye on his tail lights heading for the freeway. When we got there people were hanging out and dancing in a backyard patio. Chinese paper lanterns hung from a trellised roof covered with climbing ivy under a charcoal gray sky. Richie Valens was on the hi-fi. *"Para bailar la bamba se nesecita una poca de gracia."* I checked out the crowd and recognized some guy from Pico Rivera. He came over and asked me to dance. Afterwards he brought me a wine cooler. I chugged it down, watching Gerry and Angel do the Twist. Seeing them together made me feel uneasy. I danced with this guy a few more times, making small talk. I could see Angel and Gerry in a dark corner, rocking to a slow number. When it was over I pulled her away.

"It's getting late, we better leave soon." I was feeling woozy, beginning to slur words.

"One more dance," she said, smiling at Angel. She was flirting outrageously. I hated to see her do that. They stared into each other's eyes, swaying to a slow, sensual rhythm. I had another wine cooler, then teetered over to the car to wait for her.

"You better drive," I said when she came out. I was feeling dizzy and nauseous.

"I hope I see him again," she sang, sliding into the driver's seat. "He's soo groovy."

"I feel sick," I mumbled.

"Are you gonna be OK?" She said, starting the car.

"Yuk! I shouldn't have chugged the gin."

After we had gone a few blocks I said, "Pull over! Hurry!" She stopped just in time for me to get out and throw up on the curb.

"Oh ahh, shit," I muttered, weaving back and forth on the sidewalk.

"Come on, let's get out of here." Gerry yelled.

We pulled into a gas station. I felt worse, wretchedly sick under the garish glare of the flourescent lights. Just as we were driving in some jocks pulled up next to us. One of them yelled, "Hey, where you broads going? Wanna come with us?"

I stuck my head out the window, letting out a torrent of vomit, splashing down the side of the car. They backed up, hooting and jeering, and took off.

I was too tweaked to care. Gerry helped me out of the car, cracking up.

"Did you see the look on that jock's face? Ha, ha! Boy, you blew em' away, girl."

"Oh, shit," I moaned, shoving my head into the bathroom sink for a drink. It tasted terrible, rusty and stale. I threw some water on my face and staggered out to see Gerry washing down the side of the car with the gas station hose.

Gerry was spending the night at my house. We tip-toed into the bedroom so as not to wake anyone. I kept bumping into the walls and up against furniture. I flung off my clothes and flopped onto the bed. As soon as I lay down the room started spinning like a tilt-a-whirl

"Oh, my gawd," I moaned.

Maria stirred. "What's wrong?"

"I'm wasted," I muttered.

"Well, whatever you do, don't you dare throw up on the bed. Go on to the bathroom right now!" she hissed.

I got up and staggered into the toilet, standing over the bowl and sticking my finger down my throat, dry heaving and gagging.

There was a knock at the door.

"*Que tienes?*" It was my mother.

"Something I ate." I mumbled, locking the door.

She rattled the knob. "Go to bed!"

"OK," I muttered.

I turned off the light and stumbled into the dark, banging into the corner of the the dresser.

"Ouch!"

"Be quiet!" Maria said.

Gerry was already snoring lightly. I lay down with one foot on the floor, trying to control the whirling and spinning. Somewhere a clock ticked loudly.

"Oh, shit. Never again," I groaned.

I used to lie awake at night thinking of ways to make things work better. Mostly so that I wouldn't end up by myself. I'd do anything not to be alone. I had an idea.

At school one day I got a hat and put little pieces of paper in it, on which I'd written the names of all the guys we liked. I mixed up the pieces and said, "Pick one."

"What for?"

"I put all the guys' names that we dig into this hat and you pick one."

"OK, that means that each one of us will pick a name and the name we pick we scheme on that guy? Right?"

"Right."

"That's stupid," said Paula O'Brien, who was having lunch with us.

"No, it ain't."

"Go ahead, Paula, pick one," Gerry said.

"Ah, alright." Paula unfolded the piece of paper. "Yuk!" she squealed, throwing it at me.

"Yuk!" I yelled, tossing the paper at Gerry. She'd drawn Ray Lopez.

"Who is it?" she said, picking up the paper. "Barf." She waved it away. "Ga, why'd you put *his* name in?"

"Just for fun."

Ray Lopez was five feet two and weighed one hundred and fifty pounds. He wrote pornographic notes to girls on stained brown paper sacks and left them under the door to the girls' gym. The only problem was that he couldn't spell. Once I found a note that said: *"Fuk me teets cok pusie meet me for fuking and licing later."* I gave the note to him later in history class, saying, "Ray, you need a dictionary."

He blushed and shook his dumb, little head back and forth. "Hey ... too much, man. I didn't write that!"

After class he shuffled over to me, his eyebrows knitted up together earnestly. "Hey, girl, you think I'd do somethin' that low?"

"Yeah. I saw you writing it," I lied, "and it's a good thing one of the white chicks didn't find it and take it to the office."

He looked startled. "You saw me, man? That's a lie, you couldn't have, 'cause I wrote it at home."

I ripped the note up and threw it at him.

"Ease up, Cece," he said, raising his hands. "Gimme a break."

"You better be careful, Ray."

"OK, let's try again." I mixed up the names, passing the hat to Paula.

"Close your eyes," I said.

After we all had drawn I asked Gerry to trade with me.

"Why do you wanta do that?" Paula said.

"To prevent favoritism."

Gerry had picked Angel Hernandez, the very thing I was trying to prevent. I picked Bobby Cruz and Paula picked Raymond Johnston.

I could tell Gerry was pleased with her selection. We both had been watching Angel Hernandez cruising the boulevard for weeks in his candy-apple green Corvette. He had a quick flashy smile, and he was dark brown, almost black. He looked like a black man with Caucasian features. Very handsome and slick.

"I drew Bobby Cruz. You wanna trade?" I said.

"No," said Gerry, tucking the paper into her bra.

"Boy, you can tell she got what she wanted," Paula said.

"Yeah," I said dryly.

My plan had failed. I had to think of something else. I felt like a terrible schemer, but the thought of Gerry falling in love and getting a boyfriend, leaving me out, made me crazy and sick with jealousy.

Gerry and I were planning to go to the El Monte Legion stadium to see the Ike and Tina Turner Revue on Friday.

"You still wanna ride with me and Leonard Friday night?"

"Of course," said Gerry. "Haven't we already discussed this?"

"Alright."

I'd met Leonard Martinez a few months before at a sock hop and had been seeing him off and on. Of course I always

84

included Gerry when we went out.

"We'll probably be by for you around eight, so be ready."

"OK," she said. "I will."

On Friday night Leonard gunned his pipes and blew the horn of his lowered '56 Chevy. I ran out the door yelling, "I'll be home by midnight!"

Leonard wasn't what you'd call smart, but he had a groovy car and was a good dancer. He had a job at the local car wash. I jumped into the Chevy and slid across the cool tuck and roll upholstery. He took me in his arms and kissed me.

"Hi, Leonard," I said, brushing his cheek with my lips.

I guess, in a way, I knew that I wasn't going to ask him to stop by for Gerry. I knew she'd be dressed up and waiting with her hair puffed out like cotton candy, wearing a sexy tight skirt and a low cut halter top.

When we got there we sat in the car making out. After a few minutes of Frenching and stuff, his hand slid down to my hemline, creeping up my skirt.

"Don't, Leonard," I said, pulling away, straightening my skirt. "We better go in." I didn't want to encourage his advances. He was a nice guy and everything, but lately he no longer was content to feel me up and put his hands on my legs. Just the other night he had slid my skirt up above my thighs while we were making out and slowly pushed me back onto his impeccable tuck and roll, and I could feel his thing pressing between my legs. He wasn't a brute or anything, just slow and persistent. At night after he'd leave me off, I'd run into the house and masturbate.

The last time we made out I pushed him away.

"I'm not gonna do it, Leonard."

"Why not, baby?" he panted in my ear. "*Sabes que te quiero mucho, chula.*"

I straightened my blouse. "Yeah, I know, but that's not going to stop me from getting pregnant." Some of my girl-friends had gotten pregnant and had to get married or go live in a home for unwed mothers.

"If you get knocked up, I'll marry you."

"You've got to be kidding!" I said. "Forget it."

I slid over to my side of the car, patting my hair into shape and applying a coat of lipstick, while he sat there composing himself.

"Come on," I said, getting out.

As soon as we went in I scanned the crowded hall until I had spotted Angel.

"I'm going to the bathroom," I said to Leonard, heading over to where Angel stood talking to a couple of chicks.

"Hi," I waved to him

He didn't seem to recognize me, but then he must have picked up on the drift of my smile because he turned away from them and headed in my direction.

"Alright," he chimed. "I almost didn't recognize you without your sexy partner in crime."

I thought that was pretty witty of him. I smiled.

"We're not the Bobsy Twins, you know."

"So where is she?"

"Who?"

"Gerry."

"How should I know?" I knew that I didn't have much time. So right away I said, "Do you think you could give me a lift to Rachel's party? You know Rachel Dominguez?" I smiled and thrust my padded bra forward.

"So what's happening there--anything worth my while?" he grinned.

"Maybe," I said, looking boldly into his eyes.

"Ah, OK, let's go," he said.

"OK, I'll be right back. Don't go away."

I hurried back to Leonard. He handed me a Coke.

"Hey, Cece where were you?"

"I was talking to some of the chicks from the club, Lennie, and, ah, I'm really upset."

"Why's that?"

"'Cause I've got to make an announcement over the P.A. in ten minutes about a club activity, you know."

"Yeah."

"Yeah. Plus, I told the M.C. I'd play records during intermission, and--I forgot to tell you, but I promised Gerry we'd pick her up on the way over."

"Oh, wow. *Que lastima.*"

"Yeah, and she's probably all dressed up and waiting, Lennie. So do you, ah, think you could go and get her?"

"Sure." He smiled, like it was nothing to drive fifteen miles back and forth.

I pecked his cheek. "I'll go and call her and tell her you're coming."

I watched him as he got smaller and smaller and then disappeared through the door. I didn't bother to call Gerry.

Once in Angel's car, I watched the speedometer needle pass ninety.

"Oh, wow!" I said. "You're doing over a hundred!"

"That's right. Scared?"

"No," I lied. He passed me a bottle of Seagrams. I took a drink. There was no moon in the sky, just the ink black night as we hurtled down the freeway, going around cars, zipping in and out of lanes. Strangely enough it was quiet and calm at a hundred and twenty. I was relieved when we got there. I told Angel that Gerry was out with Bobby Cruz.

"She has the hots for him," I said.

"Oh, yeah?" he said.

"Yeah."

We stayed at the party for a little while, then went out and sat in the 'Vette, making out. It wasn't love, but it was fun. Afterwards we cruised over to Ernie's taco stand and he bought me a hot fudge sundae.

On the Monday after I had picked up on Angel, I ran into Gerry at school. Afterwards for years I would swear that her hair had been lopsided that day.

"Gawd, what's wrong with your hair? It looks weird! Kinda like the Leaning Tower of Pisa."

"How could you? You bitch!" she hissed.

"What you talking about?"

"You know what I'm talking about, man."

"What?" I said, stalling for time.

"I thought you were my best friend."

I smiled stupidly. I couldn't think of anything to say. She pushed me into the lockers that were lined up behind me, pressing my back against a hinge.

"I told you I wanted to trade," I said, giggling nervously.

"You broke the rules, bitch!" she screamed. I was standing close enough to take in her sweet smelling body lotion. Her eyes blazed, and she hauled off and slapped me. I flinched.

Shocked and embarrassed, I slapped her back, jarring her eyeglasses. Carmen Estrada pressed in between us, pulling her away.

"Come on, Gerry. It's not worth it. You'll get in trouble."

Gerry turned around moving through the group of students that had gathered around gawking at us. I wanted to run after her. But I didn't. I just watched her walk away. Our friendship was over. And it was my fault. I felt sick to my stomach.

That night I couldn't stop thinking about what had happened so I finally called her. She hung up. I called back.

"Just let me explain."

"OK."

"The reason I did it was because I was afraid that you would fall in love with Angel and not care about being with me anymore." My voice broke. "I'm sorry."

"But why didn't you tell me before?"

"I don't know. I just keep thinking of Chuckie and how he died and everything. I swear Gerry, I think I'm going crazy or something." I started to cry.

"Don't cry, Cece."

"You're my best friend, Gerry. I don't know what I'd do if I didn't have you."

"Don't be silly", she said, softly, "we're still friends."

"I swear to God, Gerry, I won't see him again if you don't want me to."

"Oh, it doesn't matter," she stammered unconvincingly. "It was just something for, you know, kicks, man. I don't think it's worth ruining our friendship."

"OK, I'll see you at school tomorrow, and we can talk about it some more."

"Sure, Cece, bye."

I dreamt I was running through a junk yard, past a bunch of broken down cars, torn apart, rusted, layered with years of dust. Rusty cans, broken bottles and old newspapers were strewn everywhere. Someone was running behind me, panting, gasping for air. It was Chuck Valdez. Blood gushed from his face. "Cece!" His voice sounded muffled, far away. Men wearing black coats and brandishing butcher knives were chasing us. They were going to kill us! I tried to scream, but couldn't.

Maravilla

"Cece, Cece,!" Maria was bent over me. "Wake up! You were moaning and kicking! What's wrong?"

Chapter 9

I called Gerry on Friday and we decided to get together. Marcos lent her his car, and we cruised Whittier Boulevard.

Around eight o'clock I spotted Angel in the 'Vette. He waved us down, asking us to follow him to Ernie's. When we got there I went over to talk to him. He asked me if I wanted to ride with him. I said I did. Then I went back to tell Gerry. Bobby Cruz was standing there talking to her, arranging something. I was glad to see them together because I was feeling a little guilty about leaving.

Angel drove down the street revving the engine, looking around to see if anyone wanted to drag. We came to a stop and he gunned the motor. A guy in another car opposite us, nodded and Angel peeled out leaving him behind, zig-zagging in and out of the heavy traffic, slamming on the brakes at the next red light. It was fun. Sort of like rocking back and forth on a horse.

After a spin around the boulevard, challenging a few more cruisers, we slid back to Ernie's and ordered banana splits. After we'd eaten them Angel pulled out a bottle of Seagram's Seven. Angel had money. His father was a land developer and had accumulated real estate all over L.A. county. When he divorced Angel's mother, he arranged a trust fund for Angel, his only son.

"Wanta blast?" he said, handing me the bottle.

"Sure." The whiskey was warm and stung my throat going down.

Gerry pulled in with Bobby Cruz in his lowered, white Chevy Impala.

I stuck my head out of the window and yelled, "Hey, Gerry, come over here."

She jumped out of the car and clattered over in her high heels. She was wearing a spaghetti strap dress that revealed her soft, chocolate brown cleavage.

"Want a hit?" I said.

"Seagrams," she said, impressed, holding the bottle up to take a small sip. It knocked me out the way she could make drinking whiskey out of a brown paper bag lady-like.

Angel had gone over to another car. Then he and a couple of guys disappeared into the bathroom. After a few minutes they came out heading toward the 'Vette.

"Hey, man," Angel said. His voice had changed. It was thick as syrup, "I want you to meet my *primo*, Jonesy. Jonesy, this is Gerry and Bobby."

Gerry said, "Hi." Bobby and Jonesy shook hands.

"And this here is Cece, my chick---for now," he said, smiling big, flashing his teeth like the black joker. "Ain't that right, baby? Cece doesn't like to be owned, right, Cece?"

"I guess, if you say so," I drawled, looking into the liquid, dark eyes of this guy, Jonesy. He looked familiar. But I knew I'd never met him before. I thought maybe I'd seen him cruising the boulevard or something. I could tell right away that I didn't like him.

"Hi, Cece," he rasped. "Don't I know you?"

"I doubt it."

"Hey," Gerry said, running her hands through Bobby's hair, "let's go. You ready or what? We've been waiting forever," she said, smiling sweetly at Angel. I wondered if she was flirting with him. She knew I'd never trade Angel for Bobby Cruz.

"Come on, let's go," I said. Somehow I felt like I would never come off as sweet as Gerry.

"OK," Angel said. "Jonesy's gonna take my car and the rest of us can go to the party in Bobby's car."

"Whose party?" Bobby asked.

"Some chick, you know, Rachel's, over by the J.C."

"OK, let's go," I said, impatiently.

We slid into the back seat of the Impala. Angel squeezed my knee as we cruised slowly down the street. I wondered who would be at the party. I pulled out my prong from my purse,

91

lifting my bouffant which was ratted and sprayed into a beehive.

"Ger, how does my hair look?"

"Looks bitchin'," she said.

"It's not sticking out or anything weird?"

"Don't worry about it. Ga, you're always bugging me about your hair."

"Yeah," Angel said, looking right through me. "You look gorgeous, baby." He patted my hand and looked out the window. His eyes were narrow slits. I didn't care. I cracked my gum thinking how cool it would be for us to come cruising into the party in Angel's green Corvette and Bobby's Impala.

We got there and parked. Bobby lit a reefer and passed it around. James Brown was wailing on the hi-fi as we walked into a dark room that smelled of cigarettes and booze, past some vague faces, into the electrical buzzing of a dirty kitchen. I hoped that the bright light wouldn't emphasize my two new zits.

Bobby handed me a tall glass of whiskey and water.

"Thanks, Bobby," I smiled at him. If Gerry could flirt so could I.

She must have noticed, because she came right over and asked me to dance. We wove our way through the room to where several other couples were dancing, and started doing the "Mashed Potato." Gerry began showing off with some fancy moves. People were watching her. She looked very sexy as usual. I felt envious as I watched her brown body sway to the music, knowing I'd never look that good. I regretted that I hadn't bought that girdle with the fake butt at Frederick's of Hollywood. At the time, I was afraid that Gerry would have seen me doing it and might have told someone. I was thinking of maybe going down there by myself someday and buying it.

When the dance ended Gerry and I went back to where Bobby stood holding a drink. Angel was in the bathroom again. Jonesy asked me to dance. Little Richard screamed, "*The girl can't help it that she's in love with me!*" There was an exciting tension in the air as he led me to the dance floor. I noticed it as soon as he touched me. He wanted to dance fast and I let him lead me. Afterwards we stood there talking. Then he looked directly into my eyes and said, "You look like Nefertiti with you hair all pushed up like that." His voice sounded dif-ferent, huskier, or something. I almost blushed.

I felt funny so I said, "Yeah, so who's that?" pretending not to know.

"You know, the Egyptian princess." He glanced down the front of my blouse. I was wearing a scoop neck purple leotard over a padded bra.

"Oh, yeah," I said, nervously looking around the room.

"You know, the chick with the big head and the long straight nose."

"Yeah, so what's wrong with my nose?" I said, smiling.

I wanted him to touch me.

"Just a tiny bit too long and straight," he said, pressing his forefinger against the tip of my nose. "Not really hooked, but definitely what I would call prominent."

I thought he was smart. Cocky and smart.

"Oh, sure," I said.

"You ever thought about getting a nose job?" he asked, smiling at me like he was in love.

"Who do you think you are, Dr. Kildare?" I said cockily. *Touch me,* I thought. He drew me into the darkened hallway. "You're beautiful," he whispered.

I could smell his after-shave lotion and a hint of whiskey on his breath. He wrapped his brown hand around my jaw, looking into my eyes. Then he reached down, stopping at the curve of my back. I moved at an angle so as not to bump noses. Just before he stuck his tongue in my mouth I giggled, turning my face so his mouth brushed my cheek.

"You gonna let me in, Mama?" he whispered.

My body flushed, my heart began to pound. His lips brushed against my lacquered hair. I pulled away embarrassed.

"Wait, don't go," he said.

"I better get back. Angel's waiting."

"Not yet." He held onto my arm, pulling me towards him. When he kissed me, I could feel the length of his body against mine. I moved closer to him, feeling a warm glow run all through me.

Someone came by, and I put my head down. Then I walked away, purposely swaying my hips (what I had of them), then turned around and smiled. "See you later."

Maravilla

When I went into the kitchen, Angel was leaning against the sink talking to Gerry. I walked over and linked my arm through his. Bobby offered me a drink. Angel patted my hand while he talked. I could tell he was stoned, getting more so by the minute.

Jonesy came into the room. I pretended to ignore him. He was talking to this chick with gigantic tits. I felt my nipples rigid against the toilet paper in my bra. I was sick with envy. I glanced down at the bulge in his pants, hoping he wouldn't notice, and at the same time I wished that he would. I was crazy.

I let go of Angel and went into the bathroom to check my hair. Taking out my lipstick, I dabbed my mouth, flicked eye shadow on, then stood on the bathtub rim and checked myself out in the mirror. I could almost hear him saying it again, "You're beautiful," could almost feel his hands all over my body. I stood there wondering if I should take out my falsies. Without thinking I reached up under my skirt and began rubbing my clitoris.

Someone knocked, "Hurry up." *Do they know?* I glanced out the window wondering if anyone had seen me.

"Just a minute, I'll be right out." I straightened my skirt and looked in the mirror. My face was flushed and strange. My eyes were glazed, my beehive collapsing.

Angel was still in the kitchen talking to Bobby. Jonesy and the girl were gone. The rest of the evening I felt bored and distracted.

On the way home Angel passed out next to me on the back seat. Bobby dropped me off.

"'Night, Cece. Don't worry, we'll take care of Angel," he said.

As soon as I got into bed, I started thinking of *him*. I touched my breasts, felt between my legs. I was with him, he was sliding his hands down my body, kissing and caressing me all over. When I came I was thinking of him, imagining that he was in bed, making love to me.

Was this love? I'd never felt like this before. Or maybe I had. I couldn't remember. I was weak with need, with desire. I thought about him constantly. Jonesy. No one else knew about it. I wouldn't dare tell Gerry, for fear of being ridiculed.

94

Besides I didn't want her to get any ideas and find someone too.

I was frightened that the feeling wouldn't go away. And scared that maybe it would. I'd never felt so out-of-it before. I was thrilled with the idea, thrilled with his boldness. Over and over again I thought about the way he had reached for me, and touched me, precise and smooth yet intense. Experienced-- that was it. He had experience. And the way he ignored me later and left (I thought) with that chick only seemed to excite and torment me at the same time.

I kept my secret. When we cruised now I always looked for him, hoping to catch a glimpse of him in a car, hoping to see him at a party. I was too embarrassed to ask Angel about him. Afraid I'd betray my feelings. Once, when we were cruising the boulevard, I saw him go by in a green Plymouth. He looked at me and waved. I turned around with my heart pounding, embarrassed, pretending like I hadn't seen him.

"You going to the party at so-and-so's?" he yelled to Angel.

"Yeah, sure, man," Angel said. I thought about seeing him there. I thought about how he would ask me to dance and then we'd go outside in the dark and make-out and I'd feel that warm, liquid glow rush through me again, feel his dark, warm hands all over me. Before we got to the party, I took out my falsies, just in case. I waited for him all night. He never did show up. I felt disappointed and humiliated. How could I be in love with someone who didn't even know I was alive?

It was a hot, muggy afternoon the day that Angel took me to meet his mother. We walked up the blank concrete sidewalk, with Angel guiding my elbow, towards the house. The afternoon sun blazed against the molten asphalt in waves of heat like water. A faded picket fence surrounded the large wood-framed house, enclosing a sloping, well-kept front yard. Flat topped hedges lined the path to the porch. All the shades in the front window were closed. We walked into a living room that smelled like lemon furniture polish and, for an instant, I thought no one was home. Dark, heavy drapes were drawn, and all the furniture was covered with plastic.

Mrs. Hernandez came into the room carrying her tea-cup poodle with a white rhinestone collar. She wore a yellow and white floral house dress, accentuating her sallow brown skin. Her large arms were fleshy and hung loose and saggy from her shoulders. A couple of wiry, black whiskers stuck out of her chin. Her hair, dyed fuchsia, was set in a neat little fluff around her flat, round face.

Angel introduced us. She stroked her poodle and swept her eyes down, stopping at my hemline. A picture of a voodoo doll with a bouffant, looking like me, with pins stuck through its heart, flashed through my head. My neck stiffened.

After a few seconds she said, "Are your parents alive?"

What? I cleared my throat. "Ah--yes. Boy, it's nice and cool in here," I said nervously.

"Yes, isn't it," replied Mrs. Hernandez, distractedly, putting her poodle down. "Go on, Boo Boo, you go play while Mama fixes supper for Angelito." She looked at me and asked, "What does your father do?" in a voice squeaky with concern.

"He's a gardener."

"Oh--how nice," she said, glancing disapprovingly at Angel, and asked, "What does Angelito want for dinner?"

"I don't care, Maw," he slurred.

I sat in the living room on the large, overstuffed chair, aware of the plastic sticking to the back of my legs, feeling regretful, almost melancholy. I began searching my mind for an excuse not to stay.

"I'm not really that hungry," I whispered to Angel. He shrugged and went into the kitchen and said, "Cece's not hungry."

Mrs. Hernandez waltzed into the living room waving a spatula in her hand. "What? Oh, no, no," she wailed. "You really have to stay for dinner, dear." She seemed almost gay now. "You know Angel told me you would be coming and I'm making something especially for you."

"Well--". I was all flustered.

"Besides," she continued with an air of finality, "you certainly look like you could use a few pounds."

I looked over at Angel, slumped into the couch, just about nodding out. Mrs. Hernandez sailed back into the kitchen pretending not to notice.

Maravilla

"I guess I am hungry," I murmured.

I couldn't enjoy the spicy enchiladas and refried beans which stared out from my plate begging to be eaten. Angel sat across the table from me, pushing his food around, picking at it now and then, while Mrs. Hernandez spoke exclusively to him about relatives and money. Occasionally he nodded his head and mumbled something.

After dinner Mrs. Hernandez suggested we watch television and switched on the Lawrence Welk Show. Angel kept nodding out and coming to, while Boo Boo the tea-cup poodle tried to hump my ankle. I discreetly pushed him away.

"Isn't he a sweetheart?" cooed Mrs. Hernandez, smiling at the thing. When she went into the other room, I hissed, "Get back, you little turd, before I flush you down the toilet!" shoving him back with my foot. He let out a yelp, charging my ankle again.

She was back. Angel had passed out. I felt hot and claustrophobic. "Excuse me." I belched. My stomach rumbled and felt like it was on fire. "I have to go to the bathroom," I said politely. When I got back the Lawrence Welk bubble machine was going full blast. I sat down quietly and mustered up the courage to say, "Mrs. Hernandez, it's getting late and I really have to go home ... er ... I think Angel fell asleep." Angel was snoring with his mouth wide open.

"Oh, poor thing," she sighed. "He works so hard."

Works? "Oh, yeah," I smiled. "Anyway, could I use your telephone to call and see if someone can pick me up?" I was considering hitchhiking the ten miles to get out of there.

"Of course, dear, go right ahead."

Frantically, I dialed my parent's number. No answer. Then I dialed Gerry's number. Her little brother answered.

"Who? Who is?"

"This is Cece. Let me talk to Gerry."

"No Gerry."

"What about Marcos?" I said quickly before he hung up. He hung up.

"Shit." I dialed again.

"Hawoo."

""Listen, Ernie, don't hang up! Let me speak to your Mama."

"Mama home no--"

"Who's this?" another voice said.

"Cece. Who's this?"

"Marcos."

I could tell Mrs. Hernandez was listening. I felt like Ingrid Bergman in "Notorious"; she was Claude Raines' mother.

"Marcos, please, do you think you could come and pick me up? I'm at Angel's house," I said, smiling at Mrs. Hernandez.

"Ah, man," he sighed, and I could tell that he didn't understand the gravity of the situation. "Naw, I don't have wheels."

"Can you borrow a car?"

He chuckled, tuned into my discomfort, and said, "My parents aren't here, Cece. I have to stay home with Ernie."

"Well, OK," I sighed. "But look, I'm gonna give you this number and, if anyone comes home, you call back and then come and get me, OK?"

"*Chale*," he grunted. "No one's coming back, man, so don't count on it."

I hung up and reluctantly went back into the musty stale living room. Lawrence Welk was doing the Hungarian Fandango. *I'm too young to die!*

"Would you like a cup of Ovaltine, dear?"

Ovaltine! Jeez, I'm almost eighteen, not a pre-teener, lady!

"No, thanks."

"What about a Coke?"

"OK."

"I always have Coke. It's Angel's favorite drink," she said, smiling maternally.

Junkies' favorite drink, dumbie! Everyone knows that!

Lawrence Welk was over and *Outer Limits* was on.

"Is you father or someone going to pick you up, dear?"

"No, no one's there."

"Oh well, then you may just have to spend the night here."

No! I'll never make it through the night in this tomb!

"Yeah, but I have to go home to do some homework and feed my cat." I hoped she'd offer me a ride.

"Well, it's just fine with me if you stay here. Next week I hope you can come early and spend the whole day. We'll go to Mass together."

We sat staring at the tube. As I watched I was aware of her heavy profile, her jaw rigid as concrete. It seemed as if time had stopped for Mrs. Hernandez, that there was nothing beyond these four walls for her. I could tell that no one besides Angel had ever lived here, and few people ever visited. I had the feeling that no one ever came by. The loneliness was overwhelming. I shuddered, thinking about it.

"You can sleep here on the couch. It opens into a bed. Is Cece your nickname?"

"No, it's my real name." I was damned if I was going to let her call me Consuelo.

"What a cute name."

"Uh-huh."

Somehow she managed to drag Angel off to bed, then brought in some blankets, smelling like mothballs, and made up the couch for me. She handed me a pair of neatly folded and ironed pajamas.

"These will probably be a little too big for you, dear. You're so thin."

"Thanks," I whispered, too depressed to protest. I heard her pee, then run water into the sink. The toilet flushed and the light flicked out.

Peeking in the door, she said, "Good night, Cece. By the way, we usually wake up at seven-thirty."

I lay in bed, hoping I wouldn't think much and go right to sleep. But I couldn't. A street light was shinning through the front window and somewhere a clock ticked loudly. I could hear cars cruising by outside. Horns honking. A siren went off. Once in a while voices came through from the sidewalk.

I was thinking about what Gerry had said--that Maria Hernandez, Angel's cousin, told Carmen Estrada, who told Gerry, that Angel was to come into a fortune as soon as he married. Until then, his father had complete control of his trust fund, that is, until he turned twenty-five. I knew Angel was deeply in debt. The month before he had had an accident driving while drunk and was now facing a jail sentence if he didn't come up with a whole lot of cash. He also had a bad drug habit. I stared at the ceiling chewing gum, making an effort not to crack it.

I wondered what Angel and Mrs. Hernandez had in mind for me. I guess I realized right then that it was only a matter of time for Angel and me.

Hey, did you hear about Cece? No, what? She and Angel Green Corvette are no longer a gruesome twosome. Wow, really?

I could just hear it. All of a sudden I had an idea. For the first time all evening I relaxed, tucking my arms behind my head, chuckling softly. He probably wouldn't even notice the difference--everyone had always said that Gerry and I were so much alike they couldn't tell us apart. Perfect.

I reached for my purse and looked into my wallet for the five dollars my mother had given me for my school annual. Then I slid out of bed and very quietly tiptoed over to Mrs. Hernandez' bedroom. I heard a light snore.

"Mrs. Hernandez?" I whispered twice, to make sure she was asleep. Then I tiptoed back into the living room, picked up the phone and dialed the operator.

"Give me the Yellow Cab. This is an emergency!" I said. The cabby answered.

"Send a cab to the corner of Dozier and Marianna Street."

I dressed hurriedly, flinging the pajamas down, sneaking out the door and down the steps to the corner.

A few minutes later the cab pulled up.

"You called, miss?"

"Yes." I slid into the back seat, giving him my address.

I began rehearsing in my mind what I would say to Gerry. I must have said something out loud, because the cab driver turned around and asked, "What ya say?"

"Oh, nothing. Just thinking out loud."

"Yeah, sure, I know what you mean. I do it all the time."

I rolled down the window. I could see his eyes in the rear view mirror, reflecting lights. I popped my gum, leaned back, enjoying the cool night air blowing against my face.

"Ger, do you still have the hots for Angel?"

"Why?"

"I was just wondering."

"Yes."

"Would you like to trade Angel for Bobby?"

"Why, what happened?"

"*Nada.* I'm just ready for a change, I guess."

"OK," she said, smiling.

"Great. He's going to the record hop on Friday. I won't be there. Ask Bobby to see what he thinks. Then call me on Saturday and let me know what happened."

"Alright, but I'm sure Bobby will go for it."

"Really?"

"Yeah, but ... I have something to tell you, Cece."

"What?"

"I've already been seeing Angel. Last week, we went to the drive-in."

"What! You traitor!" I yelled.

"I'm sorry. You know I've always liked him."

"I know it, Gerry," I said, linking my arm through hers. "Anyway, listen, my cousin loaned me two new records, Fats Domino and Mary Wells. Do you wanna borrow one of them?"

"No, I don't like Fats that much. Maybe Mary Wells. I gotta run. Meet me at the gym later."

"OK."

Chapter 10

Bobby and I went out a couple of times before I ditched him at a party and left with Jonesy.

It was my first chance to be with him and I wasn't going to pass it by. When I saw him going into the hallway I followed him.

"Excuse me, Bobby," I said abruptly. "I have to go to the bathroom." I'd been thinking of him all day and had a feeling I'd run into him. I was wearing Gerry's low-cut, pink spaghetti-strap dress and four nylon petticoats underneath. I had just had my hair cut into a Sassoon--one side longer than the other, hanging over one eye. The top was ratted to a point.

When he came out of the toilet, I deliberately bumped into him, smiling, "Oh, hi," as though I was surprised to see him.

"Hi, Nefertiti," he said, as if he were expecting me, and we immediately started where we had left off the first night. My hands were trembling and I could hear my heart pounding like an African drum. He touched my arm gently and it tingled all the way up to my neck.

"Have you been thinking about me, like I've been thinking about you?" he asked. God! I couldn't look at him. "Look at me," he whispered.

I looked into his eyes and giggled nervously. It was insane. We were both grinning from ear to ear. He stood in front of me with both arms around my waist and slowly pushed me against the wall, pressing his leg into my petticoats. I moved closer to him. He looked into my eyes and kissed me, first gently, then harder, sticking his tongue into my mouth. I could smell his Canoe after-shave lotion, feel his chest pressed against me.

We left the party, going out the back door, our arms wrapped around each other. I didn't bother to say goodbye to Bobby. I didn't think he would mind. (He didn't. A week later I saw him cruising on the boulevard with his arm around Gloria Escobar.) We walked down the street and slid into a blue Ford that was parked in the dark. We were madly touching and stroking each other and sighing. We kissed so much my face got chapped.

He kept whispering, "I want you, girl, I've been wanting you a long time."

I could feel his thing stiff against my leg as he tried to make his way through my petticoats.

"Christ, why are you wearing so many layers of clothes?" he panted in my ear. We were wrestling in the front seat. I pulled around, hitting my back against the gear shift.

"Ouch!"

"What's wrong?"

"The gear shift is stabbing me!"

We slid up on the seat and I bumped my head against the door handle.

"Owww!" I yelled. "My head!" I reached up and felt the top of my hair flattened out. "This isn't going to work."

He straightened up. "Let's get in the back?"

"Alright," I said. My head and back smarted, but I was too excited to care. He climbed over the seat and offered me his hand. I tumbled over, falling on his lap. I tried clumsily to move over and accidentally hit his thing.

"Oww," he moaned.

"Oh, god, I'm sorry," I said, feeling stupid and awkward. He recoiled but only for a moment. Then we were going at it again hot and heavy. Every nerve in my body tingled as he touched and caressed me.

He was pushing my petticoats up when I heard a voice say, "Hey, who's that? Oh, yeah... Jonesy, the party's over. We wanta leave."

A couple got into the car, barely paying attention to us, and we drove away. I gave them directions to my house. All the way there Jonesy and I were making out. Once we got there we stood in the shadows embracing until the guy honked his horn.

"Can I have your number?" he said, kissing me.

"Sure." I wrote it down and handed it to him.

He kissed and hugged me and said, "I'll call you tomorrow." Feeling ecstatic, I ran into the house, got in bed, and masturbated.

I heard the phone ring early the next morning. My mother had just gotten out of bed, thank God. She hated to be wakened by a ringing telephone. Whenever it rang early morning, say when we were all asleep, she'd pick it up and, if it wasn't an emergency, she'd slam it back down. She didn't mess around. Once, I had been talking to Gerry for a long time and she had asked me to get off four or five times. I was lying sprawled out on the dining room table, laughing so hard I was crying, when she walked over with a pair of scissors and snipped the wire off. There I was with this dangling telephone wire, saying, Gerry, Gerry?" My mother had left the room, swearing, "*Hijo de la chingada, madre.*"

I had to plead and cry for another phone. She made me promise in front of her St. Anthony statue that, if we got another phone, I'd never stay on for more than fifteen minutes. I felt stupid doing it, but I had to.

After that I never talked over my time limit, except when she was gone. My father never seemed to care one way or the other. But my mother was another story. Whenever I got on the phone, she'd come in and point to the clock or leave it sitting in front of me. "Fifteen," she'd say.

One night Gerry called and we talked for four hours straight. I finally fell asleep with the receiver flipped over next to my ear. I was lying on top of the dining room table again--since we had a wall phone with a short cord, it was the only comfortable place to have an extended telephone conversation. Afterwards, my father told me that he had walked in and had hung up the receiver before my mother could see. He didn't want to have a scene, he said, at three o'clock in the morning. My mother walked in just as I was waking up and said, "Ay, *Dios*, Cece, why are you sleeping on the table?" She acted as if it were perverse to fall asleep on the table. I could see that it was a touchy situation so I acted incoherent, rubbing my eyes and yawning.

"Let me smell your breath," she ordered suspiciously.

"For heaven's sake," I said, irritated. "Don't get hysterical. You're overreacting. I merely fell asleep." I had a certain way of talking to her when I was caught in the act, as it were. I acted haughty and used words that I knew she didn't understand. She looked at me, then turned around, dropping the subject. First chance I headed into my bedroom. I heard her say, "What's gotten into her? She doesn't even know what she's doing?" Then she continued mumbling in Spanish. My father never said much. Mostly he ignored us.

The morning Jonesy called, my mother answered the phone. "Cece?" she said. "Cece's sleeping."

I bolted out of bed and ran into the living room.

"No, I'm not," I said, scrambling for the phone.

"Oh, here she is, Lady Godiva in her PJ's," she said, handing me the line and tweaking my nose. Thank God she was in a good mood.

I cleared my throat and croaked, "Hi."

"Hi, baby," he said.

I smiled. I could see my mother watching me out of the corner of her eye. "Jonesy?" I asked quietly.

My mother said, "What happened to Bobby and Angel and what's-his-name?"

I ignored her. "Nothing, I was talking to my mother. She's working for J. Edgar Hoover."

"Did you sleep OK?" he asked sweetly.

"Yes." I felt my face blush. My mother raised her eyebrows. I turned my back to her.

"When can I see you? I miss you."

"I don't know." I hesitated, then said, "What about this afternoon?"

"Where? At your house?"

"OK, I mean, no," I stammered, glancing back at her. "Where?"

"What about the park?" I said softly.

"Where? I can't hear you."

"The park?" I said.

She interrupted, "You promised to watch Eddie today, Cece."

I nodded. "I have to bring my little brother. I promised my mother I'd take care of him today."

"That's alright with me, as long as I can see you."

I looked up at her, "OK."

"What time?" he asked.

"About one o'clock... by the pond?"

"OK."

"'Bye, Cece."

"'Bye."

My heart was pounding when I hung up.

"Well, you finally met someone you like."

"Yeah," I shrugged nonchalantly, "kinda."

"Kinda! Your face is beet red, honey."

"Is Eddie sleeping?" I asked, trying to change the subject.

"Yes. Listen, Cece, you better watch out, girl. I don't want you to get burned."

"I won't, don't worry," I said, heading into the other room.

It was a cool afternoon and a low fog had been hanging on all morning. Eddie and I were fooling around on the grass next to the pond. I looked up and saw him coming towards us. He walked over, looked directly into my eyes, and kissed me. He seemed steady as a rock. I felt myself trembling.

"Cold?" he asked, putting his arm around me.

"A little," I said, nervously pulling my sweater around my neck.

He was wearing a brown and tan Pendleton and neatly ironed, tan pants, and looked as if he had just bathed and shaved. There was a nick on his chin. His face was somehow different from the night before. He wasn't that good-looking really. His skin had a few pock marks and his eyes were bloodshot. However, it was his odor that affected me more than anything. He smelled good. Also his sense of assurance turned me on.

Unlike the night before, there was a distinct separation between us, an awkwardness. We sat on the grass watching

106

Eddie swing back and forth and play on the slide. I felt relieved that he was there.

"Wanna smoke a joint?"

"Now?!"

"No one's around."

"What about Eddie?"

"He don't care. Besides, he won't even know."

"OK," I shrugged. I hated to be a prude. I actually liked his boldness. I sat watching him roll the joint. He had large square hands that were slightly calloused and he moved them with a fine precision.

I used to love to watch him walk, taking his long, loping forward strides. Later, I found out that he liked to act clumsy to attract attention. He'd trip over his feet or accidentally drop something, but always managed to make a smooth recovery, which created a hair-splitting type of tension. It was an interesting, if jolting, combination. The dancer and the oaf.

After we'd spent time in the park, he drove me home and kissed me. saying, "I'll call you soon."

When he came by a few days later, he didn't honk his horn. He came up and leaned on the door bell. My sister Maria answered it, letting out a yelp and snorting like a barking seal. I went over to see what was going on, bumping into my mother. We both peered out the door, to see Jonesy wearing a Frankenstein mask and grunting, "Ce-Ce."

"Ga, who's that?" Maria said, disgruntled, when she realized it wasn't for her.

"Ay, *Dios*," my mother pshawed.

When he pulled off the mask, his face was wringing wet.

Another time he came over wearing a Groucho Marx nose and glasses. He used to wear his watch on his ankle. He'd sit with his legs crossed, waiting for someone to ask the time. Then he'd look down at his ankle and say something corny like, "A couple of hairs past seven."

Eddie loved it. Maria hated it. My father ignored him. My mother seemed to enjoy him, even though she thought he was a little on the dark side. Whenever he came over, we'd usually take a ride in his car until we found a place to make-out. Or we'd go to a movie and make-out. Or to a party and make-out, or to the park and make-out.

Maravilla

There seem to be only a few people in life that make you feel complete. When you're with them, everything seems to be perfectly in focus. Even thoughts slow down or cease altogether. And, for a fleeting moment, life is exquisite.

Jonesy was like that for me. Later I would regret that I ever met him. But in the beginning everything was perfect-- except for one thing. I hated his car. He had a 1950, faded green Plymouth. I mentioned to him that I thought he ought to get a groovier car, or at least have his customized. "Why bother?" He said he thought cruising and dragging was a stupid waste of time.

"Oh, well, I happen to think it's fun."

"Then you do it," he said.

"OK, I will." After I had thought it over, I said, "Let's make a deal?"

"What's that?"

"I get to cruise with anyone I want to."

"And?"

"So do you," I said.

"Yeah, alright," he said, down shifting and stripping the gears. "If that's what you want."

"Stand over there," my father said, moving Maria, Tony, Eddie and me around to take a picture of us. We were standing in front of the high school auditorium in the shadows of the setting sun. I had just graduated and was still in my navy blue robe and cap, holding my diploma.

"OK, smile," he said, shooting the picture.

"Come on, Terry, it's your turn." My mother came over and stood next to me. And he snapped it. Then he took one of me and Maria alone. Then my mother took one of father, Eddie, and Tony. Then we discovered that no one had put the film in the camera.

By this time, Eddie had started to cry and Tony had run off somewhere.

"I refuse to paste another smile on my face," Maria said, watching my father load the Instamatic.

"Oh, come on, *mija*, don't be like that," he said.

Maravilla

"Listen, if she doesn't want to smile, she doesn't have to," said my mother. "Let everyone know what she's like, huh."

"Forget it!" I said.

If it hadn't been for Jonesy getting there just in time, we probably wouldn't have taken any pictures at all. He took the camera from my father. "Come on, you guys!" He gathered us together. "You can do better than that! Say cheese."

He shot the whole roll.

Afterwards, we went to look for Gerry and Angel so we could follow them to Carmen Estrada's graduation party. They were around the corner taking pictures too. When they finished, the four of us walked across the football field to the cars.

Angel and Gerry got into the 'Vette. I slid into Jonesy's car, struggling with the faulty door handle. "Ga, Jones, why don't you get this fixed?" I said. "This car is so raunchy, I don't see how you can stand it!"

"Just get in," he said. "I'm gonna take you for a ride you'll never forget." He had this weird look on his face. We took off and a blast of wind hit me.

"Jonesy, what happened? There's no window!"

"I know," he said. "It broke and I had to take it out."

"You're kidding!"

"No. Hey, baby, just pretend that you're in a convertible with the top down," he laughed.

"Very funny," I yelled, holding onto my hair.

It was a warm, balmy night and, once I'd gotten used to it, the wind felt sort of good. I looked over at Jonesy and laughed.

He picked up my hand and kissed it. "Let's go park and make-out?"

"Alright," I said.

As soon as we walked into the party, Carmen came over and said, "What happened to your hair, Cece?"

"Why?" I said, heading for the bathroom. I looked in the mirror to see one side of my bouffant smashed flat and the top sticking straight up. I fixed it and went back into the living room.

Chubby Checkers was on the hi-fi. *"Come on, baby, let's do the twist!"* Angel and Gerry were dancing. Jonesy stood by a table, sipping beer and dipping potato chips into a dish of refried beans.

Bobby Cruz asked me to dance. We twisted around the floor. Afterwards, I went over to the table for something to eat. I wolfed down two fat enchiladas, smothered with guacamole and sour cream, a bunch of black olives, a handful of Granny Goose potato chips, and those little goodies speared with toothpicks, that tasted like weenies wrapped in tiny biscuits, followed by a tall glass of punch spiked with vodka. I danced some more and had another drink, then Bobby offered me a beer. After that I lost count, forgot when to stop, got really drunk, and passed out

Jonesy carried me into the house and left me on the living room couch with a quilt thrown over my legs.

The next morning, I woke up to Bullet, our albino boxer, barking and yapping in my ear while Eddie jumped up and down on my legs, baiting him.

Around eleven o'clock, Jonesy called. "How're you, honey?"

"Hung over," I said

"Can I see you today?"

"Sure, come over this afternoon."

I had started to see him every day.

Jonesy was the first guy I went all the way with. At first we just fooled around, making out and feeling each other up. And for a while we never went any further than that. But Jonesy was older and more experienced than any of my other boyfriends had been. He was almost twenty-one. We were both living at home with our parents, so there was never really a time when we could be alone except in the car. Once before, just as it was about to happen--we'd been fooling around and making out for hours, so I was pretty turned on, a cop came by and shined his flashlight in the window and told us to move on. After that, I chickened out.

A few weeks later, we drove up the San Bernardino Freeway, heading into the mountains to Big Bear. It was late summer and the soft, brown hills were bare and stark above the green forest. We drove up the windy road past the woods and into Lake Arrowhead.

Then we got out and hiked up a dirt path. The air smelled fresh and clean. Tall pine trees rustled in the breeze. The ground was covered with little, brittle pine cones and needles. We sat on a dock, watching the small boats rocking on the flat, glassy surface of the water. It was very still and quiet except for the creaking of the dock. We slid down and leaned against the rail. Jonesy slipped his arm around me, and we sat gazing at the sun's reflection on the lake. Somewhere a dog barked and a kid yelled. The sun beat down on our heads. After a while, my nose began to sting and my cheeks burned, so we got up and started back.

As Jonesy walked ahead of me, I picked up a pine cone and threw it at him. He turned around and started chasing me. We tumbled to the ground, laughing and squealing, and he kissed me. I could see the trees towering above us, dark shadows shading the sun, sticking up in a patch of blue sky. I felt Jonesy's weight on top of me. My body tingled, flushed with heat and excitement.

"Come on, let's go." He offered me his hand, helping me up.

After lunch, we cruised up and down the narrow dirt roads as the setting sun, a gold mauve, slipped into the hills beyond the forest. Jonesy pulled off the road.

"Where are we?"

"I don't know," he said, getting out of the car.

I could see his outline in the dark, walking towards a solitary, little cabin. He trotted back saying, "Come on, Cece."

"I don't want to. What for?"

He grabbed my hand, pulling me out of the car. The door to the cabin was old and rotting. He had barely pushed it, when it cracked open. It looked as if no one had been there for a long time. Jonesy struck a match. I saw a candle on top of a dusty old table. He lit it. Then he drew me towards him, slipping his arms around my waist, kissing me.

"Do you think anyone will come by?"

"Naw," he whispered. The candle light flickered, casting shadows on the ceiling and walls. Jonesy laid our blanket over a musty threadbare carpet, laid down and pulled me next to him. He took a bottle of brandy out of his jacket pocket and handed it to me. I took a sip. We started making-out, rolling around on the floor. He was on top of me. "Come on, honey. Please, let me." He pleaded in my ear. "It won't hurt. I promise I'll be careful," he whispered, pulling down my jeans. Then he was pressing and probing into me slowly. Then faster, then slower, then faster.

Then it was over. At first I couldn't believe it! All that fuss, for just that! God! It seemed stupid. I was disappointed and started to cry. He put his arms around me. "Sorry," he said, "I blew it. I promise next time will be better."

I didn't say anything, just lay there staring at the dancing flame of the candle, casting shadows like black wings, fluttering against the walls.

After a while we gathered up our stuff, blew out the candle, and left.

It was a jet black night and the sky lit up with a mass of brilliant stars. I had never seen it so clearly or so close. I felt like reaching up and touching it. A brisk evening wind rustled the trees, pitch black shadows in the light of the half moon. I could hear dead pine needles crunching beneath our feet as we walked down the dirt path and slid into the car.

As we rolled down the winding road, and around the hairpin turns, a sadness crept through me, an indescribable loneliness.

Chapter 11

On Thursday night, after a movie, Jonesy and I went to Concha's Mexican Restaurant on Atlantic Boulevard. We walked into the long, narrow, dimly lit room and slid into a booth. *Vacquero* sombreros, along with Mexican flags and pictures of Aztec Indians, hung from the walls and ceiling. Serapes covered the chipped, candlelit tables. Tacked up next to the cash register was a Coca Cola calendar of a girl wearing a peasant blouse, pulled down low around her shoulders. She looked like Sally Field, smiling ecstatically: "*Bebe Coca Cola.*"

Julia, the waitress, peeked out from the kitchen, shoving a hairpin into her ratted French twist. She sauntered lazily over to our table and handed us menus. Jonesy ordered a beer and a Coke for me. She smiled, bent over, revealing her plunging neckline and tremendous breasts. I could smell her Tabu perfume. Her long, fire-engine red nails clicked over the smooth surface of the menus. The week before, Jonesy had picked a carnation out of a bouquet on the counter in the front of the restaurant and, when Julia had come to wait on us, he handed it to her. "Thank you," she had said. Her bright red mouth had widened into a smile, revealing a gold capped tooth. She had brought us chips and salsa. "On the house," she said, glancing seductively at Jonesy. At the time it didn't bother me, because she seemed so much older than either of us. At least thirty. Later, I found out from Slow Freddie that Jonesy had been seeing her on the side.

While we sat there having our drinks, a couple of young boys, around seven or eight years old, came through the restaurant barking, "Shine, meester, shoe shine." No one seemed to want one. When I mentioned to Jonesy that I felt sorry for them, he immediately went over and asked for one. He tipped the kid fifty cents and came back.

We ordered another couple of drinks and were holding hands when Slow Freddie came in. He kind of loped when he walked and his back stooped over as if he were carrying an invisible burden. He had a sweet, pretty boy's face. Jonesy introduced us. He shook my hand limply and looked at Jonesy. His eyes were soft brown, like a deer's.

"What's happenin', man?"

"Nothing much. Me and my love here are just hanging out," Jonesy said, smiling at me.

"Oh, yeah," Freddie said, looking around nervously.

"Sit down. Come on and join us."

"Alright," Freddie said, sliding into the booth. He kept staring at me with this funny look on his face.

"I think I've seen you around somewhere."

"Really," I said.

"Yeah, man, you probably have." Jonesy said. "She gets around. Doncha, honey?"

I didn't say anything

"Didn't you used to go with Angel?" It wasn't that he was being tactless, you could tell that. It was just that he wasn't too smart.

"Angel who?"

"You know--Angel with the green Corvette." He grinned like he knew I was putting him on.

"Oh, that guy," I said, looking at Jonesy. "I only went out with him so I could get close to Jones." I felt the tension slip away. I moved closer to Jonesy, resting my hand on his leg. Miguel Acevez Mejia wailed out a Ranchera over the speakers above our heads.

Jonesy slipped his arm around me and kissed my ear. Freddie turned away, embarrassed.

After a few minutes, Jonesy said, "Hey, man, how about a beer?"

"Me?" he said, pointing to himself.

"No, your shadow."

"Yeah, awright."

I guess, in a way, I fell in love with Freddie that night.

Not like the feelings I had for Jonesy, sensual and intimate, but more like a friend. He and Jonesy were a good combination.

One night the three of us went to the movies to see *Bonnie and Clyde*. Afterwards, I mentioned to Jonesy that Freddie reminded me of Michael Pollard, the guy in the movie, who was always smiling with a dumb grin. Jonesy agreed.

When we cruised, Freddie would sit quietly in the back seat. If we stopped at the store for booze or cigarettes and goodies, he always was happy to run in for us. After we got to know each other better he'd come to my house and help me do the dishes or vacuum. Or he'd play with my little brother, Eddie, in the back yard for hours. Of course, my mother liked him. She'd fuss over him offering him food, drink, laugh at his dumb jokes. Sometimes they'd play gin rummy or hearts, or just sit and watch the tube.

It seemed like every time Jonesy came over or called Freddie was here. I think it made him jealous, although he never came right out and said so. When I noticed it, I tried to explain that Freddie and I were only friends and that he actually came over to visit my mother.

"Hey, man, I don't care," he said. I dropped the subject. He had stopped calling as often, maybe once or twice a week. Not like before when it was five or six times a week.

Jonesy hadn't called for over a week when Freddie and I decided to go to Sarah McKenzie's Halloween party. I went dressed in a shiny blue majorette costume, with blue sequined shorts that I'd found at the Salvation Army, black fishnet stockings, red, spiked high-heel shoes with ankle strap, a bouncy, ash-blonde wig ("Clairol-blondes-have-more-fun" variety) that I'd borrowed from my Aunt Helen who was a beautician, false eyelashes, and gobs of makeup. I stuffed two scarves into my 36C cup padded bra.

Since Freddie didn't have a costume, my mother and I concocted an impromptu creation out of an old, purple chenille bathrobe, a shower cap, and a pair of my father's old tennies. We smeared a facial mask, that turned grey after a few minutes, on his smooth hairless face. We used coercion to get him to take off his pants. Since my father wasn't there to protest, we managed to talk my mother into letting us use the car. She made Freddie promise her in front of her Saint Anthony statue that he wouldn't drink. I assumed it was consent when she didn't ask me to.

There was a crescent moon in the cast-iron black sky. The Beatles greeted us at the front door, resonating into the night:

> *Rocky Raccoon checked into his room*
> *only to find Gideon's Bible.*
> *Rocky had come equipped with a gun*
> *to shoot off the legs of his rival."*

In the house Jack O'Lanterns glittered, casting amorphous shadows. Orange and black crepe paper streamers hung suspended from the ceiling, spider webs and skeletons danced from corners and under doorways. The bathtub was filled with water, ice, beer, and blood-red food coloring. A bowl of punch smouldered in a cauldron of dry ice. Lorraine, dressed as a witch, stirred it while gibbering an incantation. Rapunzel handed out chocolate chip marijuana cookies and brownies, while Count Dracula passed around blotter acid. I declined. Things were spooky enough and I'd heard all the horrible reports that were going around about bummers. Besides, I was incognito. No pressure to prove myself.

Freddie and I didn't recognize anyone except for a few of Sarah's friends from the J.C. where she was taking classes. We hung out together drinking Purple Jesus (that's what they called the punch), ate a brownie and retired to the green living room (each room had a different color lighting) with the rest of the ghouls, trolls, and fairies. Someone was circling the room in a long, black cape with wild, white hair streaming out, an ashen, grey face, and blackened eyes. An eerie noise followed him around. Lorraine told me later that he had a tape recorder under his cape.

For a minute I thought I was at the haunted house at Disneyland, until the front door swung open and two Roman soldiers carried Jesus (in a loincloth, tied to a cross made out of two-by-fours) into the green room. The brownie I'd eaten earlier was beginning to have an effect. Little Richard was shouting, *"Tutti Fruttie or rutti, a womp bab a dooba, a womp bam boom."* Freddie and I danced the jerk. Someone in black slipped a rubber spider down my back. I screamed, and it fell out.

After a while I went over and slumped into the purple vinyl couch in my stockinged feet. I had no idea where my shoes were. I was only happy not to have gotten a slipped disc from stumbling around in those spikes. The blonde wig lay wilted in my lap. Bozo the clown had mischievously fished it off and turned it into a ball, tossing it into the air, then back and forth to his friend Bubbles. My Aunt Helen's horrified face flashed through my mind for a moment, but I was too stoned to move.

By this time, my false eyelashes felt like two large sties. But for some reason it seemed impossible to remove them. My fevered brain tried to make sense out of what was going on. Thinking about that made me giggle. My thoughts were like translucent water bubbles, bursting and disappearing, faster and faster, until there were hundreds of them all strung together, coming and going, more visual than anything else. Amazed, I sat there watching them.

Thigh to thigh, Freddie and I sat next to each other. He was like my raft on the high seas. He handed me a bottle of Jose Cuervo Gold Label. It went down, burning and smooth as silk. I felt a warm glow that started somewhere in my throat and spread like a mushroom of heat into my stomach and down my legs. Junior Walker shouted, *"Shotgun!"* I drew closer to Freddie. His arm was around my shoulder. He looked at me, saying something. What was it? His voice was thick as syrup. I noticed the way it rose and fell. The music blared on.

"You know how I feel about you, Cece," he said. Each word was separate and disconnected. Then his mouth was on mine. He was light as a feather. Somewhere deep inside me something recoiled, but it didn't matter. No sooner had I thought of it than it was gone.

Freddie's robe was open and his hairless legs were exposed. He had on blue and white boxer shorts. He had long since removed the shower cap, but there were grey smudges from the

117

facial mask on his cheeks. I laughed and he followed suit. We both were hysterical.

Through the haze I thought I saw a familiar face. It was Jonesy. Wow! I realized for an instant that I had a vise-like grip on Freddie's arm. After a second or so, I thought I heard him say something like, "Hi, man." I glanced up to see Jonesy standing there. He was cold sober. When he looked at me my face felt like a piece of crinkled tin foil. Freddie was watching me with those deer eyes. But now they were fox-like, slanted and cunning, with yellow specks that swarmed and jumped around in the green light.

I turned around and Jonesy had disappeared. Freddie moaned, "Oh, oh." I said something equally stupid, like, "Too much." I could see Jonesy in the yellow light of the kitchen, holding a drink. His face was taut and looked jaundiced. I realized that he wasn't in costume, and I sat for the longest time, wondering how he had gotten in without one.

While I sat mulling this notion over, I heard a voice say, "I wanna talk to you, Cece." It took only a few seconds for me to understand this. It was Jones, insistently tugging at my arm. It seemed ludicrous that anything could have been that important. I didn't resist as he literally towed me away. Little Richard was wailing, "*Long Tall Sally, she's built for speed, she's everythin Uncle John needs.*" Count Dracula grabbed me as I sailed by, nuzzling my neck. Jonesy glared at him and pulled me out the door.

The night air cut through me like tiny electrical currents. I took a deep breath. For some unknown reason I was deliriously happy.

"What's going on?" he said. He sounded angry.

But why? What's going on? I tried to speed up my thought processes. What does he mean? I wondered, gazing down the street in awe at the way the street light glared intensely on the cars, lined up all the way to the end of the block.

"A party," I said, giggling.

"You with Slow?"

Slow? What? I groped for an explanation. But why and what for? How stupid. The evening star blinked hello.

"I'm wasted," I said, as if that summed up everything. "Freddie and I ate a brownie and some dope cookies." He

118

seemed preoccupied, staring at something up the street, so I turned and looked, wondering just, what was distracting him. We were standing almost directly beneath the street light. Suddenly I felt grotesque, aware of my bizarre make-up. I was barefoot and beginning to get cold. Coming down. Jonesy seemed to be contemplating something.

"Did you come with Slow?"

"Yeah," I said, yawning. I was about to put my arm through his and ask him to take me home. Grateful that he was there. He seemed so solid. I moved towards him. He pulled away.

"You better see what happened to Slow. You came with him, you might as well stay with him," he said abruptly, crossing the street. I stood riveted to the sidewalk, shivering.

"Wait, Jonesy!" I started after him but he was gone. "Bastard!" I hissed at the exhaust fumes.

When I went back in, Freddie was leaning on some chick who was dressed like a Girl Scout selling cookies. I felt like crying.

"Let's blow. Come on," I said.

"Oh, wow, Cece, I was jest thinkin' 'bout buying some cookies from Susie here," he said, following the girl scout into the other room.

I sat on the plastic couch and peeled off the eyelashes. The music sounded scratchy, the lights looked stupid and garish. I must have fallen asleep, because the next thing I knew Freddie was shaking my arm. "Wake up, Cece, come on, it's late, we gotta get the car back."

I rubbed my eyes and looked round. Susie was standing behind him. He had on a pair of black pants and no shirt. The place was just about empty. There were cigarette butts on the floor and empty bottles and cups strewn everywhere. The streamers were ragged and some of the skeletons were dismembered.

"OK," I croaked. "What time is it?"

"Almost four," said the girl scout.

"Oh man, my father's gonna kill me!"

"Yeah, that's what I mean. Let's boogie!" said Freddie, helping me on with my coat.

He drove Susie home. Thank god it was on the way. He

kissed her in the car and didn't bother to walk her to the door. Afterwards he told me he was afraid that her parents were waiting for her.

"Ga, Freddie," I said, "I hope mine aren't."

Dawn was breaking as we drove up and parked on the curb instead of in the garage, so as not to make noise and get caught. Luckily everyone was asleep. We tiptoed in and I threw a blanket at Freddie, pointing to the couch. I went to my room and wrestled out of the dress and fell into bed without taking off my stockings. My mouth felt like cotton but I didn't dare get up. I fell asleep wondering what had happened to Aunt Helen's wig, and whose pants Freddie was wearing.

Chapter 12

Jonesy called a week later and apologized, saying that he'd had a bad day the night of the Halloween party. He asked me if I'd like to take in a movie. I felt myself smiling automatically.

"Um, when?" I said.

"How about Friday?"

"I don't know," I said. "I have to babysit Friday." I lied. I didn't know why I was lying. It seemed crazy. I knew that I wanted to be with him and at the same time I felt he was slipping away from me. I wanted proof that he really wanted to see me.

"Well, maybe I'll call you some other time."

"Wait! What about Saturday?"

"Ah ... I can't make it Saturday."

He had another date. I knew it! "Why not?" I said, trying to sound casual.

"Because I got something I have to do."

"OK, 'bye," I said quietly.

"Bye, Cece." Click! He didn't even care. His voice sounded so nonchalant. I felt like crying.

My father walked into the room. "What's wrong?"

"Nothing." I went into my bedroom, to find Maria and Lorraine McKenzie cracking jokes. I grabbed my coat and said, "I'm going to the library."

"Ga, what's wrong with her?" Maria said, as I ran out the front door.

At the library I couldn't concentrate. But I forced myself to stay late enough so I could go home and go right to bed,

121

instead of having to hang out with the rest of the family and have them pry. In bed I tossed and turned for hours. I sobbed, biting my lip so as not to make any noise and wake Maria up. "Shit!" I screamed silently.

After what seemed an eternity, I got up and pulled on a pair of Levis and threw a coat over my pajamas and went stealthily out the back door. I knew that my father always kept an extra set of keys in the glove compartment. Sure enough they were there. I slipped the car into neutral and started pushing it down the driveway. Thank God it was downhill. I knew that I was taking a big chance but I felt desperate. Besides, Maria and I had done it before and hadn't gotten caught. Everyone was asleep. My parents' bedroom was at the back of the house and I knew both of them were sound sleepers.

When I'd gotten the car into the street I jumped in, started it, and took off. Wolfman Jack was on the radio doing requests. I lit a cigarette, trying to calm down. No such luck. On the freeway, I watched in the rear view mirror for cops. Getting off at Whittier Boulevard, I finally calmed down a little because there was more traffic and things sort of came to life. I sped around a couple of blocks (I was relieved to see that he was home), pulled up, and parked behind his car. From the street the house looked dark and quiet. I walked around the side of the house to his window and rapped.

"Jonesy," I whispered. The window sill came to my chin, I tried looking in but couldn't see a thing. I thought I heard a snore. I rapped harder.

"Jonesy," I hissed persistently, tapping against the pane. Finally I saw him staggering to the window.

"Eh, wha'?," he said, rubbing his eyes.

"Hi," I said, trying to sound nonchalant. All of a sudden, when he did open the window, I felt stupid and embarrassed.

"Hi, baby," he said, surprised. "What time is it?"

"Oh, around two, I guess," I said calmly, even though my heart was going faster than a speeding choo-choo train.

"How'd you get here?" He seemed so composed in contrast to me.

I couldn't help it, I burst into tears, blubbering something about not being able to sleep.

"Oh, man," he sighed. "Be quiet."

"I can't help it," I sobbed.

"Come in," he whispered. I scrambled up while he helped, pulling me up under my arms. He was in his jock shorts.

"Man, Cece, I swear, you're too much," he said, running his hands through his tousled hair. "How'd you get here?" he asked after we'd stumbled over to the bed.

"My father's car."

"Does he know?"

"No."

"Wonderful," he sighed.

I was beginning to regret having come.

"I'm going crazy!" I said. "I haven't slept in a week, and you don't even care if I die."

He didn't say anything. Just sat there looking at me. Then he pulled my hand back, leading me towards the bed, and kissed me. I jumped a foot.

"Now what's wrong?"

"Nothing," I said.

He reached into my coat and under my pajamas. "God, you even have your jammies on."

I giggled, pushing his hand away. "Do you love me?" I asked. He sighed. "Tell me!"

"What?" he said with his arm around me, trying to pull me down onto the bed.

"I know that you don't."

Silence.

"Say it," I hissed.

"Say what?" he whispered. We were rolling on the bed.

"Fucker," I whispered in his ear. We were trying to be as quiet as possible. We got under the covers and he was trying to pull down my Levi's, then unbutton my top, while yanking off my coat, all at the same time. It was crazy. We were making-out wildly, all tangled up in blankets and clothes Panting and pulling and tugging my pants until they finally came off, he rolled over on top of me, pressing his thing into my stomach. Then lower.

"Wait a minute," I whispered.

"What?"

"Do you have anything?"

"What you mean?"

"You know."

"Oh, yeah," he said, stopping and going over to his dresser. He brought out a white limp-looking rubber and started rolling it on. It looked horrible. Sickening. I was beginning to lose my desire. "Oh, gawd," I sighed. "Maybe I should go." I sat up.

"No, wait," he said, caressing and stroking me. He started kissing my thighs and began to eat me. That was the first time he'd ever done that and I loved it. I came right away.

"Did you like that?" he said.

I couldn't even answer him. I lay on the bed writhing in ecstacy and we made love for a long time. He came, and after a minute or two, kissed me on the forehead and rolled over. In a few seconds I heard him snoring.

I couldn't seem to relax. I started to feel resentful. How could he just go to sleep like that! I was furious. I knew that he had worked that day. But still. I rolled off the bed, scrambling for my clothes. I felt come rolling down my legs. I grabbed his shirt and wiped my thighs with it. I wondered if he'd notice it in the morning. Probably not.

I climbed out of the window and stumbled down, scraping my knees on the sill. God, why did I do that! Never again. I was hoping I'd never see him again. Shit! I got in the car and drove home, forcing myself to stay awake.

It was almost daylight as I drove into the driveway and tiptoed back into the house. I jumped into bed fully clothed, feeling as though I hadn't slept in a year. Just before I fell asleep, I heard my father get up and leave for work. I was hoping there was enough gas in the car.

It didn't dawn on me until the following day that the rubber had broken.

In the morning, I cringed, filled with remorse. I paced the floor. I thought he hated me. But why? He said that he wanted to see me. Why wasn't that enough? Why didn't I believe him? I should have never gone over there! Should have never let him fuck me! That was it. I decided not to see him anymore. I'd forget about him. Somehow. That was it. I'd forget about the whole thing.

All day I tried forcing it out of my mind. That evening I masturbated in the bathtub until my mother rapped on the door, "Are you OK, Cece, or have you drowned?"

Later the phone rang, and my heart leapt. It was for Maria. I fumed while she talked to one of her friends, pacing the floor in front of her. Finally, I said, "I'm expecting an important call, Maria."

She glared at me and turned her back.

After she hung up, I relaxed but only for a minute. It rang again. This time it was my aunt Cora. I answered it and almost lied to her about my mother being home. They talked a while.

At nine it rang again and my mother called, "It's for you, Cece." My heart was pounding.

"Hello." It was Gerry. I barely could talk, I was so disappointed.

"What's the matter, Cece?"

"Oh, nothing. I have a headache." I'd never tell her the truth about Jonesy. "Listen, I'll call you tomorrow."

At ten it rang again. I answered it.

"Hi, Cece?"

"Yeah." It was him.

"What's going on?"

"Oh, nothing," I said casually.

"You make it OK last night?"

"Yeah," I yawned. I was shaking.

"Wanna go out somewhere this weekend?"

"Umm, I guess."

"OK, I'll come by Saturday night, and we can decide."

"Alright," I said, trying to sound nonchalant.

I went to bed smiling. In the morning it began again. The doubt. If he really cared, he'd want to see me before the weekend. He probably didn't have another date, so he called me. I was sure he was going out with someone else. The chick with the big tits. The one I'd seen him with at the party the first night I met him. I saw Gerry the next day and pretended to be interested in something she was talking about, but actually never heard a word. I made small talk and, as casually as possible snuck in, "Remember the night we first met Jonesy? Do you remember the chick he was talking to at Rachel's party?"

"When?"

Maravilla

"At that party by the J.C."

"Gawd, that was ages ago."

"I know, but it's important."

"You mean the chick with the great body."

"I don't think she was that great," I said.

"Yeah, that was Bonnie. Angel said it was Jonesy's cousin."

"Oh, really," I said. Well, it wasn't her. Then who was it?

Chapter 13

On Saturday a horn honked and I ran out to see Gerry driving Angel's Corvette with its top down, sporting the new Snoopy hat that he'd bought her. Angel had been taking her shopping ever since she started going to mass with his mother, Mrs. Hernandez.

She was wearing nice clothes now, cashmere sweaters, gold chains and bracelets, leather boots instead of the vinyl kind.

I tied a scarf around my head and jumped over the door, and we took off.

At her cousin's house in Boyle Heights, Gerry insisted on going into the bathroom before she took off her hat. She sat on the toilet seat while I stood over her, ratting, combing and spraying her hair. After that she did mine.

Around dusk we headed for the freeway, up the Santa Ana, going ninety over to Hollywood, got off at Sunset Boulevard just when it was beginning to buzz and come to life.

Sitting in the 'Vette, with the engine humming in the bumper to bumper traffic, Gerry turned to me, grinned, and hit the steering wheel. "Power, don't you love it!" she sang.

It was a balmy evening. Neon signs lit up the streets as we inched our way through the traffic, past the forty foot billboards (Liberace in glittering regalia at Harrah's, Frank Sinatra crooning at the Sands, Elvis in white and gold, studded and fringed at Caesar's Palace), past the nightclubs and the lighted marquees of movie theatres, the transients, winos and drag queens, past McDonald's, Texaco, Chevron, Standard, passing the prostitutes and pimps, Bob's Big Boy, runaway teenagers, businessmen, and high-heeled women that paraded up and down

127

the boulevard.

Gerry let me have the wheel. I zipped back on the freeway to the Santa Monica over to Venice. We were drinking Cokes and smoking Salems, tearing along Highway One, singing "Gotta Ticket to Ride", along with the Beatles.

"Not so fast!" yelled Gerry into the wind.

I slowed down, checked for cops. Out of town now, the sky was a dark, cast-iron gray. The headlights shot across the highway, casting shadows on the black hills. Salt air scent permeated the air.

I pulled over to put up the top, then headed back for the Strip. Stopping at a liquor store to buy a bottle of vodka, I used my cousin Vera's I.D.

At the Whiskey-a-go-go, we danced the jerk and watched a girl in a fringed bikini doing the go-go in a raised cage.

Gerry bought two glasses of orange juice at the bar. We took a few sips and, from under a table, I slipped the vodka out of my purse and filled them.

Later we went to the Peppermint West and danced until they closed, then waited for Carlos McGuinnes the door-man to get off. He was a friend of Marcos, Gerry's brother. He had black, greasy hair and wore a powder blue, double-breasted coat with white pants and matching blue contact lenses that shone like jewels, a white carnation in his lapel, and a lapis lazuli on his pinkie.

He invited us to his apartment, a complex of four hundred units, that was flat and stark as the moon and made us salty margaritas, served waxy jalapeno dip and rolled joints--all the time talking about the famous movie stars he'd met or almost met because he knew someone who worked for someone who knew someone.

Gerry acted impressed. Later she made fun of him. I shuffled through his record collection, putting Smokey Robinson and Little Junior Walker on the dusty hi-fi.

Gerry and I danced together, and then we sat on the bed with Carlos telling stories, smoking a joint, and dipping Doritos into the jalapeno dip.

Later we went to Mel's Drive-In and Carlos bought us scrambled eggs and bacon.

Gerry had told her parents that she would be spending the

night at my house and I told my mother that I was staying at her place. So we could stay out all night.

With the sun rising in streams of smoky orange and dusky brown, and me sitting on Carlos's lap, we drove back to his apartment and the three of us crawled into bed. Wrapped around each other like pretzels, we fell asleep.

Once or twice I felt his hand reaching for my hip and I pushed it away.

"He was like a piece of baloney between two slices of french bread," said Gerry as we drove home the next morning.

"He tried to feel me up," I said. "Can you imagine?"

"Me, too," Gerry said, giggling.

We stopped at a gas station bathroom to change our clothes and wash up before going home and taking the car back.

After Mass that afternoon, Gerry borrowed Marcos's Chevy and we cruised Elysian Park, pulling up next to where some bikers had congregated. We sat in the car with the sun on our faces checking out the scene.

Bikers were streaming in and out. One of them pulled up close to the Chevy and started rubbing his chopper with a chamois.

"How's it goin'?" he grunted.

"Alright man," Gerry cooed, flicking an ash out the window. Another biker rolled up and mumbled something, then turned and nodded his head at us.

"Nice machine you got there," Gerry said.

I could tell they were getting ready to ask us to ride. I blasted the radio up and looked in the mirror checking my lipstick.

"That guy's a twerp," Gerry said.

"Shut up, he'll hear you. Don't you want to ride?"

She looked over her shoulder and smiled at him. He grunted and kept wiping his flashy paint job.

"Wanna ride?" he said. He was wearing a brown, leather aviator jacket and mirror sunglasses. His chopper was metallic blue and opalescent white with red pin stripes. It had a long, narrow body sloping up towards high handlebars. The back seat was done in the shape of an open hand, palm up.

Gerry and I conferred about which one of us would ride it. The other guy's bike was flourescent yellow with bright orange flames.

They were revving their engines.

"Comin'? he said.

"Go on, Gerry," I said, shoving her towards the bike with the open hand.

"OK," she said, carefully straddling the narrow, little seat.

I jumped on the bike with the flames.

"Hold on, honey, I ain't gonna bite," he grunted as we took off.

I clutched the back of his leather jacket, smiling and nodding at Gerry as we spun around the park. After a couple of rounds, they took us back, pulled over, grunted, and took off.

"Fantabulous!" Gerry squealed, waving at them. We got back in the car and put on a few coats of lipstick and combed our hair.

It was after dark when we drove up to Ernie's Taco Stand looking for Angel. Gerry was restless and distracted until we'd found him. He pulled in about half an hour later. She jumped out of the car and ran over to him. I waited for about fifteen minutes before going over there. They were making out like crazy, climbing all over each other.

"What are we gonna do, Ger?" I said. She ignored me.

I stood there feeling stupid.

"Gerry," I said, rapping on the window. Some guys cruised by whistling at me and making cat calls.

"Hey!" I yelled. She turned around. Angel rolled down his window.

"How's it goin', Cece?"

"Alright," I said, hoping he wouldn't roll up the window and leave me standing there.

Gerry leaned over him. "How about something to eat, Cece?"

"OK."

"We'll get out and join you in a minute," she said, smiling at Angel. He was obviously enjoying himself. I felt left out and awkward.

130

After we'd eaten, Angel offered to take us to the movies. I wasn't that crazy about going but it was better than being home alone. I found myself wishing Jonesy was there. But I probably wouldn't see him until Monday night, as he was working swing shift on weekends at the San Pedro docks.

On our way out, we ran into Slow Freddie and I talked him into coming along so that I could bear sitting in the front seat while Gerry and Angel wrestled and panted in the back.

Gerry acted different when she was with Angel. She was coy and ladylike, not ballsy and bold as she'd been earlier in the day with the bikers. Seeing her change made me wonder if she was sincere about Angel, not that I blamed her. She looked great behind the wheel of the Corvette, flashing those little gold chains in the sunlight, wearing the new leather coat with the fur collar that Angel had bought her. But then again, I'd never actually seen her making out with other guys. But I had seen Angel with other chicks. I'd caught him fooling around more than once with Esther Ochoa. Esther wasn't the only one. I used to catch him leaning on chicks at parties and being a whole lot friendlier than was necessary. I never told Gerry though. I was afraid it would antagonize her. She was my best friend and I wanted to spend most of my time with her. I was hoping that, if we got married (I was sure that she would marry first), we could live next door to each other or something like that--even though I had no intention of marrying any of the guys I knew then. Most of them were into petty crime, burglary, dealing and doing heavy drugs.

I knew that Jonesy was stealing from the docks where he worked, then selling the stuff. TV's, radios, pots and pans, small appliances, anything he could get away with. I also knew that Slow Freddie and Victor Jimenez passed bad checks, dealt weed, and traded counterfeit money.

In November Angel got popped for possession of heroin. It was his second offense and he was going to have to do time. He was sent to an honor farm at Norco, California.

He left Gerry the Corvette and every Sunday she would get dressed up in high heels, a mini skirt, and a tight sweater (that's what he liked her to wear), put on her blonde wig and drive over to see him.

A few times I went with her. We drove out of the city limits, past the suburbs into the rural area of Norco. Entering the flat, gray building, we click-clacked in our high heels across the concrete floor to Inspection, where armed guards searched us, and continued down the long corridor. Then we waited in a long room with barred windows, surrounded by guards and relatives and friends visiting inmates. Angel came ambling out in blue denim work clothes and sat at a table with a thin screen between us and we talked. At first, he looked bloated and dragged down but happy to see us. The last time I'd gone to see him, I could see that he had changed. He was nervous and gaunt, but more aware and clear-eyed than I'd ever seen him before.

Jonesy called me on Friday. "Wanna go see a movie?"
"I don't know--I don't feel well," I said moodily.
"What's wrong?"
"I'll tell you later."
"Oh. Maybe you'll be feeling better tomorrow night. Victor is having a party. You wanna go?"
"You know I don't like Victor!" I said.
"Oh, man," he sighed.

After I hung up, I was sorry I'd been bitchy. But I couldn't seem to help it. My period was late. I thought I was pregnant.

It wasn't the first time. The last time I thought I was pregnant, it turned out that I was only late. I'd been depressed and cried a lot. This time I didn't want to say anything until I knew for sure.

The next day I called him off and on into the evening. But he never showed up. That evening Lorraine McKenzie phoned, wanting to know if I'd like to go to the drive-in with her, Paula, and Corky Cruz.

"Why not?" I said.

Rebel without a Cause and *East of Eden* were playing. I'd already seen both of them five times. When we got there,

Corky passed a reefer around. Paula was in one of her crazy moods.

"I love you, I love you, I love you!" she panted at the screen, which was lit up with a full shot of James Dean.

"You can put your shoes under my bed anytime, big boy!" Lorraine chortled, pounding her fists on the dashboard.

"He's sooo groovie!" I sighed.

"You guys are crazy," snorted Corky. "That guy's dead."

"No, he ain't," said Lorraine. "It was only a publicity stunt, man. My sister saw him on Hollywood Boulevard just the other night."

"Oh, sure," Corky said.

"Be quiet. I can't hear," said Paula.

At the end of the movie, when Dean kissed Natalie, we screamed raucously, jumping up and down in our seats.

Someone knocked at the window. Paula stashed the reefer and cracked open the wing.

"Yes?"

"Would you girls please keep it down? We can hear you all the way over at our car," said this older man. Lorraine tittered.

"Shuu," Corky hissed.

"Sorry," Paula said. "We'll try to be quieter." He left.

"See," Corky said, "you guys are too rowdy."

"Oh, who cares!" Lorraine quipped.

"Don't be such a *viejita*, Corky," I said.

During intermission, Lorraine and I went to the snack bar and bought a bucket of popcorn and a pizza. On the way back some guys made cat calls, trying to get us to join them.

"No way, Bozo!" Lorraine shouted. "Not after Jimmy Dean, man!"

Before we left, Paula took out her hair spray and gave the car a couple of shots to kill the smell of weed.

On the boulevard on the way home, I caught a glimpse of Victor's car. Jonesy was in the back seat sitting next to Mary Lou Gomez, his ex-girlfriend.

"There goes Victor and Jonesy," Lorraine said.

"Yeah," I said. "I saw 'em."

"Are you still going with Jonesy?" Corky asked.

"Ah--yeah," I said.

"I thought you two had broken up."

"Why?"

"I saw him with Mary Lou the other night."

Out of the corner of my eye, I saw Paula poke Corky.

"Oops," Corky groaned.

"Where'd you see them?"

"At the Palladium, the night Tito Puente was playing."

"How do you know they were together?"

"He had his arm around her."

"He probably was jes dancin' with her," Lorraine interjected.

They were all looking at me. I felt hot and nauseous and mumbled something about not knowing anything about it.

Paula changed the subject. I didn't hear a word they said after that.

I couldn't sleep so I got up in the middle of the night and called him. His father answered and I hung up. I wondered if he was spending the night with Mary Lou. I knew she had her own place. I started to cry, muffling the sounds into the pillow so that Maria wouldn't hear.

In the morning I wasn't feeling well enough to go to Mass. After the family left, I tried going back to sleep. But I kept thinking about Jonesy and Mary Lou, together in bed, and me big, fat, and pregnant--and alone. No! I pounded my fists on the bed.

"Shit," I cried. How could he do this to me! Everyone had seen them together. They made a fool of me. A picture of Jonesy and Mary Lou kept going around in my head. I tried calling him again, letting it ring at least forty times. No answer. I went back in the bedroom and grabbed Maria's stuffed dog, one of those purple things, banging it against the wall until one of its ears tore. I was taking rapid, strangled breaths. They were coming faster and heavier. I gasped for air. I couldn't catch my breath! I ran into the kitchen and got a paper sack and slowly exhaled into it until I'd calmed down. Then I called Gerry, asking her to come over right away.

As I was taking off my nightgown, I had another flash of Jonesy and Mary Lou. In a rage I began ripping it into strips. Then I picked up a glass that was on the dresser and flung it at the wall. I started pulling clothes off the hangers and throwing them on the floor. I sat on the bed crying and scrambling through my wallet. Taking out a picture of Jonesy with his arm around me, I tore it up, ran into the bathroom and flushed it down the toilet, screaming, "Bastard!" at the swirling bowl.

"Ga, Cece, what's wrong?"

I turned around to see Gerry.

"Jonesy!" I cried.

"What did he do to you, beat you up or what?" She looked alarmed.

"No. Corky saw him with Mary Lou, his ex," I cried.

"Is that all?"

"He was kissing her," I lied. I couldn't tell her that I thought I was pregnant.

"Oh, man, big deal. Don't you think you're over-reacting?"

I fell across the bed, deflated.

"Come on, Cece," she said, looking around at the mess. "I'll help you clean up before your parents get back."

"OK," I sniffled, picking up the torn nightie and blowing my nose on it.

After we'd straightened up, Gerry said, "I think you'd better come home with me."

"Alright," I said, putting on a black turtleneck, a pair of black stretch pants with stirrups, and slipping into my black high heeled ankle boots.

"Ga, girl, you look like you're going to a funeral."

"That's what it feels like."

I cried off and on all the way to her house.

At Gerry's we watched the tube. It was all a big blur. Later, Marcos sat next to me on the couch, playing the blues on his guitar, singing, "_Ya got me hidin', ya got me peepin', ya got me doin what you want._" He got me to sing along to _Bright Lights, Big City._ I was feeling more relaxed. Gerry went to bed. Marcos lowered the T.V. and we sat in the glare of it, watching the Steve Allen Show while he strummed his guitar into the late night. I fell asleep on the couch and woke up in the middle of the night to find a blanket thrown over me. I went back to sleep.

Jonesy called during the week and we arranged to go to the drive-in to see _Dr. Zhivago._ I didn't say much, just sat quietly, even though I felt like a hurricane was going on inside of me.

He slid over, put his arm around me, and kissed my cheek. I tensed and looked away.

"Whatsa matter, baby?"

"Nothing," I said, staring at the screen.

"Come on, tell me," he said a few minutes later.

"Mary Lou," I said in a strangled voice.

"Who?"

"You know what I'm talking about," I said, pushing him away.

"What?"

"You've been seeing her, haven't you?"

Silence.

On the screen, Dr. Zhivago wandered the desolate landscape, torn by the ravages of war. I felt like throwing up.

"I have to go to the bathroom," I said, sliding out the door.

When I came back, he snuggled up, nuzzling my neck, and sliding his hand down to the V in my pants.

"Don't!" I said, pushing his hand away.

Why not?" he whispered in my ear.

"Because," I said, biting my lip, trying not to cry.

The screen was a flat, white field of snow in the background of a deserted house with icicles everywhere.

"What's wrong, honey?"

"Did you do it to her?"

"Do what?"

"Screw her!"

"Shuu! Not so loud!"

"Why not? You can't stop me," I shouted. I could see that he was enjoying himself. I felt like killing him.

"I thought we had an agreement--like you can do anything you want, cruise with anyone, and so can I, right, baby?"

"You bastard!" I shrieked, pounding my fists on his chest.

"Don't," he said, grabbing my wrists.

I began to cry.

"Hey, baby," he drawled, "I'm sorry. She doesn't mean a thing to me."

Maravilla

Dr. Zhivago was making love to Lara for the last time. The screen lit up with a field of yellow daffodils. I sat there, rigidly staring straight ahead.

"Come on, honey," he pleaded, kissing me, gently.

"Everyone saw you with that goddamn whore!"

He gathered me into his arms, rubbing my cheek. "You're the only one I care about. She's nothin' next to you, mama." Then he reached under my sweater, feeling for my breast, rubbing my nipple back and forth, whispering into my ear, "It's you I love, baby, just you."

"What if I'm pregnant?" I whispered.

"Don't worry, honey, I'll take care of you," he said, pushing me back on the seat.

I melted into his embrace and we did it right there on the front seat of his Plymouth while Lara's Theme came in over the scratchy loudspeaker.

The next day I noticed a spot of blood on my pants. By that evening I was flowing heavily.

A few days later he called, asking if he could come by.

"Come now," I said. I couldn't wait to see him.

As soon as we had gotten into his car, he pulled out a little box. "I got you something," he said. It was a small, heart-shaped gold locket attached to a thin, delicate chain, with "Te amo" inscribed on the back.

"It's beautiful," I said, as he clasped it around my neck.

"I love you, Cece," he whispered, holding me.

When I told him that I had started my period and that we had nothing to worry about, he said, "I'm glad to see you smiling, but I wasn't worried. I would marry you in a minute, if that's what you wanted."

"I don't think either one of us is ready for that," I laughed, relieved.

"You're right, honey, but I just wanted to put your mind at ease, in case you were worried." Then he said that he had told his mother about me and she wanted us to have dinner over there that weekend.

"Do you think she'll like me?" I said nervously

"Of course," he said, pushing me gently back on the seat.

"Oh, please, please, love me," I whispered, as he pressed the full length of his body against mine.

Maravilla

At home the light from the full moon flooded the darkened bedroom. I looked in my dresser mirror and saw the gleaming reflection of the locket around my neck and touched it.

I lay in bed wide awake, thinking of Jonesy, feeling his body warmth and his essence, still with me, and snuggled into the blankets. It was strange, I thought, the way things seemed so mixed up, and then something happened, and everything became perfectly clear. Like the first night I met Jonesy and knew absolutely how I felt. There had been something so familiar about him. Everything seemed right when I was with him. Somehow I knew for sure that we would be together for a long, long time.

Chapter 14

There were a lot of things happening that summer. It was the year after the Watts riots had erupted and went off like a time bomb. I remember seeing the smoke rising in billowing black clouds high into the hot, muggy sky all the way from 97th Street. You could feel a sense of pulsing rage and paranoia in the air. Stunned, I watched the looting, stealing, and fighting on the news at night. When it was over, the city was occupied by troops like the defeated in a war zone. For us, Watts was another world. It might as well have been another planet, even though it was only twenty miles or so away.

But that summer following the riot you could feel the tension and stifling anger rising steadily like a pressure cooker in the barrio. It ran through the neighborhood like a palpable electrical current, a humming and gathering of explosive compression building to a fever pitch.

On top of it all Marcos was being drafted. It seemed like he had just graduated from high school the day before yesterday. Actually, it had been over a year. He was dead set against going, but saw no way out. His family gave him a going away party. His mother made enchiladas and mole, and Gerry baked him a cake. A few friends and the family were there. Marcos was subdued and quiet through the whole affair. But then, he'd always been introverted at parties and social events.

Afterwards, when most of the guests had left and Gerry and her parents were cleaning up, Marcos and I sat in the den and he played his guitar. He played, inspired, low and sad, starting with the blues, then a few Wes Montgomery riffs, gradually building up to some fast and furious flamenco. His

139

father had been a flamenco guitarist and had taught him to play when he was just a boy. His fingers danced over the strings incredibly. I sat there amazed, awed. I had never heard him play so intensely.

He stopped for awhile and I asked, "When are you leaving?"

"In a few days."

"Too bad. I'll miss you. You know, your dumb jokes."

"Yeah." he said, "A bummer to say the least."

"Scared?"

"Yeah--fuckin A."

"Don't go." I said. We were sitting in the gathering shadows of the night. A dim light shone in from the kitchen. I could only see one side of his face.

"You're crazy," he said.

"Don't you wish you could run away?"

"Where to?" he asked, turning his head toward me in the dark.

"Oh, I don't know. Mexico. Canada."

"You gonna come with me?" he joked.

"No", I said quietly. "I hate the cold. And I can't speak Spanish, except for *orale pues* and *con safos*."

He guffawed. I didn't mean to be sarcastic. Marcos and I always made a joke when we felt uneasy or bad.

We sat there for a while, silent in the dark room. It seemed stupid and awkward to say anything. There were just no words. Then he started playing, the low-down rambling blues, a little Howlin Wolf, some Muddy Waters. *"Got ma mojo workin,"* he wailed, *"but it jest doan work on you-whoo."*

Right before he left, the three of us, Marcos, Gerry and I decided to go to the show at the Golden Gate on Whittier Boulevard. It was a gross, smoggy day. Hot and muggy and claustrophobic. There was a tension hanging in the air, a tangible feeling of agitation and anxiety. I attributed it to the fact that Marcos was leaving soon. As we walked toward the theater I saw huge clouds of black smoke rising above the buildings. I was thinking that there must be a fire somewhere. Then I heard the sounds of screaming sirens. We turned the corner and saw squad cars darting by one after another, four cops in each car, armed with high powered rifles, tact helmets pulled down over their faces. I felt the adrenaline rush of fear shoot through me. You could see their black and white cars and eerie, flashing lights blinking all up and down the street. They were moving fast. There must have been over a hundred of them, turning both ways up the street, blocking off exits, stopping traffic.

Instinctively, we rushed forward, pulled by an overwhelming surge of energy. My blood was pumping like crazy. I felt as if we were being swept into some awful swirling vortex. As we approached the Boulevard it looked like the end of the world. The whole place seemed to have burst into flames. And the entire L.A. tact squad and police force had descended like an invading army in some kind of science fiction nightmare. There was a terrible clamor of screaming, shouting and shattering glass, people running down the street, gunshots going off. Fire trucks lined up on the road and firemen were spraying torrents of water from their gigantic hoses onto the smoldering, burning buildings as looters scrambled by. There were pockets of angry people everywhere. I saw a woman in high heels trying to stop a cop from dragging off some guy. She was knocked down and shoved into a squad car. Groups of shouting, jeering people stood in clusters, yelling at the police who were randomly arresting passersby who ignored or defied their orders to disperse. One man ran down the street, tossing a molotov cocktail into a store front whose window had been shattered. It burst into black and orange flames.

We were being jostled and shoved through the crowd toward the sidelines where cops patrolled, ordering, "Move on! Don't loiter!" Shocked and stupified, we stood watching the horror. Someone ran by saying that Ruben Salazar had been shot down in a bar on the corner. A woman started to cry. We shifted down the street to see if we could get a glimpse of something, but all we saw was the insane melee of firemen and cops swarming the place. A woman who had fallen and hurt her knee bumped into us, asking if anyone could get her out of there. She had her two kids with her, and her car, she said, was blocked off on the street nearby, in flames. We pushed through the throng of people and headed to where Marcos had parked, a couple of blocks away. The woman was crying. Her kids were wide-eyed and silent as we drove them home.

On the news that night we heard that earlier in the day a man had been arrested for a minor offense. Instead of ticketing him, the police tried to take him to jail. His wife had vehemently protested, struggling to wedge herself between her husband and the cops, yelling to passersby about what was going on. The cops handcuffed her and threw her into the squad car in front of their three children. A couple of men took notice and angrily approached them, disputing the arrest. They were ordered to leave and threatened with "disturbing the peace." A few more people quickly gathered around and within moments a hostile, enraged crowd had congregated and surrounded the squad car, demanding the couple's release, rocking it back and forth, threatening to damage it. The cops pulled out their guns. Someone started a fire in the squad car, and before anyone knew what was happening the whole thing had erupted out of control.

Afterwards, people got together to march and protest. Maria and some of her friends were attending a candlelight vigil at City Hall in memory of Ruben Salazar who had died from a gunshot wound the day of the riot, and to protest police brutality. My mother and I joined them. We marched around City Hall in a solemm procession, then over to the civic center carrying placards and lighted votive candles in paper cups, singing and chanting "*No venceremos, no venceremos!* Justice now! Justice now!" Before it ended there was a long silence dedicated to the life and memory of Ruben Salazar. Maria told me that he was a committed Chicano activist who had stood up and fought for his rights and those of his community. Now he was dead. I found it more than odd that one of the most outspoken and radical people in the Chicano community had died accidently from stray gunshots.

Two days after the march at City Hall Marcos left for boot camp.

After the holidays, I got a job at Prudential Life Insurance Company, where Gerry worked. Every weekday morning we'd catch the RTD at six o'clock, go downtown, file papers, run the duplicating machine, sometimes do light typing. It was so boring I had to drink coffee all day to stay awake. At lunch time I'd go in the bathroom and splash water on my face and pinch my cheeks. But for the first time in my life I was making my own money on a regular basis.

By February Gerry and I had saved enough to rent an apartment. We found a vacancy at the Lanai Gardens, two hundred yellow, sooty units overlooking the Santa Ana Freeway.

It was a second floor apartment with one little bedroom, which we shared, and a small living room with a breakfast nook. We had to borrow and scrounge for pots and pans, mismatched dishes and cutlery to get started.

I slept with ear plugs the first week because of the noise from traffic that rattled by night and day. Then I got used to it.

At the end of the month, Gerry found out that Angel was being released. His father had pulled strings and gotten him a job on a construction site out of the county. He was going to serve the remainder of his sentence on weekends.

"Angel and I are going to look at engagement rings," Gerry said as we drove home from work in the bumper to bumper traffic of downtown L.A. (She had given the 'Vette back to Angel and her father offered her money for a down payment on a used car.) "Then we're going to Carmen's for dinner. Do you want to meet us there? I could leave you the car."

"No, thanks," I said. "I have to do my hair tonight."

I figured she was inviting me only because she felt obliged. We had made plans earlier in the week to go to a movie and dinner together that evening.

Lately she seemed to be interested only in Angel. She bought books and magazines for brides and talked incessantly about their wedding plans. She asked me to help pick out bridesmaids' dresses and patterns of silverware and china. But she never seemed interested in what I said. It seemed stupid to try to talk to her when she wouldn't listen. She acted like she was in her glory, talking about how wonderful everything was going to be after they got married. I had my doubts. The week after Angel got released, I had seen him cruising the boulevard with Esther Ochoa and Sarah McKenzie. They were all stoned out of their minds.

When Angel came to pick her up, I stayed in the bedroom. Right before they left, I went into the bathroom and slammed the door.

On Wednesday, during lunch break, Gerry handed me her keys, saying, "Go ahead and take the car. Angel is going to pick me up."

When I got home, the phone was ringing. It was Gerry. Angel hadn't shown up and she wanted me to come back and get her.

She was standing in front of the insurance building when I arrived.

"I'm gonna find that bastard if it takes me all night," she hissed, grabbing the keys out of my hand.

We got off the freeway and drove past his house, then over to Ernie's Taco Stand. We were heading for the J.C. when we passed Sarah McKenzie's house and saw the Corvette. She slammed on the brakes.

"I'm going in," she said.

In a while, they both came out. They were arguing. She was walking back to the car. He grabbed her by the arm. She pulled away, swinging her purse around, hitting him. He held onto her wrist.

"Let go!" she shrieked.

"Ah, come on, Gerry," he said. She let him lead her to his car, where they sat talking.

Then she came over and said. "I'm gonna go with him. You take the car home, OK?"

"Oh, wow, just what I wanted to do, drive home alone," I said, glaring at her.

"Oh, by the way," she said, turning to leave, "Jonesy's in there."

Sarah McKenzie opened the door when I knocked. I could see him slumped on the couch. His eyes were bloodshot slits.

"Hi, man," he rasped. He was wasted.

"I just wanted to see what you were doing," I said. I felt nervous and uncomfortable. Sarah lay on the floor watching the tube. I knew that she dealt coke. But whatever they were on, it wasn't coke.

After a few minutes, I said, "Well, I just wanted to see what was happening with you." I was repeating myself. Sarah ignored me.

"We're jes hanging out, man," Jonesy said, smiling stupidly.

They stared blankly at the television set. *Let's Make A Deal* was on. A woman had won a washing machine and a dryer and a fur coat. She was jumping up and down, screeching and grabbing the host and shaking him.

"I'm leaving," I said

"Yeah, awright," Jonesy drawled.

I went out, quietly closing the door, got in the car and drove home.

On Sunday afternoon, Paula O'Brien and I were riding through Los Nietos past La Tiendita when I saw Jonesy's Plymouth. He and Victor were sitting in the front seat. I waved to them but they didn't see me or pretended not to. Ever since Jonesy had lost his job at the docks a couple of weeks before, he'd been spending more time with Victor. Everyone knew that Victor was a junkie, a dealer, and a petty crook. He reminded me of a weasel.

Right after I got home that evening, the phone rang. It was Slow Freddie.

"Wanna hang out?" he said.

"I don't think so," I said, hoping Jonesy would call.

"You waitin' on Jones?"

"Why?"

"Because he's with Angel and Victor."

"How do you know?"

"I saw 'em. What ya say?"

"Alright, I guess." I thought if I went with him I'd run into Jonesy.

He drove to a liquor store and bought a quart of Bud, opened it and passed it to me. I took a hit and passed it back. We cruised over to Ernie's and parked.

Cece, when are you gonna give me a break?" he said, rubbing my shoulder. His voice had an irritating, nasal tone. I

145

pushed his hand away.

"I don't know," I said, looking out the window.

"Ah, man, you know how I feel about you. I wish you were my girl."

I felt lonely and depressed.

"Come on," he said, pulling me towards him.

"No," I said. "Don't, Freddie!"

When I had told Gerry that Slow Freddie had told me that he loved me and was willing to wait for me until I was through with Jonesy, she had said, "He told me the same thing. He's a con, Cece. Everyone knows that."

He snapped me out of my reverie.

"You must be crazy, girl."

"Why?"

"Being in love with a junkie."

"What do you mean?"

"Come on, man, get hip. Everyone knows that Jones is into smack."

"Liar!"

"I ain't lyin', I swear to God," he said dully.

After a few minutes I said, "I wanna go home."

As I got out of the car, he said, "You mad at me? Oh, wow, Cece, don't be pissed, man." He was slumped low in the seat, his head hung down.

"That's OK," I said. "Forget it."

A few nights later, Jonesy and I went to Concha's for dinner. I was distracted and moody. Afterwards we sat in the car in front of the restaurant. I decided to ask him.

"Do you have a drug habit?" I said, looking into his eyes.

"Who told you that?"

"Slow Freddie."

"Yeah,"

"How long has this been going on?"

"Just a couple of months," he said, sniffling.

"Can you quit?"

"Don't want to," he said, looking at me blankly. Sounds of a fast mambo drifted out from the Boom Boom Club. The pulsations of the conga drums filled my head. A green and red

146

sombrero neon sign blinked off and on. A tear slid down my cheek.

"Don't cry, baby, please," he pleaded. "Hey, man, no one's ever cried over me before."

"Take me home," I whispered.

We drove back to my apartment in silence.

"Good bye, Cece," he said as I got out of the car. I could feel him watching me as I climbed the stairs.

That night I dreamed a black hawk perched at the foot of my bed. I woke up before dawn to see it still and solemn, its yellow beak opening and closing. It was saying something. Something simple and clear.

When I woke up in the morning, I forgot what it was.

On Friday night, Gerry and I cruised the boulevard, stopping at Ernie's. Jonesy, Angel, and Victor pulled in around ten o'clock. Gerry got out of the car and went to talk to Angel. She came back in a few minutes saying that she was going with him in Victor's car and that Jonesy was going to take her car.

"You can follow us to a party in Montebello if you want," she said. The three guys had gone into the bathroom. Then the door flung open and Jonesy ran out. Victor and Angel were right behind him. He jumped in the car and we took off, laying rubber.

"Hey, what's wrong?" I said.

"There was a narc in there!"

In a flash the sounds of sirens were screaming down on us. I looked back to see flashing red and yellow lights. Jonesy pulled over.

"Get out!" he barked.

Gerry was running toward us.

"They won't take you. Go on!" He was shoving me against the door. I was paralyzed with fear. Gerry yanked my arm.

"Hurry, Cece!" she cried.

Something made me get out and we headed down the street at a clip. As we turned the corner, I looked back to see a cop holding a gun on Jonesy, frisking him. As soon as we were out of sight, we started running. It took everything I had not to dive to the ground as we sprinted down that dark street. After a few blocks, my lungs were on fire. Panting, we slipped into an alley cutting through a back yard. The light from a TV glowed as we passed a window. I held my breath. I felt the chill of the night air against my damp, sweaty body and shivered. We turned up and down a few more streets until we came to a phone booth and Gerry called someone to come and get us. Then we walked to the Beverly Bowling Alley and sat in the restaurant waiting. The reverberations from bowling balls clattering down alleys rumbled through the building. A waitress came over and we ordered Cokes.

"Wow," said Gerry, sipping her Coke. "That was really weird. I wonder what was going on?"

Before I could answer, she went on nervously, "Whatever it was, it was probably Victor's fault. I hate him. He's nothing but a trouble maker."

I felt like slapping her.

"What about Angel?" I said

"What? Angel's clean, man!" She cut off the end of her sentence looking away, signaling that she didn't want to discuss it.

"I don't believe it," I said.

"What do you mean?"

"That's not what Jonesy says."

"What does he say?"

"He says that both he and Angel are into junk. And that he's not quitting and, if you ask me, neither is Angel. Just look at the dude."

"Jonesy's a lying pig!" she spat.

"Oh, sure. You're so stupid you can't even see what's going on right under your nose."

"And I suppose you think you're so smart," she said, glaring at me.

"At least I know the truth when I hear it."

"Shut up!" she shrieked.

Some people sitting at a nearby table turned around

"Do you understand?" she whispered hoarsely.

I lowered my voice. "I guess it doesn't really matter to you. Angel has enough money to support you and a habit. But Jonesy doesn't. What do you care, as long as you have the

Corvette and all those flashy clothes? That's all you care
about!" I was trembling. She got up, threw some money on the
table, and walked toward the exit. I waited a few minutes,
then headed out the door.

Before we got home, I asked Gerry's cousin who had come
to pick us up if he had any downers.

"All's I got is a Darvon," he said.

"I'll take it."

At home I fell into a woozy, thick sleep. When I woke,
Gerry was gone. I called in sick. After breakfast, I got dressed
and went to the bus stop. It was drizzling and traffic moved
in a steady stream as I walked with my umbrella propped open
over my head. I got off the bus and walked the couple of
blocks to Victor's. Jonesy's Plymouth was parked in front.

When I went in, he was on the couch covered with a dirty,
old blanket. His hair was tousled, his face red and blotchy.

"I guess you didn't get busted," I said.

"Naw," he grunted. "We weren't holding, so they couldn't do
anything."

"That's good."

"Yeah, man," he said, yawning. "What do you want?"

"I've come to tell you I'm not going to see you anymore."

I could hear Victor in the kitchen. I knew he was listening.

"OK, if that's what you want," he said, scratching his leg
and sipping on a beer.

I felt a wild, white hatred surge through me. I wanted to
sock him, slap him, throw something at him. But all I could do
was get up and quietly walk out the door.

A rancid odor hit me as I walked into the apartment on
Monday night after work. Gerry hadn't been home for days.
Neither of us had cleaned in over a week. The place stank.
There were dirty dishes piled up in the sink. Cigarette butts
filled ashtrays, clothes were scattered all over the floor. Empty
Coke cans and half-filled, dirty glasses sat on the coffee table

and breakfast nook. The wastepaper basket was spilling over. It made me sick. I felt weary and depressed.

So I cleaned up a little, then took a bath and went to bed. Around midnight, someone knocked at the door. It was Jonesy. He looked awful. His eyes were bloodshot and watery, his face was haggard.

"Can I come in?"

"Yeah," I whispered.

He sat on the couch sniffling and wiping his nose with the back of his hand. I sat next to him in the dark. Voices drifted in from outside. A door slammed. Sounds from the Beatles' "Happiness is a Warm Gun" came through the walls.

"I'm in bad shape, Cece," he said.

"Do you want something to drink?"

"I gotta see you. I need you," he said.

His eyes were like two burned out craters. I looked away. He put his hands to his face and started to cry. I put my arms around him.

"I got some codeine, you want it?"

"Yeah."

I gave him two pills. He washed them down and we crawled into bed. He must have left sometime during the night because when I woke up he was gone.

He called on Thursday saying that he was doing better. His voice sounded clear.

"Guess what?" he said

"What?"

"I got a job driving a truck."

"Oh, wow, that's wonderful, Jonesy."

"Hey, baby, let's go somewhere this weekend. Just you and I."

"OK."

"What do you want to do, honey? It's anything you say."

"Let's go to the mountains." Maria had just come back from the High Sierras raving about them.

Chapter 15

The wind howled as we drove through the Mojave Desert, pitting gusts of sand against the windows. Sagebrush and scrub trees scattered out in lonely tufts in the flat, grey light spreading across the desolate horizon and into the dark mountains. Only static came through on the radio.

"Man, I bet nothin' lives out there except rattlesnakes, coyotes, and jack rabbits."

"And bears," I said. "I bet bears do."

"Brown bears," he said.

The lonely road stretched out before us like a dream. We fell into a long silence, awed by the magnificent range of gigantic mountains, cascading above the clouds into towering, white peaks. I rested my head on a pillow and fell asleep.

I woke at daybreak, as we inched up a steep grade toward an orange sherbet sunrise, fanning out in soft undulations across the pale sky, casting its spectacular light over the snow-covered mountains and forest.

After checking into a room and sleeping for a few hours, we went to the lodge and rented cross country skis, then hiked out of town and up a trail into the hills. Neither of us had skied before. The snow was mushy under the bright sunlight.

"Hey, wait for me!" I shouted, hobbling up a small hill. Lifting my pole, I lost my balance and fell over. I got up, staggered, and fell back on my ass.

"Oh, shit!"

"Come on, Cece!"

I trudged on like a sick turtle through the slushy snow, panting and perspiring.

"Whose idea was this, anyway?"

"Come on, you can do it!" Jonesy yelled.

We came to a clearing and peered down a steep hill.

"You *can't* go down there," I said.

"Come on," he said. As soon as he started down he flipped over, sliding on his side. Close behind, I panicked and skidded forward, crashing into him. We lay there, tangled up in a jumble of skis and poles, grunting and laughing hysterically.

"Forget this shit!" Jonesy said, unbuckling his skis.

"Really, man," I said, relieved.

We planted our skis in the snow and hiked the rest of the trail on foot.

At the summit we sat on a rock under the cobalt blue sky, eating our lunch and gazing at the beauty of Mono Lake, surrounded by the mammoth white peaks that were shrouded in transparent, drifting clouds. We hiked back to the lodge in the late afternoon shadows. It was like a wonderful dream come true.

After dinner we sat in front of the fireplace holding hands and drinking brandy.

"I'm gonna get me a rig," Jonesy said. "A semi."

"You mean one of those huge trucks?"

"Yeah. My uncle Louie has one that he's gonna sell in about nine months. By then I should have enough saved for a down payment."

"That's great, if that's what you want to do."

"It is. I want to work outdoors. You know, be on the road. I wanna travel all over the country. I've never been anywhere besides California. Except for once when I went with my mother to visit relatives in New Mexico. But that's about it."

"I know what you mean. The only place I've visited out of California is Arizona. I went with my parents to see my grandmother. One place I'd like to visit is Hawaii."

"When I get my rig, I'm gonna go all over the states. You know, the Midwest, New England, New Orleans, the Badlands. I want to see the town in Texas where my grandfather was born."

"That would be fabulous. I hope you get to do it. I'd like to go to Europe someday. Europe and Africa."

"You gonna save money working at the insurance company?" he said derisively.

"Oh, come on," I said. Then, I said, "You're right. I'll never be able to save enough money on my salary. But that's OK, 'cause I'm gonna be an actress," I said.

He guffawed.

"Listen, I'm taking theatre arts at the J.C. It's actually the only class I have time for. I'm so wiped out after work."

"Hey, honey, by next year I'll be able to save enough money for both of us to take a trip together."

"I don't know about that."

"Why not? I guess you want to get married first," he said, smiling like he wasn't serious.

"No, that's not it. I don't want to get married."

"What do you mean? Oh, you want to wait until you're older."

"Maybe," I said. "And maybe I'll never get married."

"You're crazy, girl!" he said, tweaking my nose. "You'll get married. You were meant to be married. You'll have five or six kids and love it."

"Maybe," I said, "but I doubt it."

"Hey, honey, how about another drink? You want the same thing?"

That night after we had made love, I rested my head on Jonesy's chest, listening to the pounding of his heart as he slept. I was thinking of my aunt Clara, my mother's older sister who had been an actress and traveled all over the world. I only met her once. She had never married. I was thinking of what it would be like to travel through Europe, Africa, to see the Nile River, the great pyramids, faraway exotic places.

I woke up in the middle of the night. The room was hot and stuffy. I kicked off the blankets. My chest felt tight and I was having a hard time breathing. I got up and went over to the window. Lights from the motel reflected on icy sheets of snow. The trees were ominous black shadows. The mountain looked barren and alien as the moon. I tried prying open the window, but it was stuck, packed with snow. Jagged icicles clung to the top of the sill. I went and sat on the edge of the bed.

"Jonesy," I whispered, touching his shoulder.

"Wha'?" he groaned, rolling over.

"I can't breathe," I said. "I feel like I'm choking or something.

"It's the thin air up here, honey. Relax, don't worry." He patted my back.

In a minute, he was snoring again.

I lay there feeling the wild pounding of my heart. I felt claustrophobic and crazy. I wanted to go out into the snow-filled night and run up into the hills and never come back. Before I fell asleep, I thought of the herd of deer I'd seen on the way up the mountain, loping gracefully across a long open meadow in the sunlight.

We left early the next morning, reaching the Mojave Desert by dusk. The foothills of the Sierras were huge, looming black shadows in the light of the half moon.

"I hate to go back," Jonesy said.

"Me, too."

He slipped his hand onto my leg, squeezing my knee. I smiled in the dark.

"Stick with me, mama, 'cause we're goin' places."

I could tell he was high as soon as he walked in the door Saturday night. We went to the drive-in. Halfway through he nodded out. I stared at the screen feeling angry and restless. After a while, I went to the snack bar and called Maria. She wasn't there. As I started towards the exit, a chick I knew from high school cruised by with some guy on their way out and offered me a ride home.

I was through with Jonesy. He was never going to change. I felt like I was stuck on the same dreary merry-go-round, futilely going round and round. One day everything was wonderful, the next it was horrible again. I thought about moving away. I had some relatives in Arizona. Maybe I could go there. Anything to get away from him. Anything.

As I was drifting off to sleep, someone knocked. It was Jonesy.

"What happened? Why'd you leave?"

"Because."

"Oh, yeah," he said, sitting down. I could tell that he didn't care one way or another. He just needed someplace to hang out.

"I'm sick of you. You're just a down and out junkie!"

"You're right," he said. "So what's new, man?"

"If I'm pregnant, I'll kill myself! I hate you!" I shrieked.

"Hey, Cece, calm down, someone will hear you."

"I don't care. Get out of here. Go on, get out!"

He got up and slowly headed for the door.

"Wait," I said.

He turned around heavy and slow, his eyes hooded slits.

"Never mind," I said. "And don't come back!"

I don't remember anything except that I was standing there in my pajamas with four strange men surrounding me. One of them was pointing a gun at me. Was I dreaming? It can't be true, I thought. It was like T.V. only real.

"What do you want?" I asked, tugging at my pajama top collar. Gerry was scrambling around, groping for her glasses.

"We're from homicide," said the man with the gun, flashing a badge.

The other men began going through our closets, throwing clothes on the floor, dumping out drawers and looking under furniture. In the bathroom, I could hear someone rifling through the medicine cabinet.

"What's wrong? What do you want?" I said, trying to sound nonchalant. I figured they'd made a mistake.

"You know Daniel Jones Martinez?"

My first thought was that he was in trouble.

"Yeah, why?"

"He's dead. Someone dumped his body in front of the county hospital."

"You must be mistaken--He only left here a few hours ago." Two things were going on at once in my head. I knew Jonesy was alive and, at the same time, I knew the cop was telling the truth. I felt dizzy, lightheaded as if I had no body weight. I felt nothing. Or I felt like nothing.

"We know that. His mother told us he was here. When he left his house, he said he was coming here. You're going to have to get dressed and come down to the station."

A big, hulking man in plain clothes came out of the bathroom and said, "You got any drugs? You might as well tell us 'cause we're gonna to tear the place apart. If you tell us, it might save all of us some time."

"No, no."

"Let me see your arms." He looked at them.

"No tracks," he grunted.

A man wearing a black duster cocked to one side, picking at his teeth with a toothpick, said, "You have the right to remain silent. Anything you say may be held against you in a court of law. Better get your coat, miss."

I scurried into the bedroom like a scared rabbit. I had on red flannel PJ's with a T-shirt underneath. Dazed, I went over to the closet scrambling through the clothes that were piled together in a lump, pulled out my coat and put it on over my pajamas. I went into the bathroom to comb my hair and bumped into Gerry. She was ratting her hair. Everything seemed weird and fuzzy. The strangest thing popped into my mind. We had just seen *A Place in the Sun* on TV the week before. And I kept thinking I was Elizabeth Taylor in the movie. I felt like an actress. If I'd turn my head a certain way, I'd think, that's the way she turned her head. Even my voice changed. I was speaking in a low husky whisper.

Gerry left and I closed the door to pee. There were opened bottles on the floor, a box of Kotex and tampons had been ripped open and gone through. They lay there looking like dead animals. They confiscated all our prescription drugs. My bobby pin jar was tipped over, junk scattered everywhere.

I spaced out for a minute and forgot what was happening. I had begun to clean up when someone with an official voice knocked. "You 'bout ready?" We filed out the door. The cop with the duster was whistling some Sinatra tune.

He smiled at me, exposing one gold-capped tooth and said, "You like to hang out with junkies, huh? Anyone can tell you there's no advantage in that--young girl like you." Then he smirked. I thought maybe it was only a joke and they were just putting us on. Why did he smirk? God, is this really happening? I felt as though I were suffocating. Gerry sat next to me, shocked, not saying a word. Out of the corner of my eye, I could see his profile, the cop with the duster, and I felt a shaking hatred. The funny thing was that it wasn't in my body. It was somewhere outside of me. It hovered and hung in the air like an essence. Only you couldn't smell it, just sense it out there.

We were in an unmarked, green sedan. Two cops in the front and Gerry and I in the back handcuffed to another one. The two others followed behind us. I was having a hard time wiping the tears that were streaming down my face. I felt disconnected. As if it was someone else who was crying. Gerry was so still it looked as if she wasn't breathing. A voice in my head kept repeating, *It's not true, it can't be true.*

We arrived at the police station and were taken into separate rooms.

A policewoman took me into the bathroom and stayed there watching me while I peed. Then she checked my arms for tracks, emptied my purse, went through the contents of my wallet, frisked me, looked in the pockets of my PJ's. Nothing but a rolled up, old piece of Kleenex.

We went back into a small room. I could hear the whine of a tape recorder.

The big hulk asked, "Was he set up?"

"No. I mean, I don't know."

"Was he connecting at your place?"

"God, no," I said, being really scared for the first time.

"Do you know if he was with anyone if and when he left your house?"

"Not that I know of." My head was bent and my nose had started to run. I was staring at my shoe. I wiped my lip so snot wouldn't roll into my mouth. He handed me a Kleenex. I blew my nose. My head was on fire. I was trying not to show any signs of life, hoping they would leave me alone. I felt like screaming! They had no feelings. No feelings or understanding for me and what I was going through. I hated them. Finally, the hulk got up and left.

Another man came in. Reminded me of Jimmy Stewart. He looked nice enough, a reasonable man acting paternal. I felt relieved.

"I'm Detective Dereck," he said, handing me his card, then stuck his hand out. I sat there for a moment not knowing what to do. He smiled kindly while his hand hung in the air with assurance. I reached up and limply shook it. If this is TV, what's my line? I was thinking of Elizabeth Taylor. Be quiet, subdued, fluttery. I was terrified. I wondered just how I was supposed to act to get out of there.

"Don't worry, Consuelo. We're not going to book you. We just want to ask you a few questions."

"OK," I said, lifting my head to look at him.

"What was your relationship to Martinez?"

"He was my boyfriend."

"You were in love with him?"

What would Liz say? "Yes," I whispered.

"Ever tried scag?"

"What?"

"Junk, honey, heroin."

"No."

"Well," he said after a long pause, "I think you're telling the truth, Miss Contreres." He smiled paternally. I was thinking that he was very handsome. Polite, handsome, and assured, he looked into my eyes.

"Did you know that Daniel had a habit?"

"Yes."

"A bad one, there were tracks all over him."

OK, OKOKOKOKOKOKOK ... My head had started reeling like a broken tape deck. I stopped it, thinking, boy, you couldn't really murder a junkie, could you? And even if you did, no one would care.

"You know what happens to young girls who run around with addicts?" I didn't answer. "Most of them end up going down the same road, becoming addicts themselves. They usually go into a life of petty crime, prostitution. They end up here, or worse. A lot of them end up like your boyfriend. Understand?"

"Yes," I whispered.

We went into an office. One of the cops was typing up some papers.

"Have a seat, Miss Contreres," Detective Dereck said. "We'd like you to sign some papers before you leave."

My nose was still running. I wiped it with my coat sleeve. I imagined what I looked like sitting there in my pajamas and overcoat, my hair all frizzed out and wild, my face pale and tear-stained. I put my head down on the desk in my arms and stared at the floor. The cop came over, showing me where to sign. It was a big blur. I signed stupidly, pretending to read, since he insisted that I should. Then, like a retarded child, I sat there, waiting for them to tell me what to do next.

In a few minutes, Detective Dereck came in, saying that Officer So-and-so would take us home.

"Thank you for your cooperation, Miss Contreres."

I got up to leave and he added, "One more thing. You're not to leave the county without notifying us first. We'll try to inconvenience you as little as possible. Good night."

Outside, I looked for another bathroom. I went in and looked in the mirror. I felt numb. I almost laughed out loud. There were dark circles under my eyes and the light cast a yellow-greenish glare on me. I was thinking of Montgomery Clift in *A Place in the Sun*.

Chapter 16

A light, balmy breeze swayed the palm trees, scattering dead leaves along the road as we drove into the cemetery in a solemn procession of Chevies and Fords, past the mausoleum with the Middle Eastern design attesting to grander days, and the hundreds of gravesites on the circular road. I had always enjoyed going to Calvary. I loved the bright flowers scattered over rolling, green manicured hills and the old fashioned tombstones standing dramatically upright and defiant. Even the park wasn't as beautiful. There were never flowers growing in the park. But in the cemetery, any day of the week, you'd drive by and see a whole spectrum of color splashed across the landscape--red, white and pink carnations, purple and yellow daisies, golden marigolds, white calla lilies, sweet peas, geraniums, poppies. In contrast, the rest of the city seemed decayed and dirty.

At least one Sunday a month, our family would go with bouquets to visit the deceased. We took baby roses to the grave of Aunt Vera's stillborn baby who had died thirty years before. I was always fascinated with the miniature grave and its ornate headstone with cherubs and the one little angel in the middle. Then on to Uncle Louie's, my mother's brother who was killed in World War II, with a few straggly geraniums and so on until we'd reach the gravestone of Great Grandpa, Tata Contreres. We'd kneel down on the damp grass and my mother would clear off the plaque with a Kleenex. Most of the modern graves were stark plaques on the ground. We'd cross ourselves--In the name of the Father, the Son and the Holy Ghost. The boys would begin squirming and squealing and hitting each other. Every few minutes she would reach over and pinch one of them or shush them. My father would be standing fidgeting, dressed in his Sunday gabardine suit, black, shiny shoes, his hair parted and slicked back like a seal. He never knelt, just stood there nervously, squinting into the sun with his hands in his pockets. Every once in a while my mother would glance at him and he'd grunt, "OK, quit it" to silence the boys.

It wasn't ever an occasion for sadness or emotion, but more like a ritual. My mother hated sentimentality--what she called *sentidos simplones*. She would be dressed up, wearing a tailored suit and crepe blouse, a bow tied at her throat, her black hair done in a slick page boy, nylons with seams running straight as arrows up the back of her slender legs, black pumps (in the summer, white open-toed sandals), smelling of White Shoulders.

She always insisted that Maria and I wear starched organdy dresses, and stiff nylon slips, that made me itch all over and sweat. After we had dressed, she would drape a towel over our shoulders and brush our hair out, making fat curls and pinning our bangs back with plastic barrettes. She would get upset if either of us squirmed or scratched. When she was seven, Maria stuffed her organdy and lace Easter dress and her new Mary Janes into the trash can outside. Then she went and flushed the barrettes down the toilet. Mrs. Hernandez found her dress and shoes and brought them back. Then my father discovered the barrettes lodged in the toilet when he took it apart to fix it. When my mother asked her about it, Maria glared at her, turned around, and stomped away. That was the last time Maria ever wore her hair in curls. Maria was the only one who had ever gotten away with defying my mother when we were children. I never had the nerve, so I wore my hair in sausage curls until I was ten.

By the time Maria was ten, she had memorized every prayer in the Catholic Church, and every question and answer line in her Catechism, going over every issue, arguing about the contradictions and pointing out what she considered errors.

At the grave site, mother began, "Our Father who art in---"

"*Which* art, mother," Maria corrected.

"Which art in Heaven," she continued, "hallow be thy name."

Maravilla

"*Hallowed*, Mother," Maria sighed.

"Hallowed," she responded. Maria would continue to correct her until she snapped, "*Ay, callate*, let me finish!" But Maria never flinched or faltered with her fat, round face expressionless and her beefy, little body solid and implacable.

At the next gravesites, we would make an abrupt sign of the cross, stuff the flowers into the hole and move on. By the time we'd gotten to Tata Contreres' grave, my mother would be straightening her skirt, pulling up her little, white gloves, enraged and screaming at us or stiff and tight-lipped with anger. Maria would be pouting. Eddie and Tony would be disheveled and whiny. My father would either be waiting in the car or over a drink at the corner bar, having left the car keys on the floor under the seat. And I would have escaped into my sci-fi fantasy where I was Wonder Woman flying over the city restoring order and peace.

Now, Jonesy was telling a joke, his face crinkled up into laughter. He wore a yellow T-shirt and Levi's. His hair combed in a DA in tight, little waves over the top of his head into a waterfall on his forehead. I couldn't make out what he was saying, we were both under water.

We turned a corner and rolled past Great-Grandmother Contreres' grave which was up on the hill. I remembered that she had always taken those small religious pictures and stuck them onto the bouquets with a hairpin or safety pin. Little pictures of the Virgin holding the baby Jesus or of Christ with His hand over His heart. The last time we visited the cemetary, I had seen some of them still there, faded and frayed. She had died earlier that year, having spent the last days of her life in a wheelchair crippled from arthritis. My father said it was because of Uncle Eddie, her youngest son, that she was sick and finally refused to walk. During WWII, he was declared missing in action somewhere in Italy and was never heard from again.

"Who knows?" said my mother. "People get sick and they die. That's the way it is." Up until her dying day, Great-Grandma Contreres was fiesty and mean as hell. She used to keep a belt coiled in her lap to protect herself, she said, from Blackie, the neighbor's doberman.

162

Maravilla

"*Ese perro, horible, ojala, que se muere!*" she would hiss. Just before she died, she started lashing out at everyone. One day, before she had grown too weak to move about, she had wheeled herself into the living room where the family was talking about her in hushed voices.

"*Nunca me van a matar! Esos chingados, cobardes!*" My father went over to her and wheeled her into the room.

"Those bastards cannot take my property!" she cried.

"Her mind was wandering," my mother said. Back to the time when the government had bulldozed the rambling old Victorian where she had lived for forty years to make way for the first L.A. freeway. "The house was built in 1898," my father said, "solid as a rock." The whole neighborhood was gone now.

"Excuse me, Cece, do you have a tissue?" asked Emma, Jonesy's sister, snapping me back to the present.

I scrambled through my purse and found one, handing it to her. The car pulled over and we climbed out.

It had rained the night before, clearing the air. Ragged, white clouds drifted across the clear blue sky, golden sunshine dappled the trees.

As we came over the hill, I saw the shiny, gray casket coming into view next to the deep hole. Every line and angle was sharply focused and clearly defined against the dazzling light.

Jonesy's mother, in black with a veil over her head, quietly wept. She had broken down and aged into an old woman overnight. His father, in a navy blue, shiny suit, stood next to her, looking tired and shaken. Next to them were his two brothers and sister. The youngest brother was crying. Behind them, Grandmother Martinez stood next to the rest of the family members.

A priest reciting in Latin sprinkled incense over the casket. Unable to watch, my eye circled in on Gerry and Angel standing arm and arm, then on Slow Freddie in a wrinkled, black suit and a green string tie. He looked pathetic. I felt crazy and almost laughed out loud. Stop it! I glanced down clearing my throat, watching numbly, but giddily, as they lowered the casket into the deep hole and began shoveling clumps of dirt onto it. I kept thinking of how I had yelled at him not to

163

come back. Going over and over the scene in my mind, until it was all strange and confusing and I wondered if I possessed some awful, destructive kind of power, like black magic, and all the horrible things I said and thought would come true.

I felt numb and exhausted from trying to control myself and stop the crazy thoughts that were flooding my mind. I began to imagine that I was watching a movie I had seen many times before, with the family standing around while the casket was being lowered. Mrs. Martinez had fallen across the box before they lowered it, and now she flung herself onto the earth that covered it. One of her sons pulled her away. She moaned and clutched his arm. She looked like a stranger. I wondered who she was. This crazy old woman. It seemed like only a few days ago Jonesy and I had visited her. Her hair had hung around her shoulders loose and sensual. She had been carefree and happy.

Her younger son held her up by the arm, as the rest of us straggled back to the cars. I rode back with Emma and her husband. I had only met them once before. They ignored me and I wondered if they blamed me. Of course, they had no way of knowing that I had told him to go away and not come back, did they?

My mother was waiting for me in her car in front of the house. Out of politeness, they invited us in. Tamales, menudo, beer, whiskey, and Seven-Up were spread out on the table. I introduced my mother to the family. People milled around talking in hushed voices. Mrs. Martinez clung to her son's arm, fingering a large, black rosary. As she walked past us, she reached out to me feebly. I had to force myself not to pull back.

My mother signaled me that she wanted to leave. As soon as we got into the car, I burst into tears.

"Please don't," she said, pulling out a bottle of Jack Daniels and handing it to me. "Here drink some of this, Cece," she said. "It'll calm your nerves."

By the time we reached the house, I was drunk. I staggered into my old bedroom, closed the door and fell on the bed. It was Maria's room now and I knew that she would resent my being there. *So what!* I thought. *Screw her.* I looked into the mirror and was surprised to see that my face was about the same. It was strange because I felt so grotesque. I had always suspected that I was freaky but now I knew for sure. And no one would know except for Jonesy. He knew. But he was dead. It was incredible that he was here one minute, then vanished the next. Gone. No, I knew he was out there, I could feel his presence hovering around in the air. I got up and went into the bathroom and tried to throw up, gagging and spitting into the bowl.

Pulling out Maria's toothbrush, I brushed my teeth, splashed water onto my face and checked my complexion in the mirror. I looked yellow. I took out a jar of pancake makeup and smeared a glob of it onto my face, circled rouge on my cheeks, flicked black mascara on my lashes and dabbed a splash of my mother's dark red, iridescent lipstick across my mouth.

Maria walked in as I was ratting my hair.

"Ga, are you weird!" she said, stomping out.

She was right, I thought as I continued to pat my hair into shape. Why was I so concerned about my looks? I slunk into the living room and switched on the TV. In a stupor, I watched Robert Young in "Father Knows Best."

Around ten o'clock, Angel and Gerry pulled up. They walked into the living room, hand in hand, offering condolences. They made me sick. It was easy to see their sympathy was shallow and contrived. The fact that Jonesy was dead didn't matter to them. They were in love and that's all that seemed to count. I ignored them, staring at the tube, mumbling something about being wiped out.

"Why were you so rude to them?" my mother said after they left. I got up and slammed out of the room feeling rummy and hung over. Came back in a few minutes and asked, "Can I borrow the car?"

"What for?"

"I wanna go buy some cigarettes. I'll get you some too," I said, hoping to convince her.

"*Ay, Dios*, why don't you go lay down! You look terrible. Go on."

"I can't sleep! I'm not tired!" I screamed. "Just loan me the car for a little while, I swear I'll be careful and come right back. Please, mother!" I begged, about to break into tears.

Maravilla

"Oh, go ahead," she said, rifling through her purse for the keys.

As I went out the door, I heard her tell my father that she thought I was crazy.

I drove to the closest liquor store and bought a six pack of Bud. The guy didn't bother to ask for my ID. I must have looked thirty years old. I felt like a hundred. Getting back in the car, I headed for the Santa Ana Freeway, pressing down on the accelerator until the speedometer hit eighty. I got off at the Whittier Boulevard exit and slowed down when I saw the law. I had no idea where I was going. I drove up and down, cut around back streets and alleys until I almost ran out of gas. I had drunk a couple of beers and was high when I saw the 1950, green Plymouth coming towards me on the opposite side of the street. It was Jonesy! I honked the horn and sped around the block to catch up to him. After that, I saw four more cars just like his.

When I got back home, my mother had left for work and the kids were watching the tube. My father was sleeping. Maria, with her eyes never leaving the screen, said monotonously, "Boy, mother is pissed at you."

I let out a belch and swayed into the bedroom, quietly closing the door and fell in a heap to the floor and passed out.

I moved back into the house. My mother was working a few nights a week at a local bar and grill. They closed at two and she usually didn't get home until three or four in the morning. I talked her into letting me have the car at night by promising I'd watch the boys. After she'd leave, I'd hang around until they went to bed and get Maria, who was usually half asleep and too groggy to refuse, to keep an eye out for them. After getting gas, I'd drive up and down the street over and over, drinking a couple of beers and chain smoking mentholated Salems. Once in a while, I'd pull over and pass out. A couple of times I woke up to find myself parked on the curb with a puddle of vomit next to my feet. Every once in a while I'd cruise over to Jonesy's, but the house was always dark as if no one lived there. Later I heard that his mother was in a psych ward. Right before Jonesy died, his father had run off with a younger woman and, after the funeral, his mother had a nervous breakdown. When I heard that I stopped going by.

After the funeral, Freddie and I cruised together a lot, drinking booze and blowing weed. A couple of times I got drunk and puked all over the front seat of his car. He had to carry me home and put me to bed. Whenever we were together, we talked about Jonesy, Jonesy, Jonesy! He followed us everywhere. Freddie and I clung to each other, sleeping together like children afraid of the night, trying to keep him out.

Right before I went back to work at the insurance company, Freddie came over, shaky and irritable. I could tell that he needed a fix. I wanted him to tell me how Jonesy had died.

"I got some money you can have, Freddie. You can borrow it if you tell me what happened."

I had asked him before but he had sworn he didn't know. I knew he did.

"Come on," I pressed him. "Freddie, tell me!"

"Naw, I don't know, I already told ja," he said, sniffling.

"You look terrible, man."

"Cece, I swear I'd give it up for you. I'd do anything for you, if you'll just say you'll be for me."

"Just tell me what happened and I'll let you have the money." I pulled out the wadded up bills. "Come on, Freddie, I won't tell anyone, I swear. Only I have to know."

"OK," he sighed. "But don't tell anyone, man, swear that you won't tell." He reached for the bills. I held onto them.

"Tell me."

"It was Angel."

"Yeah."

"He scored some bad stuff. Sold it to Jonesy. Victor and I were going to split it with him. As soon as he fixed, he went down."

"What did you do?" I was trying to hold back tears and keep from gagging at the thought of Jonesy dying like that. "Why didn't you do something?"

"We were scared, man. Scared of the heat."

"Who else was there?"

"Victor and Chuy, that's all. Man, it was heavy. We all were hurting except for Angel. We tried to revive him, honest we did. We shot milk into his veins, someone said to do that.

Nothin' helped. It was too late. I swear, Cece, I was down on my knees praying the whole time. So we put him in Victor's car 'cause Angel was scared and wouldn't take him in his and Victor drove him to the hospital and dumped him. That's all, I swear it's the truth, Cece."

I was crying.

"Give me the money," he said.

I passed him the bills. Fifty dollars. I knew I'd never see it again. It didn't matter. Nothing mattered.

Chapter 17

When the pregnancy test came back positive, I was elated, imagining what it would be like to have a baby growing in my belly. I went home from the Planned Parenthood office in a daze, thrilled about having my very own child. Someone that I would always have and no one could take from me. I began wondering if it would be a boy or a girl, have curly or straight hair. I imagined a child with a bright smile, straight, white teeth and honey brown skin. In my mind, I held this cuddly, loving baby in my arms. I spent the rest of the day wandering around in a dreamlike state.

A few days later, I woke up feeling queasy and bloated and ate a light breakfast. I had made an appointment for a job interview a few weeks before doing filing and light typing.

On the day of the interview, I got dressed up and borrowed my mother's car. Halfway there, I pulled over just in time to get out and throw up on someone's front lawn. I got back in shaking, hoping no one had seen me, and drove away. I felt nauseous and faint so I pulled over to rest and immediately drifted off to sleep.

I woke up sweating and dizzy, with my hair and makeup a mess. I drove back home and got in bed.

When my mother came home, she asked me if I had had any luck with the interview.

"No," I said, "I don't feel good. I think I might have the flu."

"Oh, really? Too bad. If I would have known, I wouldn't have left the car. I'll get you a couple of aspirins," she said, closing the door.

Maravilla

In the evening, I felt better and ate some cottage cheese and drank a Seven-Up. I stayed home, in and out of bed for the rest of the week.

After Jonesy died, I had moved back into Maria's bedroom. I had missed so much work I got fired from my filing job at the insurance company. Gerry and I eventually had to give up our apartment, which was a relief. While I was there, I thought of Jonesy constantly, especially when I was alone. I kept waiting for him to show up at the door. I heard his voice, saw his face. I'd wake up in the morning dreading the rest of the day.

On Friday, a week after I found out I was pregnant, my mother brought in the local want ads, saying, "Look, Cece, they need a counter girl at the Tastee Freeze. Why don't you go see about it? You can't just lay around for the rest of your life.

I waited until afternoon when my queasiness was gone to see about it. Unfortunately, I got the job.

I felt horrible. I was having morning sickness and I could barely drag myself out of bed. I was positive that I'd be fired if they found out that I was pregnant. I was on edge, beginning to feel desperate, going back and forth in my mind about what to do. My mother had told me that she and my father were having a bad spell financially and if I wanted to stay there, I'd have to work to help pay bills. I thought about how Liz Delaney had been treated when she was pregnant. Like a freak. After she went through all the trouble of having to leave home and school, she had had to give the baby up to its adopted parents before she could even hold it or find out if it was a boy or a girl. They wouldn't let her know where it was. She probably never found out. I was sure that I would never do that! I would rather die.

A week later, I called Sarah McKenzie and asked her for the name and number of the Mexican abortionist. She gave me two names, saying not to worry.

"It really doesn't hurt," she said. "They put you out and you can't feel a thing. All you have to do is call and make the appointment, and take five hundred dollars in cash."

What! I felt panicky, wondering where I was going to get the cash. If I used all the money I got from the Tastee Freeze and didn't pay my share of the rent and borrowed a little from Gerry, I'd have around two hundred dollars.

When I asked her for the money I lied, telling her I needed it for my teeth. She said all she could spare was around a hundred. Desperately, I called her back, asking her to meet me at the Tastee Freeze.

We sat out in the 'Vette and I told her the truth. She was quiet for a while, and finally said, "Cece, why didn't you tell me before? I don't know, man. All I can get is around two hundred at the most."

"That's not enough," I said, bursting into tears. "I don't know what to do."

"We'll think of something," she said.

That night she called me back with a plan.

She would tell Angel that she was pregnant and ask him for the five hundred dollars.

"Afterwards," she said, "I'll tell him the truth."

"He'll never forgive you."

"Oh, yes, he will. Don't worry, Cece. It's important to you, it's what you have to do, isn't it?"

"Yeah," I whispered.

I felt as if I were caught in an endless nightmare. Every night I'd lie awake going over and over it in my mind. Yes, I would have the abortion; no, I wouldn't have it.

When she brought me the money a week later, I took the five hundred dollar bills and hid them in the lining of a suitcase. The next morning I called the doctor's office and made an appointment.

Gerry agreed to drive. She picked me up early Sunday morning. It was warm and sunny on the way down. I was nauseated and cried off and on, trying not to think about what I was going to do. I couldn't stop myself. I was committing a mortal sin according to the Catholic Church. Killing my baby! The one that I wanted to hold in my arms more than anything else in the world. I remembered hearing Father O'Dowd preaching about how women who had abortions were no better than murderers and they would go straight to hell if they died without confessing their heinous sin. And even if they made it to confession, they might have to carry their horrible guilt to the grave. I felt like grabbing the steering wheel away from Gerry and turning it towards an oncoming car. I was shaky, my palms were damp, and I felt like screaming but I sat quietly, hardly moving. The car was hot and stuffy. I could feel my blouse stuck to my back.

"Gerry," I said, "I changed my mind, let's go back."

She pulled over at the next freeway offramp and started heading home. After a few miles I said, "Never mind, let's go on." She didn't flinch. We turned off and headed south again.

About halfway there I said, "I want to go home, let's go back."

"Anything you say, Cece," Gerry said.

Once more we got off the endless highway. After we'd gone awhile, I said, "I changed my mind."

This time I could tell she was pissed.

"Cece, please make up you mind! We're gonna run out of gas and we haven't gotten halfway there!"

For the rest of the trip, I sat rigid with fear, while Gerry, who must have thought she was cheering me up, chattered about her wedding. I nodded my head back and forth, not hearing a word she said. I felt as though I were suffocating.

When we got there, we were supposed to meet a man wearing sunglasses and a tan Levi's jacket on a certain street corner. He spotted the car and shuffled over. He looked greasy and sly as he slunk into the back seat, leaned back arrogantly, lit a cigarette, and said he wanted us to drive with him to the outskirts of town to where the doctor was. I asked him why the doctor wasn't in town. Sarah had told me that he was right in the downtown area.

"*Porque,* he's been descreet and doing eet in a *casa* outside of thee town. You know, man, becooze of thee *ley.*"

I was holding back tears. There was a yucky bile in my stomach making its way up to my throat. I gagged slightly, swallowing some spit and barf.

Gerry looked at me, then at him. He nervously flicked an ash off his cigarette and said, "Come on, maan, I haven't got all day, you know."

There was a long silence. I felt panicked.

After a minute, Gerry said, "We're not gonna do it."

"Oh, maan, what you chicks fred of, eh?" His eyes were watery and ringed with large, black circles. I could tell he needed either a drink or a fix and soon.

"No," said Gerry. "Get out!"

He stared at her without moving. She started up the car. I glanced out the window, relieved that we were in the heart of the city. Traffic roared up and down the street, people bustled around the car.

She put it in first and looked into the rear view mirror, saying "OK, adios, man."

He muttered an obscenity and banged out.

On the way back, I felt like screaming but I said nothing. Thank God Gerry was quiet. My breasts ached and my stomach was queasy. But still, I was relieved that we didn't leave town with that creep.

I went home and got in bed but couldn't sleep. I felt paralyzed. Something was keeping me from killing myself. It's a mortal sin to commit suicide and once you're dead you can't get to confession! Maybe that was it?

The following day my mother was on my back, complaining.

"Gawd, girl, you look terrible! What's wrong? Why don't you comb your hair or something? At least try to stop being so depressed. Please, answer me!"

"JUST LEAVE ME ALONE!" I shouted, running out the door. I walked down to the corner, headed over to the Tastee Freeze and ordered a banana split. I hung out there until dark, then I snuck back into the house.

Later, my father came into the room and sat at the end of my bed.

"Anything wrong, Cece?"

I closed my eyes, pretending to be a asleep. He ruffled the blankets, tugging at my leg.

"Hey, Cece."

"Yeah," I answered drowsily. There was a hint of whiskey on his breath.

"Anything wrong, honey?"

"Naw," I said. He patted me on the head and left the room. There was a sliver of light as he opened the door, then darkness.

That weekend I refused to get out of bed. Sunday afternoon, my mother came into the room.

"What's wrong with you, Cece?"

I pulled the covers over my head.

"I can't stand it anymore, Cece!" she cried. "Ay, *Dios*, put your clothes on, comb your hair, go on!" She grabbed hold of my pajama sleeve, forcing me into the bathroom. "Go on, change, do something with yourself or get out! Do you hear me? I mean it!"

The next day, I called another Mexican doctor and made an appointment for the following Tuesday.

We drove down the San Diego Freeway through the Imperial Valley into Mexicali. We cruised through the center of town, down the main street, then turned up a side street, following the directions I was given on the phone. The office was right outside the business district.

The receptionist was dressed in an old fashioned house dress. I wondered if she was a nurse or what? She spoke in a Spanish/English dialect, saying that the doctor had an emergency and wouldn't be back until that evening and we would have to come back later. I almost cried right there, thinking I would probably go crazy before he returned and end up in a hospital, or worse yet, in jail. My head was filled with horror stories that I'd heard about Mexico. Gerry soothed me by saying not to worry, we could get a room in a hotel and wait.

We found a seedy place, with old winos and a bunch of dirty streetwise kids hanging around begging for money. I was doubled up with stomach pains and was having a hard time walking. Everyone stared at us as we hobbled in, Gerry holding onto my arm, half dragging me up the stairs.

Once in the room, I lay on the bed groaning and dripping with perspiration. I was sure that I was being punished for something I had done. Something horrible. I wondered if it was the time I had stolen all that money out of my uncle Johnny's coffee can. Dear God, I prayed silently, I promise to confess to the crime as soon as I get home and give the clothes I bought with the money to some poor people. What poor people? I don't know. Maybe I'll leave them at the little Salvation Army house in front of the Market Basket or something. All of them, except for the powder blue cashmere sweater. Oh, God, I moaned. Maybe I was being punished for the millions of lies I had told. My mind raced like a ticker tape machine, thinking of all the sins I had committed. I had lied to Father O'Dowd. Maybe that was it! After all, he was a priest and it was probably a bigger sin to lie to a priest than to an ordinary person. At least that's what my mother claimed. Oh, forget it! What the hell does she know, talking to her little saint statues and reciting threatening old wives' tales? A horrible dread crept through me. All my sins were marching before me like avenging angels. I knew I would not live through the night. I was doomed. Either the doctor would accidentally kill me or I'd die after the operation of an infection, gangrene, blood poisoning. A hemorrage. Or I'd be kidnapped and sold as a slave. I had heard about girls who had disappeared in Mexico. Only last week I'd read about it in the Enquirer. Please help me, God, I prayed. I'll never do anything bad again. I'll be perfect. I'll go to church every Sunday, stop lying, stop stealing. No making-out, or anything. Let this nightmare be over with, please! My mind continued relentlessly. Even if I made it back afterwards and didn't get sick, I'd probably never be able to have another baby. My mother always talked about botched-up abortions where the womb was scarred so bad it was impossible to get pregnant again. But then, I thought, why worry about the future? I was sure I was going to die. I cringed inwardly, trying not to make noise or move too much. Gerry was resting on the bed next to me with her shoes off, reading Cosmopolitan. I didn't want to upset her any more than I had to. *Jonesy, where are you?*

I finally fell into an exhausted sleep. I dreamed I was at a carnival. Harsh, bright colors lit up the tent. An emaciated clown barked, "Come in!" I wandered into a freak show. Fat Siamese twins, joined at the spine, were on stage. One of them was writhing and moaning wildly. Purple blood and yellow mucus slid out from between its legs. People in the audience cheered and hooted. Then a bloody, long-legged black spider slithered out and crawled up its stomach. I jerked awake.

"What's wrong?" Gerry asked.

"I had a nightmare." I was shaking. I felt as though I had been plugged into an electrical socket.

"Try to rest, Cece," she said. "It'll be over soon."

Maravilla

I turned my back to her and faced the blank, filthy, cracked wall.

Finally around seven o'clock, we went back to the doctor's office. The woman directed me into a room, asking Gerry to stay in the waiting room.

It was a small, stark, but clean office. She gestured for me to lie on the single cot in the corner. The pains were excruciating in my legs and stomach. I tried to explain this to her but she was unconcerned, busily preparing instruments. I decided at that point to face my execution with dignity and keep quiet. I actually felt excited and giddy with relief that one way or another it would soon be over. My mind was screaming, do it and get it over with! I wanted it to be over before I had time to think about it again, about the baby, about Jonesy.

The doctor walked briskly into the room. I was immediately relieved that he actually existed. I could tell he was confident. Probably a family man. His hands seemed steady and his eyes, what I could see of them as he was darting around preparing things, were clear. His manner was matter-of-fact. He spoke in Spanish to the woman. She came over and asked for the money. I reached over to my purse, pulled out the envelope and handed it to her. She counted it and left, returning in a few minutes.

I lay on the cot naked from the waist down, with a light sheet covering my legs. The doctor walked over and smiled at me as if it were a routine office call--for all I knew it might have been, for him. He spoke in broken English, but his accent was refined. He said he was going to examine me. While he stuck his finger into my vagina, he asked me if I visited Mexico often. I managed a weak "no", hoping I wouldn't offend him. The woman came over with a needle, probed for the vein and shot it into my arm. Just before I went out, I saw her sprinkling something onto the instrument table, then it burst into flames.

Someone was tugging at my arm insistently. "Cece, wake up, Cece, wake up!" Every once in awhile I'd pull up, then sink back into a black hole, unable to move. Then once more the tugging and pulling, the muffled voices coming from far away as if in a tunnel. I woke and saw Gerry and the vague outline

176

of the woman. They were saying something. They looked as if they were deliriously happy. I felt wonderful. I fell back onto the softness of the bed.

"Come on, Cece," Gerry said. "It's time to leave! You've been asleep for hours. Come on!" She pulled me into a sitting position. I fell into her arms and she pushed me away, holding me up.

"Dreenk thees," said the woman. Gerry held coffee to my lips and I sipped it feebly. Yuk, it tasted like dirty water. I tried to lie down again.

"No, no, you have to get up!" Gerry wailed.

They had me by the underarms and were walking me around the room. My feet dragged and shuffled across the floor.

"You're gonna be OK, Cece. It's over, you're fine, you're gonna be just fine. The doctor said you were early enough and that there would be no complications."

I mumbled something and slipped away.

"No, Cece, wake up!" she said, jerking me up. "We have to leave. It's late and the lady wants to go home. The doctor left hours ago." They were pulling on my coat. The woman rubbed a cold washcloth over my face. Shapes were becoming more defined. I looked around the room, thinking, I'm still alive. The pain, except for a slight cramping, was gone. I felt deliriously happy.

"If I could just lay down for a minute," I sighed as Gerry dragged me out the door.

Outside I could hear noises coming from town. Somewhere Mexican music was playing. I heard sounds of guitars and trumpets. The night was a beautiful black velvet, lit up with a million twinkling stars, flickering like little candles. A balmy, light breeze swept through the streets. I was alive. The pain was gone. A liquid warmth seemed to fill me. I felt as though I could sleep forever.

Gerry shoved me into the front seat of the car, adjusted the pillow for my head and I sank into it gratefully. I had never known such peace, such tranquility.

As we drove through town, tinny music wafted out from cantinas. I looked up for a minute to see the place lit up, alive

177

with people bustling up and down the dirt roads. Then I sank back into the dream.

At the border, two customs officers shone flashlights at us, asking if we had any food or drink to declare.

"No," Gerry said.

"Why were you in Mexico?"

"Visiting relatives and shopping," she said.

Then he shone his light on me.

"You better go see a doctor, young woman, as soon as you get back home. I know what you were here for. You don't look too good. Be sure you see a doctor!"

I nodded my head groggily and we crossed over the border. Wolfman Jack was coming in loud and clear on the radio. Gerry popped a bennie into her mouth. It was a dark, moonless night and the highway opened up. The white line of the road divider shone in the headlights, the only thing visible against the blackness as we shot off into the desert.

Chapter 18

The organ bellowed "Here Comes the Bride" into the hushed stillness of Our Lady of the Angels as I watched Gerry clutching a bouquet of white carnations held together with a pink ribbon. Her hair had been ratted into fat sausage rolls and piled on her head, except for one long curl which fell demurely over her shoulders. A rhinestone tiara sat on top of her curls and a stiff, white veil covered her face. Her lacy gown hung in a flounce around her shiny white, pointed pumps as she slowly glided up the aisle on her father's arm. Manuel Rodriguez, in his black tux, looked like an older version of Rudolph Valentino, with his swept back, pomaded black hair and pencil-thin mustache.

As the maid of honor, I wore a mint green A-line dress, a la Jackie Kennedy, matching elbow-length gloves, pillbox hat and pointy, mint green pumps. The three other bridesmaids, Beatrice, Gerry's seventeen year old sister, her cousin, Lily Chavez, and Carmen Estrada were dressed in exact replicas of my outfit, except theirs were yellow. Each of us carried one long stemmed, yellow rose. At Beatrice's insistence, mine had been sprayed mint green. I had protested, but later was relieved since everyone stared at it, mercifully taking the spotlight off me, with my runny nose and watery eyes. The ushers wore black and white rented tuxes.

There was a smog alert broadcasted on KFI on the way to the wedding and I could feel my eyes watering and stinging. I exhaled, letting out my breath in short gasps so as not to hack out loud. We were lined up along the altar just as we had rehearsed the night before, backs straight, one foot extended, except for Slow Freddie with his perpetual lope. Sally, the little flower girl in mint green dress and matching Mary Janes, waddled up the aisle next to Tommy Ochoa, the ring bearer who was barely out of diapers. Tommy appeared to be in shock. About halfway up the aisle, he got a panicky look and clutched at his fly, dropping the box with the ring. His mother appeared, as if by magic, to whisk him away, and thrust the ring at Slow Freddie. His hand shook and a wan smile formed on his lips as he accepted it. His hair was slicked back like a biker's, accenting his gaunt tired face, and his tux hung loosely over his scarecrow frame. His mustache had been trimmed, but his Fu Manchu goatee looked more straggly than ever. He turned, with purply, swollen eyes looking at me, and I felt a tremor go up my spine. A nausea. Almost a panic. Then he turned his head away, so the others couldn't see, and crossed his eyes. I glanced down quickly letting out a small hack. I could feel the beginning of a sinus headache.

Stella Rodriguez sat in a front pew, her eyes brimming with tears as she watched Gerry. A pink corsage, accenting her cleavage, was pinned to the shoulder of her shiny blue dress, that rustled when she moved and changed shades in the light. Next to her, Grandma Rodriguez sat sporting a white corsage on her lacy mauve shoulder, blinking through her rhinestone winged glasses. Her face had long since collapsed into perplexity and its crevices were streaked with a chalky pink powder. A little, brown hat with a short veil perched on the tight ringlets that framed her bewildered face. She nervously fingered a shiny black rosary. Next to Stella and Grandma Rodriguez were two of Gerry's younger brothers, Ernie and Chano. Marcos was on his way to Viet Nam. Behind Grandma Rodriguez and Stella sat the extended Rodriguez and Ochoa families. The rest of the church was filled with friends of the families. A few of our friends from school sat in the back. Everyone was dressed in their Sunday best. Eddie Ochoa, a former Rams linebacker, all two hundred and seventy pounds of him, sat sweating and breathing heavily, wiping his face and forehead with a white handkerchief. A few others used church bulletins against the muggy heat.

Father Lopez, the new pastor, appeared from the door off the side of the altar, looking robust in his purple and white

180

vestments. Performing the ceremony of the Mass, he offered the body of Christ from a golden chalice to the bride and groom. Gerry and Angel were kneeling within the boundaries of the alter as if in special dispensation. I watched Gerry taking the host into her mouth, inhaled the odor of incense and burning candles and wondered what stupid lies she had to tell Father Lopez. She got up and sailed over, placing her bouquet at the feet of the statue of the Virgin. I was thinking about how it had always been easy for her to fake it. I felt a contempt towards her. I hated both of them, especially Angel. I was filled with a shaking disgust.

When it was our turn to receive communion, I wondered if I'd be the only one to refuse the wafer. I had vowed the night before to never receive communion again. What did it matter? Jonesy was dead. What difference did it make if God could snuff him out just like that? It was all so stupid and absurd. But still, I didn't want to be different. I wanted people to think that I was like them. One of them.

My eyes stung and a tear slid down the side of my face. I heard sniffles and the loud honking and blowing of noses. A baby howled. A few people coughed. I knelt at the altar railing with my eyes closed and head bent. When I heard Father Lopez' garments rustle by, I automatically began to recite, "*Bless me Father for I have sinned.*" I took a sidelong glance to see Beatrice taking the host into her mouth. Freddie refused it. Watching him with his head bent down, knowing that he reeked of stale booze and nicotine and was more out of it then I was, seemed to relax me. I wasn't the only oddball.

A few days before the wedding, Gerry had casually mentioned that she and Angel would be moving to northern California, to Oakland where Angel had family business ties. She said it would be easier for them to make a go of it, for him to stay out of trouble if they moved away from L.A. I didn't say anything. I thought our friendship was over. I couldn't see how I'd ever be close to her again as long as she was married to him. I told myself that I was happy to be done with them.

The organ started up and the wedding party followed the bride, now linked to the groom's arm, out of the church. Freddie walked beside me in that see-saw motion of his, looking a sickly yellow, as if he had the rest of his life to do this

181

one thing. I felt like slapping him. I was secretly revolted by the way I treated him, but I couldn't seem to help myself.

Outside my eyes smarted in the smog. There was a buzz of talk and gay laughter. Someone was throwing rice. A few grains pelted me in the face, falling on the concrete, and into the dirty crevices of the sidewalk. Little kids jumped up and down squealing. Older folks gleamed happily at the young couple. A camera clicked. Angel encircled Gerry in a long kiss. More clicking cameras. I inhaled the gray, sulphurous air and hacked, turning to Gerry, embracing her formally. I forced a smile. The groom hugged and kissed me, sticking his tongue in my mouth. I looked at him blankly. His face seemed strange, distorted. A large, grotesque, misshapen head connected to his stunted body. I turned around, heading away from the crowd.

Freddie put his arm around me, guiding me over to John O'Reilly's blue, '49 Ford that we had decorated the night before with mint green and yellow paper flowers strung together and tied to the bumpers. Freddie and I slid into the back seat. Beatrice got in the passenger seat. John O'Reilly drove. We started off across town to the VFW hall, honking horns in the procession that followed the bride and groom in Angel's father's black Cadillac. The Caddy was decorated with white paper flowers, old tin cans rattled off the bumper, and JUST MARRIED was scrawled in white on the back and side. A picture of Jonesy flashed in my mind, his casket being lowered into the hard, brown earth. His wailing mother. I wriggled nervously and snickered to dispel the mood.

"What?" Freddie said.

I rummaged through my purse.

"Nothing," I sighed

"Want a drink?" He pulled out a bottle of Tequila.

"Okay." I was hoping that it might clear up my sinuses more than anything else. It tasted rusty and stale.

"Ugh, I think it's a little early for that," I said, handing it back to him. I watched him take a long drink. I felt my knee brushing against his pant leg. Smelled the booze combined with the Old Spice on him. He slipped the bottle into his pocket and placed both hands on his knees. His fingers were long and slender, like a piano player's. Dark brown with flat, elongated nails. I linked my arm through his. We were cruising down

Beverly Boulevard. People on the streets waved to us or honked and smiled from their cars. Beatrice rolled down her window. A blast of air hit me.

"Too windy for you?"

"No." I looked at Freddie. He was spaced out, staring out the window.

At the hall we were given breakfast. Freddie excused himself heading for the john. He returned a few minutes later looking glazed but relaxed.

Afterwards, we stood in the reception line while the bride and groom shook hands and embraced family and friends. More beaming smiles and heartfelt congratulations were expressed. Angel was bright and clear eyed. I wondered how long it would last. Before he'd beg pardon and go to the head and shoot up. *Why didn't Angel die instead of Jonesy?* This idea popped into my head just as Mrs. Hernandez was coming towards me with a triumphant smile to shake my hand. I flashed a big, toothy grin at her. I could feel my face blushing. Okay, stop it! More people came by. *Jonesy where are you!* A roar had started in my head. I teetered on my pumps and my chest felt hot and constricted. *Think of something.* Eddie and I playing in the back yard. I'm tickling him and he's giggling. Jonesy walks over and throws him into the air. We're all laughing. Please God, let it end! I looked up at the white and purple crepe paper entwined and twisted together on the ceiling. In the middle of it hung a big purple and yellow pinata, in the form of a wedding cake with pink and purple streamers. Another one of Beatrice's ideas. In the corner was a plastic fountain, gushing pink champagne with pink plastic rosebuds and little, green leaves swirling around it. Next to that was a long, narrow table loaded with ham, cheese, roast beef, French bread, and black olives, and another one with menudo, homemade meat and raisin tamales, beans and rice, a bowl of punch, paper plates, napkins and plastic forks and spoons. Next to the table was a keg of beer. In the back of the room was a bar.

When it was over, we went into the hall. Johnny and the Dominos were on-stage warming up in blue pants, red vests, and longish greasy hair. The bride and groom two-stepped around the hall to Cherry Pink and Apple Blossom White. Wedding presents piled up next to a five-layer, white-frosted chocolate cake--Gerry's favorite flavor. There were more flashing bulbs. The parents of the bride waltzed around the floor. More cheers. Mrs. Hernandez politely refused. No partner. Afterwards we all clapped and cheered again. I sipped from a plastic champagne glass. On-stage, Johnny crooned "In the Still of the Night."

Uncle Eddie walked over, offering me his hand. He pressed my knuckles into his rotund belly and we two-stepped a foot apart. "Hang On Sloopy" came on. I started to do the jerk. Uncle Eddie joined me, surprisingly light on his feet. He was once a football hero. Not anymore; he had a bad heart. He panted and perspired, making an effort to grin at me. A *corrida* blared out from the bandstand and everyone linked arms, shuffling back and forth, bumping into one another. I was beginning to feel gay. Almost happy. I went for more champagne. Bobby Lopez and I swirled and dipped to a Cha Cha.

There was a ruckus coming from the bar. It was two men. One of them was taking a swing at the other. A women screamed, pushing between them, yelling, "Don't, Carlos, don't!" Stella Rodriguez rushed over with her shiny dress rustling, shouting for Uncle Eddie, who sauntered over and calmly put a half Nelson on the dude. The women held back the other man. Two men hustled over and escorted the troublemaker out of the hall with warnings of calling the police. The crowd straggled back into the hall. Uncle Eddie was the hero.

Freddie loped towards me holding out a plate of food. "I thought you might be hungry. I'll go get us a drink, too." He came back with a Tequila Sunrise. I ate while he watched, not touching his. I swilled down my drink. We were joined by Johnny and Bobby Lopez. Bobby sidled closer to me. I felt hot and uncomfortable. My feet burned and ached in the hot spikes. I leaned against Freddie for a minute.

They began talking about cars so I went outside and sat on the steps. It was a balmy, still night and there were no stars in the sky. I took in a deep breath and hacked. The moon was a vague half-circle. Some low riders cruised by. I could see the faint glow of a lit cigarette and hear their muffled voices. The vibrations from the band were pulsing in my head. The low riders took off, sounding their pipes, laying rubber. Two chicks and a man were walking up the steps, Gerry's relatives. I didn't feel like talking to them. I got up and headed back into the hall, spotted Uncle Eddie walking towards me, and detoured into the toilet.

Beatrice was looking in the mirror picking at her hair.

"Hi," I said. She ignored me. I bumped against the door, realizing that I must be drunker than I thought. I pulled up my long, stiff dress, pulled down my panty hose and sat on the cool toilet seat. Someone came in. A tense silence followed. I hacked. Something told me to get out, but it was impossible. I sat there for a minute wondering what to do. Then I wiped and flushed the toilet.

I heard the tail end of a conversation in a heavy Chicano accent. It was a chick with hair the color of wheat at the ends, a red-gold band next to that, and black at the roots. It hung dank and singed around her shoulders and her brown, hawklike face. Her eyebrows were two black arrows over her bloodshot eyes, pointing to her temples.

"I saw you dancing with him," she slurred, staggering towards Beatrice.

"I don't know what you're talking about," Beatrice said, still checking herself out in the mirror, adjusting her lipstick with the tip of her little finger.

"Thas my ole man," she snarled, with her head wobbling back and forth like a puppet.

Beatrice ignored her, flipping her lipstick into her little, nylon fringed bag and started out. I was washing my hands pretending not to notice.

"I saw you, man!" she persisted.

It was high school all over again.

"Well," said Beatrice haughtily, "I didn't know that dude was your old man." The way she said "dude" was an obvious put down.

The chick grabbed her by the elbow, hissing, "*Mentira!*"

Beatrice pulled away letting out a snide, little laugh. I must admit it was kind of funny. The chick was wearing a black and pink dress. It was puffed out and gathered at the knees, making it difficult to take long steps. She teetered back and forth on pink spike heels. I figured she'd hit the floor with the slightest shove and never make it up again.

"Let go. You're drunk," Beatrice said.

"*Puta!*"

"Oh, God," Beatrice sighed, exasperated. She looked at me. I shrugged my shoulders.

Just then the door swung open and Gerry came in with her train gathered up in her arms, announcing, "Wow, do I have to go." We turned to look and the chick pushed. Actually, I couldn't tell if she pushed or accidentally fell against Bee. Beatrice briskly stepped aside. Then the chick pulled back, raising her arm in a clumsy maneuver to strike at her. Bee turned to say something to Gerry and wasn't prepared for the blow so I intercepted it, pulling her arm back. I was standing with my legs apart in an effort to stabilize myself in my high heels. I felt woozy and my moves seemed awkward and slow.

The door swung open and another wild looking chick came in. I recognized her as a *pachuca* from Los Nietos. She acted startled and swept her eyes over the room suspiciously.

"I've been looking for you, Delia," she said.

Delia staggered, then raised her arm in a wobbly attempt to hit me. Beatrice grabbed it. The other chick, whose hair was dyed jet black and was wearing fuchsia lipstick, snarled, "Leave her alone!" They were right in their element. I could hear Gerry peeing. I mustered up my composure and, in a sober voice, or as sober as I could, said to the brunette, "Why don't you take her home to sleep it off?"

A mistake. Delia flipped off her spike heel and brandished it in my face, losing her balance. The heel grazed my cheek. Gerry came out and yanked it out of her hand. She crashed into Gerry. I pulled her back. The brunette lurched forward, grabbing hold of Gerry's long curls, jerking her head around.

"Let go of her!" Beatrice screamed.

The brunette spit at her. Beatrice, enraged, hauled her off and slapped her, calling her a bitch. Wild-eyed, the brunette let go of Gerry's curls to go for Beatrice. Someone was trying to get in the bathroom, imploring in a high, strained voice, "For heaven's sake, what's going on?" By now the drunk blonde had Gerry's veil clutched in her fist. Beatrice, in one last attempt at reason, pleaded, "Will you please tell her to let go of my sister's veil?"

186

Maravilla

"*Chinga tu madre,*" hissed the brunette, going for her hair, yanking her head around. Instinctively, Beatrice lurched forward, grabbing the front of her nylon blouse. We were grunting and panting, shifting towards the door, bouncing off the walls. They were strong as gorillas. Solid flesh, drunk as hell. The brunette pulled away and I heard the rip. Beatrice didn't have time to release her and there it was, her blouse torn, exposing her snow white, Playtex Living Bra against her dark brown skin. She had a handful of Bee's hair. Beatrice raked her nails down her arm. Delia was yanking Gerry's veil, forcing her head down. I was trying to pry her fingers open.

Mrs. Hernandez slithered through the room into a corner. Her eyes were wide and glittering. We staggered toward her. I felt my elbow sink into her fleshy stomach. Delia still had a grip on Gerry while I pried at her hand. The brunette had Beatrice by the hair, Bee had her by the hair too as we pressed into Mrs. Hernandez, who was beseeching, "Stop it, girls, stop it!"

A crowd gathered around the door, pushing into the room. Stella Rodriguez, followed by Uncle Eddie, squeezed through.

Uncle Eddie took hold of the brunette and we all lurched at Delia, forcing her to let go of the veil. Before we knew what was happening, she had broken away and locked herself in the stall. Everyone quieted down. Mrs. Hernandez knocked at the door.

"Come out, right now!" she ordered.

Delia was blubbering and sobbing incoherently.

The toilet was packed. I was sweating and my underarms were wringing wet. I could see beads of perspiration on Gerry's brow and upper lip. The place smelled dank. The brunette had regained her composure and was trying to talk Delia into coming out.

"Fuck you," she bawled, letting out racking sobs. "I'm gonna kill myself."

Someone suggested we call the law.

"Naw, we can take care of it, can't we?" yelled Uncle Eddie at the bathroom door. I could see one wild, dark eyeball peering through the crack of the door.

"Louie's here, Delia, and he's gettin' pissed, you better come out, man," warned the brunette.

"We're not going to hurt you," Gerry added.

The door clicked open and Delia stood swaying back and forth, with black mascara smudges around her eyes and cheeks. She looked like a scared raccoon. She was fried. Her bleached hair looked more wilted than ever. She burst into muffled sobs, throwing herself at Gerry.

"Please forgive me," she wailed.

Gerry backed away but it was too late. Delia was slobbering into her bodice. I tried to gently pry her away. No luck, she was holding on tighter than a baby chimp to its mother.

"I'm drunk and I fucked up," she blubbered, smearing lipstick on Gerry's white lace bosom.

The brunette patted her head. The crowd was shoving and pushing.

"Move back!" Bee ordered. Once again Uncle Eddie came to the rescue, firmly pulling Delia away from Gerry. She collapsed into his arms and he carried her out light as a feather. The brunette clutched the front of her torn blouse.

"I hope we didn't ruin you wedding, man. I'm sorry, *esa*," she said.

Mrs. Hernandez discreetly draped a shawl over her shoulders and she straggled out. Stella Rodriguez sighed, "*Ay, Dios Santito, Dios Santito*" as she rubbed the lipstick stains off of the bride's dress.

"Good heavens, your hair's a mess and you still have to open your wedding gifts. *Ay, Dios!*" Grandma Rodriguez stood next to them, shaking and muttering to herself.

"Will you comb my hair, Cece?" Gerry asked.

"Sure."

Someone brought over a chair and she unfastened her tiara. I patted and smoothed over the professionally done curls, sticking in the stray ends and spraying them with a can of hair lacquer. Then I brushed the one long, silky curl around my finger. I could smell Gerry's Arpege. I was hoping my headache wouldn't return. The fight seemed to have cleared up my sinuses. I kept going over the long curl. It felt so good and smelled so clean.

"Hurry up," said Stella impatiently.

"Okay, that's it," I said. Gerry got up, glancing at herself in the mirror.

Maravilla

"How do I look?" she asked her mother, ignoring me. Stella stood over her, straightening her dress and patting her hair.

"Just fine, honey, just fine. Now go on out and open your gifts. Everyone's waiting," she said nervously, pushing her out the door.

They rustled out in their noisy dresses. As I watched Gerry leave, I was thinking that that would probably be the last time I ever combed her hair.

After they left the bathroom, everyone cleared out and I decided to redo my hair and face, hoping that the gifts would be opened by then. I ratted it into tufts, smoothed it over and sprayed it. Then I dabbed on lipstick, mascara, a little rouge, and some mint green eye shadow.

I went out and ordered another Tequila Sunrise, sipping it slowly. I spotted Slow Freddie leaning against Susie Garcia's hip as if no one else in the world existed. She was smiling coyly at him. I felt a minor irritation, belched out loud and quickly looked around to see if anyone had heard. I could see Stella rounding up the bridesmaids, herding them over to the front of the stage where Gerry stood above them, flushed and appearing only slightly wilted for all the ruckus, while the drummer of the Dominos rat-atat-tated a beat similar to the kind they play at the circus before a thrilling feat. Gerry turned her back to the crowd and tossed the bouquet over her head.

As it sailed into the air, we lunged forward. I went for it like a basketball player. Just as I was about to catch it, someone pushed me hard from behind and I went sliding across the waxed floor on my ass. Looking up, I saw Bee with a smug little grin, holding the wilted bouquet. The flowers were broken and bent. The crowd cheered and hooted like they were at a football game. Bobby Lopez helped me to get up. I staggered to my feet clumsily and politely excused myself, saying that I was going to change.

Back at the bathroom, I unzipped the stiff, scratchy dress, slid it over my hips and hung it on a hanger over the door, unpinned the pillbox hat, that had somehow managed to stay on through the whole day, and placed it on the toilet seat. Slipping off my pumps, I began massaging my swollen toes. Then I unhooked the merry widow corset that had left impressions on my rib cage and peeled down the girdle. Sighing with relief, I put on my purple mini skirt and lavender sweater, squeezed into white fishnet stockings and slipped into white pumps. Then I shoved open the door and stood on the toilet seat to see what I looked like in the mirror. Someone came in and I quickly climbed down and went out.

Back in the hall, I looked for the bride and groom.

"They've left," sighed Stella beatifically, as if she had just pulled off the biggest coup of her life, then abruptly rustled off. Freddie was gone too. No Susie either. From the corner of my eye, I could see Uncle Eddie heaving towards me. Nonchalantly I made for the door. Outside I felt a chill, thought about going back for my coat, thought about Uncle Eddie, and decided not to.

I started down the street. A few cars cruised by. I heard someone guffaw. I wondered if they were laughing at me. "Probably not, I whispered out loud. They probably didn't even notice you, *pendeha!* No one notices anything you do, stupid! So what! Who cares anyway?" I was heading for John O'Reilly's car. I wanted to curl up in the back seat and take a nap. It was locked.

"Shit!" I muttered. I didn't want to go back to the hall. Oh, go on, go back and have some fun! Fun? You call that fun? Shit! Oh, shut up and leave me alone! Look, there are lots of people you know in there. Go back and mingle, dumbie. No! What are you going to do? It seemed as if everyone else was having a good time while I only wanted to mope and feel sorry for myself. What a bore! HAVE FUN! BOOGIE, *ORALE PUES!*

A tear slid down my face. Oh, gawd, I was going to cry. Shit! Tears began to flow. Jonesy, you bastard! I hissed convulsively. Saliva sputtered onto my chin. My nose started to run. I felt enraged. Freddie, that punk! Gerry, the fake little bitch, Angel a junkie and a liar. (All junkies are liars!) Beatrice a bossy, raving Amazon. That *mensa*. God, and Stella Rodriguez? What a phony jive trip she's on!--"Come along darling, fix your hair, dear; smile, honey." I was enraged thinking of the way she had rebuffed and ignored me. And Manuel was nothing but a closet alcoholic. The fool. What about you? What? Yes, you, miss smart ass! You're worse off

190

than those goddamn *pachucas* with your sniveling and whining and complaining.

I could hear the click-clack of my heels on the concrete. Up ahead, a shadow moved. A man was walking toward me. He must have heard me. Embarrassed, I quieted down and held my breath, looking away till he passed. Jonesy, where are you? I implored. God, I wish I was dead! No, you don't. OK, stupid, what if God grants your wish? Like you get in a bad accident, all smashed up by a car or someone knifes you. I felt a tremor shoot up my spine, shivering at the thought of being mutilated, crippled or worse! However, it seemed to have a calming effect on me. I changed my mind. Yeah, I'd rather live, I thought, at least until I could think of a painless way to go. Coward! My mind reeled and snapped with a life of its own. I couldn't control it. I tried giggling, that always seemed to help. The giggle escaped, swelling into a gale and I snorted, then roared out loud. I was hoping no one had heard me. I wondered if I was going to flip out. Blow it. Like my cousin Effrin, who was doing time at Norwalk State tranqued-out on Thorazine. My teeth chattered.

Looking through a picture window, I saw the glow of a T.V. I'd been walking for a while and seemed to be headed towards my aunt Cora's. I had passed the residential area and was now into the neon lights, walking past a liquor store, a dry cleaners, Chris and Pitt's Barbeque, Ernie's Bar and Grill where my mother worked on weekends. God, what a dump! How does she stand it, I wondered. The Market Basket parking lot was dark and deserted. A few desolate cars were parked behind the Montebello bowling alley. Frank's Used Car Lot was closed; little lights from the bowling alley glinted off the chrome bumpers.

At the end of the block, I turned up the street and spotted the stucco triplex. Aunt Cora was working nights at the Granny Goose Potato Chip factory. I found the key under the garbage can where she kept it, in case Vera dropped by and went in.

The place smelled rotten. Bad plumbing or something. It was furnished like a motel room with formica furniture, vinyl cushions and plastic curtains. Sounds drifted through the clapboard walls, garbled voices, the wail of a baby, someone coughing. Flicking on the tube which sat in the middle of the room, I drowned them out. "Have Gun, Will Travel" was on. What a mug on that guy. I was beginning to feel better. Cousin Vera was right when she said she liked to turn the TV on first thing in the morning, especially if she was alone, since it made her feel like she had company. It was true. I was feeling less lonely already.

Going into the kitchen, I opened the refrigerator and took out baloney, Velveeta cheese, mayonnaise, and Weber's bread and made a sandwich. Even though my stomach was full, the alcohol made me ravenous.

I walked back into the TV room taking a humongous bite. As it was going down, it swelled into a solid mass. It was the bread and the baloney gummed together in my throat. I realized too late that I should have chewed it longer. It wasn't going down! I gagged and sputtered, trying to catch my breath. I was doubled over. I couldn't tell if I was breathing or not. Oh, my God, my wish was going to be granted. I was dying! I coughed and gasped for air, my eyes were burning and tearing. How many minutes did I have? One, two? If I didn't die, I'd probably be a vegetable. Bouncing off the walls, I staggered into the bathroom, realizing that I was still high. I pounded at my chest, hopping up and down. That's what they said to do in first aid class. I bent over and struck at my back, stood up and hit my chest again and again. I was heaving violently, trying to force it to go down. Finally, after what seemed like an eternity, it moved hot and burning like a jagged piece of metal searing my throat, a huge rock slowly sinking down my esophagus.

I stood stone still. It felt like a fist was lodged in my chest. I was nauseous and shaky. Going over to the toilet bowl, I hung my head over, jamming my finger down my throat repeatedly, until I choked and gagged and my stomach lurched convulsively and it all started coming up--the cold cuts, beans, tamales, wedding cake, the Tequila Sunrises, the rum-and-coke, and champagne. Slimy yellow and snot green, it gushed into the bowl, curdled and lumpy. The rancid stench of vomit filled my nostrils. Dry heaving, I held onto the sides of the toilet seat and spit out the last of it in long, mucous strings. I took a deep breath. I was going to live after all. I had only thrown up. No big deal, dumbie, I thought.

I slid to the floor, exhausted and dizzy, sobbing with disappointment and relief. Pressing my cheek against the filthy cracked linoleum, I curled into a fetal position, gagged a few times. A tear slid across my nose and onto the floor. The slick surface felt cool and soothing against my flushed face. Things sort of came into focus. There was a wet spot where my tears had fallen and I wiped it dry, making a little, shiny circle that was cleaner than the rest. Someone slammed a door. Overhead, the electricity buzzed. There was a commercial on TV. Some happy children's voices cried "Look-Mom-NO-Cavities!" My body slumped and I relaxed for the first time all day.

After a few minutes, I got up and flushed the toilet and went over to the sink and rinsed out my mouth. Then I went back and dialed my parent's number, even though I knew no one would be home. Then I dialed Jonesy's old number. "The number you have reached has been disconnected, no for..." Click. I dialed Freddie's house. A man answered and I hung up. Satisfied that there were signs of life somewhere, I turned back to the TV.

Festus was shuffling and dragging his bum foot across the jail house floor. His brows were knitted up earnestly, as he pleaded, "I think it's serious, Mr. Dillon. Homer was at Kitty's totin' a sawed-off shotgun!"

A picture of my mother curled up on the couch and my father slumped in the stuffed chair in the corner flashed in my mind. My mother had her arm around me. We were watching "Gunsmoke", as we did every Friday night. I stared at the screen. It was a rerun. I'd already seen it. I flipped the channels. A Christian preacher, spreading God's word through the Lord Jesus Christ, testified. "Jesus heard my prayers. We were broke, now we have two cars and a washer-dryer-dishwasher! It was Jesus!"

I flipped to a game show. A woman was screeching like a banshee. She had just won a new car, a mink stole and a vacation in Miami for two. When she jumped up and down, her jowls wobbled and her body shook like Jell-O. I giggled. I was wishing Gerry was there. I flipped to a Wallace Berry movie. He was hiding ten thousand dollars under a shack, looking around furtively. The house burned down at the end with all the money in it. I spread out on Aunt Cora's rickety couch and pulled the greasy-smelling blanket around me. I flipped the channels again, stopping when I got to the Saturday night movie. "Great," I sighed. It was Natalie Wood and Steve McQueen in *Love With a Proper Stranger*. There was a scene that knocked me out, when Natalie leaned forward and her hair fell softly over one eye as she looked boldly into the eye of the camera. I was mesmerized at the way it slid over, shiny and silken, flowing down the side of her face like a waterfall.

During the next commercial I went back into the bathroom and looked in the mirror. It was depressing. The bags under my eyes were big enough to pack. Black mascara was smeared all over my cheeks. Scanning the labels in the medicine cabinet, I found some stuff that said "skin tightener". I washed my face, globbed it on, and went back to the movie. Natalie was pregnant and Steve didn't want to marry her. The skin tightener was beginning to dry and itch. It felt like a thin layer of cement. I'm going to have to stop eating chocolate and drinking so many Cokes, I thought. Then maybe my skin would clear up. Natalie was talking to a seedy, back-door abortionist. I flipped the channels. Nothing but Oral Roberts and a basketball game and some cartoons. I switched back to the movie. There was another toothpaste commercial on, so I went back into the bathroom and rinse off the mask. I was thinking that I should stop ratting my hair so much; it was beginning to look like a Brillo pad. I thought of Natalie's soft curls. With a stiff brush, I started raking through the rats. When I got it flattened out, I realized unhappily that it was too kinky.

At the end of the movie, Steve McQueen was carting around a placard that said "Better Wed Than Dead". Then he and Natalie kissed and made up. Which I took to mean that they were going to be married or something. They were happy again. I decided right there and then that I was definitely going to have to dye my hair brown instead of red, but I was sure I'd never get the kinkiness out of it. It was *Johnny Carson*. I lowered the volume. Stretching out and pulling the blanket up to my chin, I began drifting off to the lull of the TV. I bet a hairdresser could straighten it. Carmen Estrada had hers done and it looked straighter than a horse's tail. *That's it!*

194

I thought. I would call Shear Magic the first thing next week, make an appointment with Victor, get this goddamn kink out of my hair, and dye it chestnut brown or something like that. I'd look completely different. I'd change. I would stop thinking of Jonesy all the time.

I woke up in the middle of the night to the monstrous buzz of the T.V. My mouth tasted rotten. My pantyhose chafed against my thighs. Aunt Cora hadn't returned. I went into the bedroom. A garish yellow light reflected off the green walls. I climbed into the bed and stared at the ceiling, trying to relax. It was no use. I couldn't sleep. Next to the bed were several cardboard boxes filled with books. I sat up, exhausted and weary but anxiously needing to do something. I went over to look at the books, thinking they must belong to Aunt Cora's boyfriend Bruno Fevovitch. He always had his nose in a book. At family gatherings, he'd sit in a corner with his legs crossed, reading paperbacks. I bent over, scanning the titles. Wedged between two thick novels were several volumes of poetry. Pulling out a tiny volume by Gabriela Mistral, then two more, Frederico Garcia Lorca and Caesar Vallejo, I sat on the bed reading them, attracted to their names more than anything else.

On the cover of Mistral's book, I discovered she was a poet from Chile who had been an ambassador to Mexico. She had never married or had children, even though most of her poems were about children and small animals. I moved on to Lorca. I had no idea what he was talking about, but still his words excited me. Especially the ones on blood and death. Caesar Vallejo was sad and remote but his spirit went to my heart.

In the middle of a poem, I put the book down. My eyes burned, my head swirled with images. Grandfather Contreres in his casket, white satin against his ashen face, Chuck Valdez lying in a pool of yellow blood, Jonesy's stiff body, his mother sprawled over his casket, the head of a lion, the grotesque mask of a grinning, old, wrinkled man surrounded by skulls, crossbones, and long-legged spiders. I picked up a pencil that was next to the phone and wrote on a napkin:

Maravilla

In a small green room I lie waiting for
Saber-toothed panther to advance
Yellow flames of wolf-eyes flicker
In the dark, crescent moon night
Mi corazon, mi alma, mi vida
Noche de sangre amarillo
Fuente del mar y el mundo
Que no es la verdad.

I read it over and over. I must have done this twenty-five
times or so until I burst into tears, shaking and rocking back
and forth. I felt like I was drowning in air. I was losing it!
Frantically, I dialed my parent's number. No answer. Then my
grandmother's. "Hello," said a tiny, old voice. I hung up, feeling
stupid. I fell across the bed, writhing and sobbing, flailing at
the mattress. After a while, I quieted down. Too tired to move,
I blew my nose on the blanket, hoping that Aunt Cora
wouldn't notice, then fell back against the pillow and went to
sleep.

I dreamt I was surrounded by the muffled boom of rush-
ing water. A large, black shadow swam towards me. I struggled
to get away through a clotted bed of kelp but its branches
entangled my arms and legs. The shark was circling around me,
its narrow, slit eyes glowing. I began stroking frantically,
trying to get away, but instead I was swept into a torrent,
grappling at seaweed and kelp beds, hurtling into the white
water, tumbling headlong into a rip tide.

I woke up terrified. Aunt Cora lay next to me, snoring
like a Mack truck. That was the sound I'd heard. I glanced at
the clock on the dresser. It was two o'clock in the afternoon.
The poetry books lay scattered on the floor. Next to them was
the poem I'd written. I picked it up and read it. It seemed
silly now. Almost stupid.

As I sat on the toilet seat, snatches and particles of the
dream flashed through my mind. "It's only a dream," I thought,
"Forget it." I flushed the toilet and went over to the sink and
rinsed my face. Shoving the curtain back, I opened the window
above the bathtub. It was a dull, muggy day and the gray,
afternoon light cast a dismal glare against the flat buildings
and concrete sidewalk.

Chapter 19

I went back to work typing and filing at Prudential Life Insurance. I hated it. But it was the only job I could get. Even the Tastee Freeze job had been more interesting.

For months, I woke up every morning with the memory of death. L.A. was a blank landscape of endless freeways, underpasses, overpasses, on ramps, off ramps, and congested traffic in the backdrop of a dense, smoggy sky. The horizon was a filmy, gray-brown blur against concrete buildings, sidewalks, and houses. Everything was gray. Not the gray of silver or fog, but the gray of waste, apathy, and death. I could smell the carbon monoxide, the sulphurous odor of the grainy air.

Jonesy had been dead for six months, but still I thought of him constantly. I scribbled chaotic, indecipherable notes on scratch paper, stashing them in an overnight suitcase under my bed. I knew there had to be something drastically wrong with me. Why was I hoarding tattered pieces of paper with crazy words written on them? My clothes were a mess. Wrinkled and stained. I hadn't retouched my hair for months and the roots were black next to a red-gold band and faded split ends. My fingernails were cracked and ragged. I was down to a hundred pounds.

My mother accused me, in turn, of taking LSD, smoking marijuana, being pregnant, of having an abortion.

"*Dime, que tienes?* You look terrible. What's wrong?"

"I don't know, nothing," I said, too depressed to talk. She tried to force me to drink whiskey--to perk up my appetite. Sometimes it worked and I'd go on binges, eating everything in sight, later returning to my listlessness, barely eating at all.

Maravilla

In January, Maria came home from Berkeley. She was going to the university there. She'd gotten a partial scholarship the year before, with Grandmother Acevez financing the rest. Right before she went back, we had a big fight. She complained that I hadn't been cleaning up after myself. My mother walked into the middle of it, siding with Maria. She said she was sick and tired of my selfish behavior and moodiness, that I was like a poison inflicting the rest of the household.

"Why don't you just move out!" she screamed.

"OK, I will," I mumbled. Even though I had no idea of where I was going.

I couldn't seem to shake my depression. It hung over me, heavy and morose. I felt desperate. I thought about killing myself. But how? Images of razor blades, pills, guns, auto wrecks, and knives rolled around in my head.

After the fight that night, I lay in bed crying and listening to Maria snore. In desperation, I began to pray, *Hail Mary, full of grace, Our Father which art in heaven, I believe in God the Father Almighty, creator of heaven an earth. Oh my God, I'm heartily sorry for having offended Thee, Hail Mary, full of grace.*

"St. Teresa, somebody, please help me!" I whispered desperately.

Maria stirred. "What's the matter, Cece?"

I didn't answer.

"Why don't you answer me?"

I don't know," I said, trying not to cry. It seemed all I ever did was cry. I was sick of it.

"You know what I think?" she said.

"What?"

"I know how you must feel, Cece, but I don't think going around in rags, whispering prayers, and not talking to anyone is helping. You look like Aunt Becky just before she went to the nut house."

"I know it. I feel like I'm going crazy."

"You're not crazy, Cece, but you have to do something, something different."

"I miss Jonesy," I said, "I don't have any friends. I wish I was dead!"

"Jonesy is gone, he's dead. You're alive. Start acting like

it," she said. "It's sad, but you knew what he was like when you met him."

"What do you mean?"

"You told me before he died that you were going to stop seeing him, because he was doing junk and hanging out with Victor and his gang," she said. "You said you'd never really be serious about him. Do you remember?"

"Yeah--But I can't help thinking if things had been different. If the cops hadn't hasseled him all the time, if he could have bought his truck, if I hadn't yelled at him to go away. I did love him, Maria!" I cried.

After I had cried for a few minutes, she said, "You're right Cece. The cops hassel us because we're Chicanos. Especially, guys like Jones. It's hard to get a job, to make money. It's true. But you have to fight back! You have to do something! Have you thought about getting out of here?"

"It's easy for you to say, Maria, Grandma is helping you, and you got a scholarship and everything."

"That's because I asked her to. Besides, I have to pay her back, you know. She borrowed money on her house, and I have to make it good as soon as I can. Why don't you ask Dad to help you? He could get a loan."

"I don't know. Besides, what would I do with the money?"

"For one thing, you could quit that job. You hate it. Maybe you could go back to school. I know that's not what you want to do, but at least you'd be doing *something*. You could take poetry, or acting or something. You used to take acting classes, and you were good at it."

After a few minutes, I said, "Maybe you're right."

"I know I'm right! Listen, Cece, anything would be better than going around acting like a martyr and praying to your St.Teresa picture. You're not twelve years old anymore."

"I wasn't praying to a picture, Maria!"

"Yes, you were. I heard you reciting those prayers we learned in catechism. I don't know what good you think it does. All those things we learned in catechism are ridiculous, Cece! First of all, the Catholic Church forbids the use of contraceptives. In this day and age! We're supposed to get married and have a bunch of kids even though we may end up being too poor to even feed them! And another thing, as women we can't become priests either.

"So, who cares? I don't want to be a priest. And I'm not going to have a bunch of kids either! I'm not even planning on getting married, you know. I don't know what that has to do with me. I'm just trying to get from one day to the next."

"I know," she said, "but I don't want you to end up like Terry--Mother goes around praying to little plastic statues and throwing guilt trips on everyone. Or end up married to that guy, Slow Freddie, and having a bunch of snot nosed brats."

"Ok, Ok, Maria, I get the picture."

"You know what I want, Cece?"

"Yeah, to be the first female pope."

"Don't be silly. Women probably aren't allowed in the Vatican, except possibly to clean and cook and keep their mouths shut. Anyway, that's not what I want. I'm not even a practising Catholic and you know it. What I want is freedom and the power to rise to the top of my profession. I want to be able to make changes. To help people. If I can't do that, then I won't do anything. I'll learn everything I can and use it to fight back.

"Of course," she said, as if it were already true, "I'll help you. Anyway I can. In fact, if I get my hands on some extra cash right away, I'd help you now."

"You would?" I said.

"Yeah, but you have to promise me that you'll try to get away from here, or at least do something about yourself. Another thing: get rid of those pills you've been taking. They're making you worse."

"They calm me down."

"Calm you down! You look like you're half dead."

"All right, Maria. I swear I'll try, swear to God."

I lay awake for a long time, thinking of what Maria had said. I knew she was right. I had to get away, get out of my rut. But how? I wondered. How?

After going back and forth in my mind about what to do, unable to sleep, exasperated and exhausted, I began to pray the Hail Mary again.

That night, I dreamt that Maria sat on a golden throne, wearing a red cape over long, dark robes. There was a small, red beanie on her head. People gathered around, kneeling at her feet. One of them kissed the ring on her finger. In front of them, four brown bears in purple and orange tutus, pranced and pirouetted. Little bells tinkled from their wrists and ankles, as they danced and sang, "London bridge is falling down, falling down, London bridge is falling down, my fair lady."

While they danced, I rode the merry-go-round on a shiny white and yellow horse. Round and round, I went to the sound of the tinny organ music. Each time I passed by the brass ring, I tried grabbing it, but missed. Round and round, I whirled while the bears danced and the people, one by one, kissed Maria's ring. At the end of the ride, I groped for one last chance at the ring and grabbed it.

Then the bears started running on all fours. They lumbered into the street, past the neon lights, heading for the city limits, throwing off their bells, ripping off their tutus as they ran. Panting and puffing, they galloped through a large, open meadow toward the forest. Overhead, the full moon hung in the sky, beaming, surrounded by circles of blue and yellow and purple rings. "Run, run!" the moon shouted, casting beams of light, guiding them over gullys, through ravines, up hills, and over streams through the dark, back to the woods. I was running behind them.

Then all of a sudden, I was falling through a hole, flying down, tumbling and turning! I found myself in a long, narrow corridor with a high ceiling and stark, white walls, lit up with a brilliant light. At the end was a long brown door. I walked toward it and it got farther and farther away. I was getting younger and younger. I was ten years old again, carrying a notebook, dressed in my old Catholic school uniform, the pleated, navy blue skirt, the white, peter pan blouse beneath a cardigan, and black-and-white saddle oxfords.

At the end of the hallway, I opened the door and entered a large school room--which I recognized immediately as St. Alphonsus, my elementary school. Children's desk were lined up in neat rows, facing a gigantic black board. One side of the room was a mass of tiny, six-sided windows flooding in a blinding, white light. I squinted, making out at the front of the room what looked like a tremendous, old oak tree, all gnarly and silver gray, barren as the dead of winter. But, as I got closer, it changed into an oak desk. Someone was sitting, writing. It was St. Teresa!

I recognized her by her shabby habit and bare feet, her clam, beautiful face. But she was younger than I remembered. She glanced at me sternly. There was a sign hanging from the front of the desk: "No Trespassing." She continued writing, ignoring me, and I knew immediately that I could not now, or ever again, interrupt her and that some invisible boundary lay between us which I could never again pass. I felt an unbearable sense of loss and remorse. Then she was gone. Her book lay open and the word RITE stood out in big block letters. I didn't understand it. I wanted to scream, "Come back! I'm all alone. I don't understand!"

Just before I woke up, my notebook turned into a white dove and flew away through the six-sided windows.

The full moon shone through the bedroom window like a laser beam, making my head buzz and hum. I felt weird, sad, and happy all at once. The word "rite" kept running through my mind like a stuck record. I got up quietly and went into the kitchen to make some hot chocolate. I threw some water in a pot and while it was heating, turned on the transistor to Wolfman Jack on low volume so I wouldn't wake anyone. The Temptations crackled out of the tinny speaker, "_The way you do the things you do, the way you do the things you do!_" I poured a packet of chocolate mix into a cup of hot water, grabbed a notebook that was on the counter to write the dream down. Before I could think about it, I began writing:

The sun was high in the sky that afternoon, when Sewa took off toward Rattlesnake hill, telling her grandmother that she was going to gather piniones and saguaro fruit. But really she just wanted to be alone. All day she had had a feeling that she wanted to walk alone in the desert, hiking up and over the foothills. Before leaving, she slipped into her thick-soled, knee-high elk moccasins to protect her from the wild nettles and prickly cacti plants, slid her flintstone knife into its sheath at her waist, secured a small pouch with her favorite shells and sacred trinkets on a leather string around her wrist, for good luck, then touched the copper amulet *around her neck, making sure it was fastened. On her way up, she stopped at a stream to fill her little water gourd, then headed toward the mountains. After she had been walking awhile, she lost track of time and noticed the sun beginning to cross over the sky into the west. She sat down by a yucca and took a sip from her water gourd. It wasn't until she got up to leave that it dawned on her that she was lost. This is impossible! she thought. She had been hunting and gathering in this desert since she was a little girl and knew every inch of it.*

"Are you lost?" the wind seemed to whisper.

She whirled around to see a tremendous coyote standing where the yucca had been.

"Who are you?"

"I have a message for you," he said. "If you want to find your way back home, you must go over the mountain, follow the creek you find there to the end, jump in and swim through the stream, out to the mouth of the river. Go as deep as you can to the bottom and you will find a black, obsidian rock, very flat and smooth. Bring it back to me."

"Why should I! Go away, stupid, old dog!" she said, frightened.

"Wait!" he said. "If you don't go and do what I tell you, you will be lost forever in the desert. You may never again see your grandmother, or your family, or your people. Even if you do find them, your life will be dull and common. You will be an empty person performing empty tasks." Then he roared with laughter.

"What if I do what you say?"

"You may die," he said matter-of-factly. "But if you die, you will reunite with your people in the underworld. And they will celebrate and dance with you for many days. You will be held up high in the circle.

"Or then again," he said licking his paw, "you may not die. If you live, you'll be back with your family, blessed by the Great Spirit."

When she looked up again, she saw only the yucca with its single tall, spiky cactus flower in full bloom. She gazed up at the mountain, thinking that there was still plenty of light. If I hurry, I'll make it back by dusk, she said to herself. She strung her gourd over her shoulder and headed up into the foothills. Just as she went past, a gigantic Saguaro, a big, brown she-bear, appeared in her path.

"Follow me, Sewa," she said. "I'm the guide here. I'll show you a short cut." She led her up a steep path, around a bend to a tremendous, hollowed out oak log, entering on all fours. Sewa got on her hands and knees and crawled in behind her. It was black as coal. She could not see a thing, so she held on to the she-bear's tail. When they got to the end, the she-bear suddenly grabbed her, shoved her into a small hole and covered it so she couldn't escape, and left her there alone. Sewa struggled and squirmed, trying to get free, feeling stupid, remembering what her grandmother had told her about she-bears. "Never trust a she-bear you meet in the foothills," she had said. "They will lure you away, save you for winter, then eat you."

"Help! Help!" she yelled, even though she knew that she was too far away for anyone to hear her.

All of a sudden, she heard a hissing sound, looked up, and saw a big rattler winding toward her.

"I'm coming to rescue you," it said, helping her out of the hole. "That will teach you to trust she-bears." Sewa was scared to death of the snake, but didn't know what else to do, so she followed it out of the log as fast as she could, up the side of the mountain, toward a big gray rock.

"Come in here. You'll be safe," the snake said, dissappearing under a crevice. No sooner had Sewa slithered and squeezed under, then the snake sank its fangs into her leg. Sewa moaned and immediately passed out.

She dreamed she was in a strange, dense forest, wandering into a sunny, woodland meadow, where a group of angels with transparent, pastel wings and silver hair danced and sang, along with fairies in pointed hats, with bells on their ankles, twirling around in a circle. She found herself in the middle of their ring while they sang: Listen to your heart, only to your heart. Sing your own song, sing your own song. So listen, listen, wait and listen. Only you know the way, only you!

When Sewa woke up, an old crone with a face like a black hawk had sucked the venom out of her leg and was bandaging it with dampened cactus leaves.

Maravilla

"You'll be fine now," she cackled, helping her up. "I want you to come with me. I'll show you the way back."

"No, thank you," Sewa said. "I'll find my way back alone."

"Wait, don't go yet," said the crone. "I know your grand-mother and she sent me for you, so you wouldn't get lost."

"She did?" Sewa asked.

"Yes, come on", said the crone, leading her up to the top of the mountain. "We must get there before dark."

When they had reached the top of the mountain, Sewa sat down exhausted and thirsty.

"Go ahead and rest dear," said the crone. "Let me help you with your things." She helped her to take off her gourd, eyeing her knife and pouch greedily.

Sewa, too tired and thirsty to notice the crone's interest in her things, said, "I wish I had some yerba manzania to make me feel better. That's what grandmother gave me when I was tired."

"Drink some of this," said the crone, handing her a drink in a cactus husk. "It is like yerba manazania."

Trusting her, Sewa drank it down and soon was sound asleep.

She woke up to the beaming light of the moon. Looking around, she noticed that everything she owned had been stolen. Her knife, her amulet, her gourd, even her knee-high elk moccasins. She fell on the ground and wept.

After a few minutes she stopped, realizing that she was very thirsty and that, if she didn't find water soon, she would die. Using the moon to light her way, she began scrambling down the mountain, scratching and scraping her legs and feet on rocks and nettles till they bled.

Finally, she found a tiny, little stream and began to follow it down and around until she came to a place where water gushed out of the side of a hill. She drank and drank until she couldn't drink anymore. When she felt rested, she continued down the hill until she came to a rushing creek.

Maybe this is the creek the coyote told me about, she thought. If I dip in and swim to the river, I'll find my way home, she thought. She wadded in slowly, then plunged down underwater, swimming steadily until she came to the mouth of the river, going deeper and deeper, until she was at the very rock bottom of the river. She reached down to what she thought was a black obsidian rock and grabbed hold of something soft and slimy.

"Got you." it said, with a voice as old and squeaky as a rusty door hinge. "You big dumby. You never learn, do you!"

Sewa was shocked and began grappling and gasping, swallowing water, desperately, trying to get free.

"It's too late for you," croaked the troll. "You're so stupid! You do what every one tells you to. You don't have a mind of your own. So now you have lost everything. Ha-ha-ha-ha!" he howled, with a cruel laughter.

Just when Sewa thought it was all over for her, a big wave came and knocked the troll off balance. He lost his grip and she swam away.

Being old and feeble, he couldn't catch her as she swam swiftly down stream, out of his sight. It seemed to Sewa that an eternity had passed by the time she reached the banks of the creek. She crawled out of the water, collapsing on the ground, gasping for air, and sobbing.

Right before dawn, the coyote came back as she lay on the ground too exhausted to move.

"Well, dear, you didn't do too well, did you!"

Sewa didn't answer him. She pretended to be asleep. Maybe he'll think I'm dead, she thought, and leave me alone. The old creep!

"I know you're awake," he said, "and I want to send you on another errand. And this time I hope you'll do better."

Sewa bolted up and looked him right in the eye.

"Forget it!" she said. "I'm not going anywhere."

"Do you want to see your people again, Sewa?" he warned. "If you do, you better do what I tell you to."

"Listen fool," she spat, "I don't care what you say. I'm staying right here till morning, then I'll find my way back by myself, without your help!"

When she looked he was gone.

But in his place was the she-bear and behind her was the rattler, the old crone and the troll. They all began to plead and cajole her to let one of them lead her back.

"Follow us! We'll show you the way, the way, the way," they cried in sing-song.

Maravilla

By this time, Sewa was too tired to be frightened or even to get angry. In fact, she thought they were kind of funny.

"Oh, go away," she said. "Don't be dumb." And she laughed out loud at them.

After that she fell asleep again.

She woke up at the break of dawn, feeling refreshed and ready to start looking for the path back home.

"Never again," she said to herself, glancing down at her sore feet that were now callused and tough as leather. "Never again will I listen to a coyote, never! Even if I don't find my way back, right away, I'm sure that the Great spirit will lead me there someday. Until then, I'll live here in the desert with the wild animals and plants. But from now on I'll take care of myself and listen to my heart." And she began to sing, "Only with my own heart, my own heart!"

Then all of a sudden, she clearly saw the path that would lead her home.

When she finally arrived, her grandmother and family were so happy to see her that they gave her a "welcome back" party and celebrated for three days and nights. While everyone gathered around her in a circle, her grandmother placed a black obsidian amulet around her neck and presented her with a pair of knee-high elk moccasins and a freshly sharpened flintstone knife.

She said, "Your new name is Sewa Flying-Eagle-Woman *because you are brave and far sighted and have traveled over the mountain and found your way back home."*

The End

It was almost daylight when I finished. Exhausted, I scanned what I had written. It was strange. I had no idea where the story had come from. I tore the pages out of the notebook, stashed them in my suitcase and went to bed.

Chapter 20

After work the following afternoon, instead of going home, I drove to Pacific Coast Highway, past Seal and Huntington Beach, looking for a place to stop. Just past Corona del Mar, I spotted an open stretch of land, parked my car, and walked through the dry, brown meadow to the edge of the cliffs. It was windy and the sun was gradually sinking into the horizon. A triangle of gold light reflected on the blue-green water. It was about a forty foot drop, steep and straight, plunging down. I stood there for a minute, hypnotized by the rhythm of the waves and the white caps crashing against the rocks. I felt woozy and strange, as if the ocean were calling to me, pulling me in. I shivered and reached into my pocket for the heart-shaped locket that Jonesy had given me and threw it into the water. Then I pulled out the last of my stash of valiums and white crosses, hesitated a minute, then flung them down too. After a second or so, I turned around, headed back to the car, and drove home.

A few days later, Gerry called. I hadn't heard from her in months.

"Cece, Angel's going to jail."

"Oh, no. That's too bad."

"I've got to see you-- Please. I've got to see you right away. Do you think you can come up?"

"I don't know. I have to work."

"Please. I need you! Please come. You're the only one I can turn to."

"Um, O.K. I'll come. Wait a minute. Maria!" I yelled. "Can you give me a ride to the airport tonight?"

Maria sauntered into the living room. "I guess. If you pay for the gas and help me type some papers," she said, leaning against the door.

"All right, Ger. Pick me up at the San Francisco airport at one o'clock."

"Thanks, Cece. I'll be there."

My mother had walked into the room. "Where are you going now?"

"I'm going to San Francisco to see Gerry."

"Just like that! What do you think you are--a jet setter or what? Sam, talk to her."

"Where you going?" my father grunted.

"I just finished telling you. To the city of San Francisco."

"Oh," he said, going back to his newspaper.

"You're crazy!" she said.

"Mother, Gerry needs me. Angel's in trouble. He may be going to jail and she needs me now."

"Big deal," she snorted. "And you need money. What about your job?"

"Tomorrow's Friday. If you call in sick for me, I can go for the weekend and be back by Monday in time for work."

"*Valgame Dios!* I suppose you're taking my car to the airport?"

"Come on, Mother. I'll pay for the gas. Please!"

"O.K., O.K.," she said, walking out of the room, mumbling "God help me, I raised a beatnik."

"Beatniks are passe, Mother," I said, going into the bedroom to type Maria's papers.

"Well, whatever you call those weirdos with old, ragged clothes and long, messy hair. *Sin vergüenzos!* They never clean themselves or wear underwear!"

"Hippies, Mother," yelled Maria. "How many times do I have to tell you they're hippies, not beatniks? And there are some things that are more important than being clean and wearing girdles and bras and jock shorts, you know."

"*Callate la boca,* Maria. No one's talking to you, *sangrona.*"

"I'll be quiet when you stop pretending to be so provincial," Maria said.

"Those people are nothing but a bunch of maa-ree-wanos," she said. "*Pelados, con sus nalgas pa hueda!*"

"Come on, Terry. It's okay for you to get tanked out of your mind on booze, which happens to be more addictive than cannibus, but you go crazy if anyone gets high off a perfectly harmless herb," Maria said in her usual, condescending manner.

"Oh, can-yurr-butt!" yelled my mother. "Is that what you're learning at college, Maria, how to be a phoney?"

"Oh, forget I mentioned it." Maria trooped by me. "She's impossible."

"Don't get her riled up before I leave," I said.

She went into the bathroom, slamming the door. I could hear my mother counseling Eddie. "Don't listen to that snake-in-the-grass, *mijo, esta loca.*"

Later, she knocked at the bedroom door, cracking it open as I typed. She stood in the doorway, smoking a Pall Mall.

"Yes?" I asked.

She flicked an ash to the floor and came in.

"I want to talk to you, Cece," she said. Her eyes were wide and watery. "I just want to say one thing before you go to San Francisco. Promise me one thing, *mija*. Can you do that?"

"What?"

"Promise you'll take care of yourself. Promise you'll eat good and, you know, comb your hair, keep clean and, you know, wear underwear." She puffed on her smoke.

"Okay, Mom."

"And another thing," she said, knitting her brows. "Please don't use marijuana and that other stuff." She mouthed LSD. "You know what happened to Effrin after he took it, Cece? He's drooling all over himself at the county nut house. *Pobrecito.* I don't worry about Maria," she continued. "She's as strong as an ox. But you, Cece ..." She frowned, came in closer, sitting at the edge of the bed.

I began folding clothes into my suitcase.

She sucked on her cigarette, blew out a cloud of smoke. Lowering her voice, she went on. "Cece, Maria thinks she's so smart. I've never said this before, but as God is my witness," she raised her hand in testimony, "I love all my children equally, believe it or not. But, Cece," now she was mouthing the words, whispering, exaggerating the vowels, "you're better off than she is. At least you have feelings. Maria is made of stone. She's smart as a whip. She can add and subtract and do algebra, or whatever you call it. But you, Cece, can sing and dance and you write all those wonderful things down on little bits of paper." She paused, then mumbled, "God knows what you'll do with them." She glanced at me. I looked away.

"It doesn't matter," she went on apologetically. "Maybe you can, you know, give some of them to me?"

I was embarrassed, wondering which ones she had read.

"I didn't think you'd like them," I said, avoiding her eyes. "I didn't think you'd understand. I mean, I don't think anyone would understand."

"Oh, I don't. But that doesn't matter. I still like them."

Maria came into the room. Mother fidgeted with the bed-spread. "I was just telling Cece that I hoped, you know," she sucked on her cigarette, squinted her eyes up, exhaled, "that she takes care of herself and doesn't take mar-ee-juana. I worry so much after seeing cousin Effrin. Maria, you should see him. He's like a *legumbre cocido*."

"Effrin was always like a cooked vegetable," Maria said.

"Yeah, but the drugs made him worse. And what about Manuel Ortiz, Bertha's son? *Ay, Dios*, look at him. He thinks he's Jesus Christ. Going around blessing everyone and wearing his long, greasy hair parted in the middle and dressing like a girl. Poor Bertha, she's dying of embarrassment. It's from the drugs, Maria, I tell you."

"That may be true, but then look at Uncle Ray. He was crazy as a bed bug and he never took drugs except for rot-gut whiskey."

"That's true, Maria, but I think it was the war that made Ray crazy. After he came back from Germany, he never was the same. You didn't know him then, but he was a handsome and intelligent man. My God, women were crazy about him."

"I have no doubt," said Maria. "People go crazy in wars. There's a lot of them going crazy right now because of the war."

"What war?"

"The one you've been watching on TV every night, Mother."

"Oh," she said, stubbing her butt out on the floor, sticking it in her pocket.

"Gawd, why don't you put it in an ashtray?" Maria moaned.

"Listen, Maria. It's my shirt, right? Not yours."

"Marcos is in Viet Nam," I said, "somewhere in the jungle. Stella Rodriguez is going crazy, too."

"*Pobrecita*," said Mother. "I thought they were only advisers or something. Not fighting a war."

"Advisers!" Maria groaned. "People are dying every day. Hundreds and thousands of them. It's horrible, for God's sake. No one cares!"

Maria's eyes blazed like two small fires. I was applying a coat of make-up, rubbing it into my cheeks and forehead.

"Cece," my mother said, changing the subject. "You don't have to wear all that junk on you face. You're pretty enough without it."

"Haven't we been through this before?" I sighed.

"But you look like a you-know-what," she said.

Maria looked up, exasperated. "It's perfectly natural for her to paint her face. Our ancestors, at least some of them, the Huichol Indians--Isn't Grandma Contreres half Huichol? Anyway, they still paint their faces, especially during their religious ceremonies, when they take their sacred mushrooms."

"Maria, we're not Indians, we're American citizens. It's normal for them, not for us. Ay, if Grandma Acevez heard you talking about taking drugs, she'd cut you out just like that." She snapped her fingers. "And you'd end up working at the Granny Goose Potato Chip factory like Tia Cora instead of being a lawyer."

"Come on," Maria said. "In the first place, I didn't say *I* was taking drugs. Secondly, I've already got the money in a bank collecting interest."

The phone rang.

"Mama," Eddie yelled.

Mother shuffled out of the room, mumbling, "Shit. I can't say anything to Maria. She knows it all."

"I'm going next door to talk to Evelyn," Maria said. "Call me when you're ready to leave."

Maravilla

She slammed out of the room as I was drawing two black lines around my eyelids.

"Okay," I said.

I flew out of the L.A. International Airport on the midnight flyer.

An hour later, I was in San Francisco, trudging down the ramp through the long, gloomy passageway, lugging my overnight suitcase.

As soon as I had pushed through the swinging doors, I spotted Gerry. She was wearing an ankle length navy pea coat and a crocheted hat with little plastic gold colored coins that jingled and jangled when she walked. A line of toilet paper hung out from the side of her hat in a long curl. (I remembered her stuffing toilet paper in her hats to give the illusion of height.)

Her face looked wan under the fluorescent lights.

"I'm so happy you're here, Cece," she said embracing me. She looked ragged and tense. Anything but happy.

"Hi, Ger." I put my arms around her. "How are you?" I said, tucking in the toilet paper.

"Oh my God, I didn't know that was hanging out."

"Let's get out of here. I left the car double parked."

We scrambled out of the winding maze of the airport, into the pouring rain, and over to a new, cherry red Corvette. There was a ticket on the windshield. Gerry grabbed it.

"Another goddamn ticket," she groaned.

She got into the driver's seat and fumbled with the gear stick.

The place was jammed with bumper to bumper traffic.

"Do you want me to drive?" I said.

"No, I'm okay," she said, bursting into tears.

Rain shattered against the windows in a deluge. Cars backed up behind us, going around, blasting their horns.

"I'm driving," I said, getting out. Gerry moved over. I pulled on the wipers and put it in first. It lurched forward like a drunken beast.

"Where to?"

"Follow the arrows."

I nosed into the flow of traffic that looked like a collage of water colors with muted neon lights and blurred motion.

Everything quivered, distorted by the downpour.

"Don't give it so much gas," she said.

I let up on the accelerator.

"It's been terrible, just horrible, Cece. I thought things would get better once we moved here, but they didn't. They got worse."

"What happened, Ger?" I said, adjusting the rear view mirror.

"Angel's going to jail again," she cried. "You tried to warn me, I know, but I wouldn't listen!"

She took the toilet paper out of her hat and blew her nose.

"He stayed away, sometimes all night long. Oh, Gawd! When he did come home, he'd call his mother. His mother! And they'd talk for hours. He was hanging out with the worst low-life you've ever seen. Worse than the *cholos* on Ford Boulevard."

"You're kidding," I said.

"Once, when I was waiting for him to come home, we'd planned on going out for dinner, he was already an hour late, which was common. I happened to look out the window and saw him going into the apartment downstairs, where this white chick that I despise lives. Anyway, I waited for a while and, when I couldn't stand it any longer, I went down there. I could see his pants as I went down the stairs, through the window. But when I knocked at the door, no one answered. Shit, man, I thought I was going crazy. I felt like Ingrid Bergman in that movie ...."

"*Gas Light*."

"Yeah. Anyway, he came up later and acted like it was no big deal that he was three hours late. And get this! He pretended that there was nothing going on, that it was all my imagination.

"You're kidding!"

"No. I threw a glass at him. It hit his head, but he was so stoned it didn't even faze him!"

"It really sounds horrible."

"It is. It wouldn't be so bad if I was closer to home. You know, to the family and my friends and stuff. God, I've been so lonely, I wish I was dead."

She thrust her face into her hands, muffling her cries. We circled around in the maze of the airport.

"Which way shall I go?"

"Follow the signs towards Oakland."

"Why didn't you tell me about all this before?"

"I kept thinking that things would get better. He promised me that he'd straighten out if we moved here."

"Wow, I don't know. Maybe you could talk him into coming back to L.A."

She blew her nose and sniffled.

"At least you'd have your family and friends," I said.

"I don't know what I'm going to do," she sighed. "I'm so mixed up. But I don't think I want to go back to L.A. There would be too many memories there. I'll tell you one thing. I'm sure sorry I ever got married. It's a trap. It's boring. I never have fun anymore. Everything is his way. His job, his money, his problems. 'What's best for Angel.' Then there's his mother--- what a bitch! Gawd, I hate it! I swear, if I could have known what I was getting into, Cece!"

I felt mixed up and sorry for Gerry, but in a strange way, relieved, feeling close to her again.

"Like I said, it wouldn't be so bad if I could be closer to you. You and Marcos are the only two people I care about being with now. And Marcos is in the goddamn jungle in Nam!" She sputtered, breaking into tears.

I pulled over to the side of the road and put my arms around her. After a few minutes, she quieted down.

"Oh, Cece, I hope Marcos is going to be okay."

"I hope so, too," I said.

"My mother's a basket case, man. That's all she can talk about. Marcos!"

The rain had slowed to a drizzle. I started up the car and drove around until I found a liquor store. I went in and bought a bottle of brandy, opened it, and took a slug, passing it to Gerry. She sipped it.

"Man, things are *soo* weird sometimes," she wailed.

"Yeah, I know what you mean," I said.

"I'm sorry, Cece. I hope I'm not bringing you down."

"That's all right, Ger. I'm glad I'm here, glad you're telling me this. I've been down too, feeling bummed out a whole lot."

Maravilla

We were in front of the liquor store, sitting in the garish reflection of neon lights.

"Let's go," I said, starting the car.

"I met a woman, Flora Dominguez. She's a checker at the store where I work. She said I could stay at her flat until I found a place. She lives in San Francisco. I'm not staying at that horrible, little apartment another night. I'll go crazy, especially now that Angel's going to do time."

"What's he doing time for, anyway?"

"Oh, you know, the same old stuff. Tickets, possession." After a few minutes, she said, "Do you think you could help me move out?"

"I guess so, if that's what you want to do."

"All I have are my clothes and a few personal things. It wouldn't be too difficult."

"Okay," I said.

We circled off the freeway.

"Now which way?"

She gave me directions and we continued.

"I was afraid you'd try and talk me into staying with him."

"Why is that?"

"When I told my mother that I was thinking of leaving, she went nuts and started to cry. She insisted that I try to work it out with him. Then she started in about Marcos again. That's why I couldn't bear living there. Then my father got on the phone and said, 'You better stick it out with Angel. He's your husband. You can't just leave him.'"

"What did you say?"

"I said that I couldn't stand it, that Angel was going to jail. And he said, 'You should have thought of that when you married him. You're a married woman now.'"

"What a drag."

"Yeah, and he was slurring his words like he was smashed. So I said, 'Okay,' and hung up. It's useless to try to talk to either one of them."

"Jeez."

"Listen," said Gerry. "I know I made a mistake, man, but I ain't gonna spend the rest of my life paying for it. No way." She took a drink and passed it to me.

216

"I don't blame you, Gerry. I think you're doing the right thing." I took a slug.

"You really think so? You have no idea what I've been through. Last month, I thought I was pregnant."

"Oh, my Gawd," I said, handing the bottle to her.

"That did it. I realized then and there I'd never be able to have a baby with Angel. I was planning on getting an abortion. I had really sunk to the bottom." She took a sip.

"What happened?" I said.

"Well, when I told him about it, he freaked. He started to push me around. Then he broke down and cried like a baby, begging me to stay with him and saying that he'd change and everything."

"Weird," I said.

"Yeah, it was. I pretended to agree with him so he'd leave me alone. Thank God I started my period right after that. Anyway, the reason I want to move now is that he's flying to L.A. this weekend. That's why I needed you to come right away. He's going to pick up his mother and drive her back. In fact, he's already left. She's supposed to stay with us until he gets sentenced, which could be weeks. Gawd, I couldn't bear it. I swear to God she hates me, Cece. She barely even speaks to me any more, especially since she heard that Angel got busted. You know what she told his cousin, Gloria?"

"What?"

"Get this, that she thought it was *me* who drove him over the edge with demands so he turned to smack! I mean is she weird, or what?"

"That *vieja* is really the Wicked Witch of the West." I grimaced at the thought of Mrs. Hernandez and her claustrophobic house.

"I think she got wind of what I was planning to do, because she said on the phone that she was bringing some papers she wanted me to sign. Something about property. Said her lawyer was advising her. I think she's trying to intimidate me. She doesn't know how desperate I am. Right now I'd sign anything, even if I ended up with only the clothes on my back."

"She probably thinks everyone is like her and can be bought," I said.

"Yeah, I bet she sleeps with her banking statements." Gerry guffawed. "I can just see her all alone, cuddling and kissing her money."

"Yeah," I said. "I can see Mrs. Hernandez and her tea-cup poodle snuggling up to her paper assets." I snorted. We both roared.

"Anyway," Gerry continued. "Last night Angel told me he'd sign the 'Vette over to me before his mother could do anything about it. He said that he was selling a piece of property that his grandfather left him and, instead of finishing the deal, he was going to sign it over to me. He said that he realized it was his fault that we couldn't make it and that he would try to help me before his mother interfered."

"That was nice of him," I said.

"Yeah," said Gerry. "I think that he means well, I really do, but he's weak. That's what's so sad. If it wasn't for smack, he'd be okay. But then it would probably be something else." She started to cry again. "Cece, I'm so afraid that something terrible will happen to him," she sobbed.

"Well, if he does time, maybe it'll clear his head and set him straight like it did last time."

"That's what I'm hoping for. It's been hell. I swear, living hell!"

"I hear you, Gerry. I know exactly what you mean."

I handed her the bottle. She took a gulp and passed it back.

We went to dinner and then to her apartment and spent the night packing.

The next day was clear. The sun shone and a strong wind blew in gusts, whipping my hair around as we shoved Gerry's stuff into a big Chrysler station wagon that one of her friends from work had brought over. Then we got in the car and took off like fugitives. Voluminous clouds scudded across the clear, blue sky. The vast body of water sparkled in the distance, surrounding us as we crossed over the Bay Bridge into the city, driving up and down the roller coaster hills to Church and Nineteenth Street.

Trudging up and down three flights of stairs, we lugged the cardboard boxes into Flora's flat, stacking them in a back porch that overlooked a tiny yard where clothes flapped in the wind from backyard clothes lines.

The living room was spacious, with old fashioned French windows that overlooked Dolores Park. Potted plants and macrame hung from the dusty sills. Tie dyed sheets sagged in soft mounds from the ceiling.

"How do they do that?" I asked.

"Oh, they tie off sections and dye them, then untie them and re-dye them another color," Gerry said.

We looked through the rest of the place, stopping in the bedroom. There was a double mattress on the floor, covered with an Indian print bedspread with little yellow elephants waving their trunks. A poster of Janis Joplin hung from the wall next to an official looking American flag.

Gerry went into the kitchen and got a drink of water. Her face was pinched and puffed up from crying. I followed her. Pasted on the refrigerator door was a picture of Martin Luther King, Jr. with "I have a dream" written under it.

"I'm getting hungry," Gerry said. "Why don't we get something to eat?"

"All right."

"We can go to Mission Street."

Ragged clouds tumbled around in the powder blue sky like fat white clowns. The wind stung my cheeks, ruffling my hair, as we walked up and down the steep hills.

On Mission Street, we stopped at a Mexicatessen and ordered green-chile burritos and hot chocolate. I tore into mine, not realizing until then how hungry I was. Hot sauce dripped onto my hand, and I wiped it off with a napkin as I watched Gerry take little nibbles off hers. I felt embarrassed for wolfing my food in front of her. She way always such a lady.

"Flora might be at Dolores Park today, passing out flyers," Gerry said.

"What for?"

"Oh, anti-war stuff."

"Oh."

I didn't want to appear naive, so I resisted asking questions, even though I was very curious.

As we approached Dolores Park, I could hear the wafting sounds of a Latin-Afro beat. Dark-skinned men were on the grass, beating their congas, tablas, and dum beks. Colorfully clad people were scattered all over the park. Children ran and played, babies cooed and cried, some of them still nursing. Girls in flowing Gypsy skirts and elaborate jewelry and guys with long, tangled hair and wild outfits danced bare-breasted under the sun. We sat on the grass, watching. A naked man walked by.

Gerry looked to see my reaction. "Too much, huh?"

"Really!"

"I thought you'd like it here," she said, smiling.

I felt as if I were at a fantastic carnival with all the wild colors and the strange, exotic odors and sounds surrounding us. Gerry talked to Flora for a while, then we started back up the steep hill. Shadows fell in angles across buildings, sharp and distinct in the brilliant light. We passed rows of pastel flats that were similar, but somehow uniquely different. Everything seemed strangely familiar. For a few minutes, I felt as if I were in a dream. A dream that made me feel completely at home with myself.

"I think you're going to be happy here," I said to Gerry.

"I hope so," she said sadly. "I don't know. What about you, Cece. Do you think you'd like to live here?"

"Maybe."

"We could get a place together! I'll have some money as soon as I sell the 'Vette, and there's that property Angel is giving to me. I could find us a flat. Think about it?"

"Okay," I said.

Chapter 21

By the time my flight touched down in L.A. I had decided that I would continue working at Prudential until I had saved enough money to move to San Francisco.

Later that month Terry helped me to get a job, waiting tables, on week-ends, at the restaurant where she worked, so I could save money.

I spent a dismal winter but managed to make enough to buy a '57 VW bug by May, with enough money left over to make my move.

When I told Terry I was leaving she said, "*Ay, que bueno.* I'm sure you'll be better off there as long as you don't get involved with *traviesos.*"

"OK," I said. "I'll be sure to hang out only with people that aren't too dark, too light, make sure they're all Catholics, drink Oly, and smoke Pall Malls."

"*Valgame Dios,*" she complained to my father. "Sometimes Cece acts just like Becky, your sister. It's her mouth. She inherited *esa boca* from Contrereses."

"Oh, leave her alone, *vieja.*"

On a Friday morning in late April of '67 I woke up early and began packing. While rummaging through boxes I came across some old photos. In one of them I was sucking on a baby bottle. Maria stood next to me looking bow-legged and paunchy in a loose diaper. She was sucking her thumb. Behind us loomed the whitecaps of Huntington Beach. There was a picture of Sam looking suave, dressed in army fatigues. (He'd been a paratrooper in World War II.) He was leaning over, with one foot propped up on the shiny bumper of a black '46 Chevy coupe. There was a picture of my mother in a stylish forties suit with shoulder pads, her hair done in a pompadour with a white gardenia behind her ear. She was squinting into the sun, holding me in a frilly baby dress and sun bonnet in her arms. Maria stood behind us frowning, her stubby knees exposed, her little jaw resolute.

I took the pictures and slipped them into a pocket in one of my suitcases. I was thinking about Huntington Beach. The way the hot white sands felt under my feet. I loved the misty blue-grey sky, the salt air scent, the grey and white seagulls and the tiny delicate shells I found. I liked to walk to the end of the pier and watch the slick black seals bobbing up and down out beyond the breakers. Mostly I loved swimming in the cold water after lying in the sun until it was too hot to take any longer.

When we were little Sam would carry Tony on his shoulders and hold me by the hand as we ran into the frothy surf. He'd lift me up and swing me around, dipping me down, skimming my ankles across the waves, then up, over and around and around, then gently set me into the shallow part while he swung Tony. I'd stand there waiting with my heels sinking into the soft wet sand, afraid with that childhood fear of disappearing or of being sucked away, letting the waves rush over me, knocking me under and tumbling me around in the salty water. I'd pop up and run out squealing, then go back again to get swung around until I was drunk with dizziness, or Sam finally had to stop from exhaustion.

When Maria and I were older we'd inch our way into the cold water, daring each other to go further, making bets as to who could swim faster or go deeper. I could swim faster but she had staying power. I'd dive in first and swim out, and she'd follow behind with slow sure strokes, out-distancing me every time. Out beyond the breakers we'd bob up and down like seals, playing tag with the other kids, doing somersaults or just floating on our backs, drifting and rocking in the rippling water.

By the end of summer we'd be dark brown. Aunt Cora called us pickaninnies because we were almost black and our hair stood out in wiry corkscrew ringlets.

In the evening we'd have weenie and marshmallow roasts.

Just before sunset we'd romp through the shore playing tag, skipping through the shallow waves that often glowed with a phosphorescence. Then we'd hike to the pier to watch the seals and throw scraps to the gulls.

After dark Sam would build a bonfire and my mother would tuck us into our sleeping bags. I'd lay there listening to the rhythm of the pounding surf, gazing up at the stars, while Sam pointed out the Seven Little Sisters, the Big and little Dippers, the blue planet of Venus and the Milky Way.

I remembered one morning waking up on the beach to see Sam frying fish that he'd caught earlier. I snuggled up next to him, close to the fire, with a blanket. Overhead gulls screeched, their wings fanned into the silver-grey lights, diving down into the choppy water. The ocean and the sky were the same color except the sea was shimmering and translucent and the sky opaque, pearl grey slashed with jagged ribbons of golden-peach with the sun rising, in the background, a silver ball of fire.

Sometimes in the late spring, after a rainfall, you could see all the way to Catalina Island, twenty-six miles away, to the soft brown folds of the rolling hills and the clear, sharp crevices and angles of the mountains.

Alongside the road, running through meadows and over hills, grew wild irises, yellow and orange California poppies, pink and purple sweet peas, in a blanket of color, spread out across the landscape.

Not anymore. That was years ago. Now it's all built up with 7-11's, McDonald's, Jack-in-the-Boxes, condos, tract homes, and shopping malls. The smog is usually too heavy to see beyond a few feet away. Except after a rainstorm or the Santa Ana winds. Then for a short while you can see the mountains and the skyline etched clearly to the horizon again.

My father and mother came out to see me off. Sam carried Eddie in his arms. He peered into the window.

"Here's the map. Be careful, honey, watch your rear view mirror for trucks. Always give them the right of way, understand?"

"OK," I said, taking the map. It was the third one he'd given me in a week.

"And call collect if anything goes wrong. I'll come get you," he said, slipping me a twenty.

"OK. Thanks, daddy."

"Cece," said my mother, sticking her head around from behind Sam, "remember what I said, stay away from strange men and don't take anything, you know what I mean. And Cece, try not to be depressed. Be happy."

"Sure."

Sam ruffled my hair.

"She's worried," he whispered in my ear. "We love you, honey. Go on, have a wonderful time. Don't worry, I know you can take care of yourself. Anyways, you know, you won't be too far away from Maria. You know Maria, she's tough as nails, you can always count on her," he said, kissing my cheek.

"Cece," Eddie cried, "don't go! I wan you take me to Dizzyland."

"OK," I said. "When I come to visit we'll go to Disneyland, OK? 'Bye."

They waved to me as I backed out of the driveway. I waved back. I watched in the side view mirror as my mother turned to go in with Eddie trotting behind her. Sam stayed there getting smaller and smaller, watching the back of the car until I turned the corner.

I drove slowly through Maravilla past the rows and rows of flat pale yellow projects, heading toward town, past Our Lady of the Angels with its old fashioned Gothic structure, past the Catholic school where kids were running and playing and shouting, past Sandoval's Market, the Shell, Chevron, Texaco and Standard stations, past the Floral Drive-In where *Una Noche De Amor* was playing, past Bertha's Beauty Salon and Wig Styling, the Peek-a-Boo Bar with its dancing girls and topless waitresses, past St. Vincent de Paul's Second Hand Store, the Highway Patrol and the Market Basket, onto the freeway through the steady flow of endless traffic, past the black smoke, through the monotonous terrain, a spread out flat line of miles and miles and miles of concrete in the backdrop of a smoggy grey skyline.

I spent the night in a motel somewhere near Salinas. When I arrived in San Francisco the next afternoon a chilly wind was blowing and a low fog hung over the bay. Flashes of sunlight broke through as I neared the Mission district.

After inching through a hopeless tangle of traffic and zig-zagging through a labyrinth of streets that ended abruptly, driving up and down impossibly steep hills (one was so steep I thought I was peering off the edge of the world, and going down that sheer vertical drop gave me butterflies), I stopped for directions and found the place.

It was just like Gerry said, an ugly fluorescent green building on 24th Street close to Noe, over a T.V. repair shop. I found a parking spot a few blocks away, walked over and rang the bell. The lock buzzed and I pushed past a wrought iron grating, entered a dank passageway and climbed the dingy staircase.

Gerry cracked open the door when I rapped, unhooking the chain.

"Cece!" she said. "You finally made it! We've been waiting for you. Come in, come in!"

I almost didn't recognize her. Her hair was different parted in the middle and hanging straight and loose. She was wearing rimless gold framed glasses with blue tinted lenses. Five or six colored antique necklaces hung around her neck.

I entered a dark sweet smelling room and set my bag down. We embraced.

"She's here," she yelled.

A guy with aviator sunglasses and long black hair pulled back in a ponytail walked into the room. As Gerry beckoned him her hand flashed with a ring on every finger.

"Hi, Cece," he said hoarsely.

There was something familiar about him. I stood there smiling stupidly.

"It's Marcos," Gerry declared.

He took off his glasses. His face was gaunt, his eyes tired and sad.

"Marcos!" We brushed against each other stiffly, touching cheeks. I could smell his pungent masculinity, felt the boniness of his lean body. The three of us stood there awkwardly grinning at each other.

"I didn't recognize you, Marcos. I thought your were at your mother's." My head buzzed. I felt a nervous edge.

225

"I got in last week," he said.

"Gee, it's great to see you. It's been a long time."

"Yeah, man. How was your trip up?"

"OK. I spent the night in a motel so I'd get here during the day. I knew I'd have a hard time finding the place. You know, with the traffic and everything. I'm not used to the city streets. They're so confusing. And those steep hills! They're something else." I was rattling on, trying to fill in the gaps which seemed to extend into the dark room.

"Yeah, I know what you mean," he said.

A narrow shaft of sunlight streamed through the small window onto a faded brown carpet. There was an old funky couch in the corner. A tie-dyed sheet sagged on the wall behind it. The rest of the room, except for a stereo, was empty.

Marcos went over and put on an album.

"Come into the kitchen, it's warmer," said Gerry.

We sat in the kitchen at a round table looking out at an alley. Bob Dylan bellowed:

> *Hey, Mr.Tambourine Man*
> *Play a song for me*
> *In the jingle jangle morning*
> *I'll come following you.*

Gerry filled a pot with water and put it on the stove, lighting it.

"Is chamomile OK?"

"What?"

"Chamomile."

"Sure, anything is OK."

I could see her breasts moving under her blouse, brown nipples pressed against old lace. Her tight Levi's were faded and colorfully patched. One gold moonbeam hung from her pierced ear.

All of a sudden I felt out of it in my plaid pants and matching red sweater and bag. Gerry must have noticed.

"Gawd, girl, am I glad to see you! You look great! Doesn't she, Marcos?"

Maravilla

Marcos had walked into the kitchen and was leaning against the sink lighting a cigarette. The light accentuated his acne-scarred face and straggly goatee. His high cheekbones were smooth and hairless, no sideburns. I remembered Gerry saying that they were part Hopi.

"Yeah," he said softly, "you look great."

"Oh, thanks," I said, fidgeting with a spoon.

Gerry was talking non-stop about the problems she was having with the landlord, an old Italian guy who didn't want what he called "Hippies and Peacenicks" living in the building. I noticed Marcos had a peace sign sewn onto the back of his army shirt. Gerry said she was having to hide Marcos until she could figure out what to do about it.

"I hope it's OK if I'm here," I said.

"Oh, sure, he knows you're coming. I told him that you're my sister, that you were a teacher."

"You did?"

"I told him you teach poetry. You're still writing poetry, aren't you?"

"Sort of. I'm hoping I can take some writing classes at City college this summer. Writing and theatre."

"Alright! Did you know Cece writes poetry, Marcos?"

"Far out." Marcos said.

"Do you still stash your poems in that little suitcase?"

"Yeah, I said, Boy I'm wired. I must have had ten cups of coffee on the way over."

"You know Emile Dickinson?" said Marcos.

"You mean Emily Dickinson?"

"Yeah. Her."

"Yeah," I said. "We studied her in a class I took."

"Who's that?" Gerry asked.

"This chick who wrote thousands of poems," said Marcos. "Far out poems. Stashed them and no one ever found them until after she was dead, man. She never left her house, either. One of my buddies in Nam had some of her stuff. It was alright, man."

"Why didn't she leave her house?" asked Gerry.

"'Cause she probably didn't want to be bothered. Would you go out there if you didn't have to?"

"Really, Marcos, of course I'd go out. What a trip she must have been. I bet she was real pale," Gerry said, lighting a joint, passing it to me. "I hope you're not planning anything that weird, Cece."

"Listen, I have to look for a job. So I guess I'll be forced to go out."

"Wonderful, *esa*," said Gerry, affecting her old Chicano accent. "Because if you stay holed up in here you'll be mildewed in no time at all." She hit on the joint, held her breath, coughed up a cloud of smoke, gagging and stomping.

We laughed. For a minute it was just like old times, cracking jokes and acting silly.

Bob Dylan wailed:

> *Oh, where have you been*
> *My blue-eyed son?*
> *Oh, where have you been*
> *My darlin' young one?*

"Listen, man," said Gerry. "You don't have to worry. Don't bust your ass."

"What do you mean?"

"I got enough money for all of us. I sold that property and the Vette. So we're fixed for a while. OK?"

"I know, you told me, but I won't feel right until I have my own money."

"Yeah, yeah, yeah," said Gerry, waving her hand impatiently. "By the way, Flora said they'd be hiring someone at the store. You know, that store where I checked. You could try there. It's OK. I mean, you know, you don't have to go around kissing ass and you can be comfortable, like you don't have to dress up in designer clothes and all that shit. I bet you'd like Flora too. Don't you think so, Marcos?"

"Sure," said Marcos. "Flora's alright. Hey, I'm going to the store to get some cigarettes." He padded out of the room.

"I gotta take Marcos to see a doctor in Mill Valley. That's why I'm so glad you got here, otherwise I was going to have to leave a note on the door. Gawd, I'm glad you're here, Cece!"

"What about my stuff in the car?"

"We can get it later."

"OK," I said, sipping tea.

"Did you know that Marcos got a medical release?"

"Yeah, I remember you said something about it. But you didn't say why."

"He stepped on a fucking mine."

"Oh, my gawd."

"Really, man, it blew off part of his foot, that's why he's limping."

"You're kidding. Gee, I didn't notice him limping."

"He's going to have surgery. The doctor said he'd be normal afterwards, wouldn't limp or anything."

"That's good."

"He's got shrapnel in his leg, though. But he's lucky. I'm actually glad it happened because it got him home."

"That's true." I said.

The sun had disappeared. Shadows began to fill the room. I felt a chill, wrapped my hands around the warm cup.

"He was in pretty bad shape when he got here. My father threw him out. They had a big fight and Marcos kicked in a door. My parents are really freaked out. I think he'll do better here."

"Well, he looks great," I lied.

"The government is giving him a pension, and pick up on this, a lifetime supply of pain killers."

"Too much," I said.

"Yeah. He's got jars of Librium, Percodan, Darvon and Valium. Except that Flora told him not to take them anymore. She says they're making him depressed."

"That's what I was taking, Valiums. I was moody as hell, too. I quit."

"That's good. By the way, how is your mother?"

"OK, everyone's about the same. Maria is going to Berkeley."

"Maybe we could drive over there next week."

"Did you buy a car?"

"Yeah, it's parked right out front. The blue Ford. It's a lot better than that gas hog. You know, the Corvette."

"Speaking of the Vette, do you ever see Angel?"

"Angel who?" said Gerry sarcastically.

"Come on!"

"Well, yeah, as a matter of fact, he was released about a month ago. Anyway, he came over here in one of his father's Lincoln Continentals. I mean, can you believe it! White on white. Looked like a pimp. It was embarrassing, Cece. Gawd, I was worried that one of my friends would see us."

"What a crack up. What did he want, anyway?"

"Who knows, man," she sighed. "I think he was trying to impress me, like he said that if I came back to him he'd change and everything. The same old stuff. Said he was clean now and that I'd have a good life, hah! Money and style instead of living in a dump like this. Can you believe it?"

"Weird," I said.

"Really. As if I'd ever go back to that bourgeoisie existence."

"So what did you tell him?"

"Hey, I like this place. My life style suits me just fine. I didn't want to hurt him. But I was trying to get rid of him before E.Z. came by."

"Easy?"

"E.Z. Those are his initials. Eugene Zanuck. He's my new boyfriend from New York City. He's Jewish."

Gerry had changed. I was glad. I wanted to forget the past. Jonesy, the projects, that garish flat L.A. light, the phonies on Hollywood and Vine, the carnivorous freeways, the oil dikes in Huntington Beach. I was glad to be done with it. I'd never go back there. Never. If I ever left San Francisco I'd go to the islands or the desert.

I went into the bathroom and brushed my hair, raking through the spray. Then, wiped off my lipstick. When I came out Gerry had picked up the dishes and was stacking them in the sink.

"What ever happened to all your things, you know, all the stuff you got when you were married?" I said, looking around at the starkness of the flat.

"As soon as Mrs. Hernandez found out I wasn't coming back she had it shipped to L.A."

"All of it?"

"Well, most of it. I was relieved. I mean, I can't be tied down to all that junk, man."

"What about all your pots and pans and those neat ceramic dishes you got?"

"I kept some things like sheets and towels, a few pots and pans and dishes. But the rest of it I was glad to get rid of. I mean, where am I gonna put a Spanish style dinette set, anyway? I hated all that stuff. It was sooo weird. I mean, fuck it, who needs it?"

"Really," I said, watching her brush through her long straight hair.

"Let me do yours," she said.

"OK," I said.

She pushed my head down, brushing my hair up and over the top. I could feel the blood rushing to my face, as she brushed and stroked it over and over. Then she pulled my head up gently and ran her fingers through my hair, lightly brushing the top of it. She made two tiny little braids in front, that hung down the sides. With a small colored pencil she drew something on my cheek and handed me a small mirror.

My hair stuck out wild and full all around my face and there was a tiny red heart on my cheek.

I smiled. "I like it." I said, handing her the mirror. She took it and drew a small blue star on her cheek.

Marcos was back.

As Gerry finished up in the kitchen, we sat in the living room in the last shaft of sunlight. Marcos started to strum his guitar. A Santana tune, "Black Magic Woman." You could see that he had changed. He wasn't the same person I'd known. I had never noticed his Indian features, his high cheek bones, his hawk-like nose, etched so clearly. He used to be chunky and boyish. That was gone. There was something about him, something indescribable, in his eyes, his manner, his voice. He seemed to be more *himself*.

"I liked that," I said, listening to the melody. "Been playing much?"

"Yeah," he said. "I got a gig at a cafe on 24th Street. Been practicing with a band too."

"Written any new songs? Remember when we used to stay up all night singing and writing lyrics?"

"Hey, yeah--I got a few new songs. I wrote some poetry, too."

"I bet you're good," I said. "I'd like to see it."

"Hey, I'll show you mine if you show me yours," he joked.

"You first."

"Same old Cece. That's what I always liked about you. You're funny and cute at the same time." He chuckled, and a little bit of the old boyish Marcos came through.

"We better go," Gerry said. She went to the living room closet, taking out a brown and white Mexican poncho, pulling it over her head.

"Here, Cece, you wanna borrow this?" she said, handing me a rainbow colored shawl with long tassles. "It's a lot colder here than what you're used to, so you better wear it."

She draped it around my shoulders. Marcos opened the door and we filed down the dark staircase. Outside a bitter wind cut through me. Tall buildings blocked out the sunlight that was left.

Gerry and I sat in the front, Marcos slid in next to me.

"I know you're going to like it here, Cece. It's gonna be great, just great! Tomorrow we're going to Speedway Meadows. Santana and the Jefferson Airplane are playing. And pick up on this, next week Janis is going to be at the Fillmore."

"Far out."

We were rolling up and down the hills over the trolley tracks, past Dolores Park and the brightly painted Victorian flats. Everything seemed bright, and clear and new. I felt excited and I was thinking anyday, any day, very soon, I was going to be happy, really happy. I just knew it.

"Are you gonna come with us tomorrow, Marcos?"

"No, I'm going over to Ray's. We're gonna march in the park."

"Marcos is going to an anti-war demonstration. Maybe we'll come with you, Marcos, then go to the park later. What do you think, Cece?"

"Sounds alright with me."

"It's fine with me," Marcos said.

We coasted down Dolores St. past the mom and pop grocery stores with their open air produce stands and Mission Dolores with its bells tower looming high into the blue sky, heading for the heart of the city.

"I'm getting some of those mushrooms," said Marcos. "You wanna try some?"

"Sure," said Gerry. "I'll give some to Cece."

"Mushrooms?"

"Yeah, magic mushrooms, they're very mellow."

As we turned the corner the sky opened up and the bay came into view. We sped past the Presidio which was surrounded by massive spruce and oak trees standing ancient and gnarled in the grey light. A thin layer of fog hung over the water. Several small sailboats swayed and pitched in the high winds. As we approached the bridge, going past the toll gate, the lane narrowed and we slowed down, entering a fog bank, engulfed in shrouds of gray mist. Dusk fell over the city, ragged orange strips of light splashed across the horizon. In the dusky sunset a lone cargo ship sailed to sea. Overhead the ochre arches of the Golden Gate Bridge towered majestically upwards. We picked up speed, plunging ahead into the stream of traffic.

La Mujer Latina Series

The Broken Web
The Educational Experience of Hispanic Women

Edited by Teresa McKenna and Flora Ida Ortiz
Co-published with The Tomás Rivera Center

ISBN 0-942177-00-2. 1988
Hardbound $32.00
Paperbound $23.95

A revealing anthology of essays on the failure of the institutions to provide for and encourage the educational achievement of Hispanic women, thus adding to the inequalities they face in U.S. society today.

Maravilla

By Laura del Fuego

ISBN 0-915745-15-1. 1988
Hardbound $25.95
Paperbound $12.95

From the housing projects of East L.A. to the lively scene of San Francisco's Haight-Ashbury district in the 1960s, Laura del Fuego's first novel tells the absorbing tale of a young Chicana making her way through turbulent times.

Women of Mexico
The Consecrated and the Commoners

By Bobette Gugliotta

ISBN 0-915745-16-X. 1988
Hardbound $32.95
Paperbound $19.95
Illustrated

This collective biography not only offers insight into the more famous and infamous women in Mexican history, but weaves a fascinating tale of how the ways and deeds of Mexico's unsung heroines have shaped both a culture and a nation.

La Mujer Latina Series

Between Borders

Essays on Mexicana/Chicana History

Edited by Adelaida del Castillo

ISBN 0-915745-14-3. 1988
Hardbound $45.00
Paperbound $32.00

The first serious, comprehensive history of U.S. Latinas of Mexican descent prior to the 20th century. Written by a team of Mexican and U.S. scholars and based on copious documents and sources from both countries, this book sheds light on the traditional leadership of the modern Latina that is both ignored and little understood.

Fiction

Bring Me A Story

By Sally Benforado

Hardbound $14.95 1986
ISBN 0-915745-08-9

Softbound $9.95 1986
ISBN 0-915745-11-9

In the eleven short tales of *Bring Me a Story*, author Sally Benforado weaves together the oral history of a family of Sephardic Jews, from their close-knit home in Turkey to their new lives in America. They are stories of a heritage that spans the globe, of centuries-old traditions transported to a different world, and of a people who held on tightly to the ways of their ancestors, who, like them, left their homes to settle in a strange new land. *Bring Me a Story* stands as a living testament to a people born of their Hispanic ancestry, Jewish tradition and immigrant experience.

Collection Development

The Chicano Public Catalog
A Collection Guide for Public Libraries

Compiled by David Gutierrez and Roberto G. Trujillo

ISBN 0-915745-03-8. 1986 $39.00 300 p.

An authoritative guide to the best and most significant writings for public, academic and professional Chicano collections with full descriptive annotations. It includes indexes, annotations and bibliographic data. An important tool for collection development and evaluation.

Literatura Chicana
Creative Writings Through 1984

Compiled by Roberto G. Trujillo and Andres Rodriguez
Introductory essay by Luis Leal

ISBN 0-915745-04-6. 1985
$23.00
210 p.

More than 750 bibliographic citations of creative and critical literary works in print and nonprint form on the Chicano experience. Organized by genre and indexed by title and author, the bibliography covers poetry, fiction, theatre, oral tradition, and other subjects and includes listings of literary periodicals, dissertations, bibliographies, anthologies, and video and sound recordings.

Bilindex & Bilindex Supplement 1
A Bilingual Spanish-English Subject Heading List

Standardized Spanish equivalents to Library of Congress subject headings including: an explanatory preface; cross references; scope notes; children's subject headings; standard subdivisions; and English-to-Spanish index; regional variants of authorized Spanish subject terms; and hard-to-find technical items.

Bilindex: ISBN 0-915745-00-3. 1983. Hardbound $65.00. 533 p.
Bilindex Supplement I: ISBN 0-915745-02-X. 1986. Softbound $55.00. 334 p.

Mexican American Studies

El Libro de Caló
The Dictionary of Chicano Slang

Edited by Harry Polkinhorn, Alfredo Velasco and
Malcolm Lambert

2nd edition
ISBN 0-915745-10-0. 1986
Hardbound $32.00
Paperbound $17.95
100 p.

This is an indispensable dictionary that is easy to use; it is a guide to understanding the
dialect popularly spoken by Mexican Amercians in the regions of the Southwest.
Includes an English-Caló concordance.

Mexican Americans in Urban Society
A Selected Bibliography

By Albert Camarillo

ISBN 0-915745-12-7. 1986
$29.95
250 p.

A specialized but comprehensive bibliographic study documenting the contemporary and
newly acquired urban experiences of Mexican Americans living in the U.S. cities as they
migrated from the crop fields of the Southwest to the newly emerging post-war
industries. The most updated and complete bibliographic control effort on writing on
regional urban developments by Mexican Americans.

Online Information on Hispanics & Other Ethnic Groups

A Survey of State Agency Databases

Edited by Roberta Medford and Eudora Loh

ISBN 0-915745-07-0. 1986
$45.00
200 p.

This is the most complete directory of state agency databases, located in the 10 states with the largest Hispanic populations, with a listing of their names, addresses, and phone numbers. This includes a wide range of statistical and other pertinent data on Hispanics, Blacks, Asian-Pacifics, and other ethnic groups living in the U.S. Complete with indexes, this book is a guide to the myriad of data collected and maintained by state agencies on ethnic groups.

Statistical Sources on the California Hispanic Population

Edited by Eudora Loh and Roberta Medford

ISBN 0-915745-01-1. 1985
$22.00
210 p.

A comprehensive directory of state documentary sources on the Hispanic population of California on a wide range of subjects, from consumer patterns to population, health and housing. This directory describes and evaluates the data sources. Includes index.

LECTOR

Lector: The Hispanic Review Journal
Lector: Mexican American Writers

$45.00

Focus on Mexican American Writers

Floricanto Press • 16161 Ventura Blvd., Suite 830 • Encino, CA 91436

LA RED/THE NET

The Hispanic Journal of Education, Commentary and Reviews

1989

Volume 2, Number 2

Published by Floricanto Press, 16161 Ventura Blvd., Suite 830, Encino, CA 91436-2504 (818) 990-1885

Gisella K. Caballis, Editor,
University of California, Los Angeles
Roberto Cabello-Argandeña, Publisher
Translation, Typesetting & Graphics, Production
IAD, Inc., Exclusive Distributor
17337 Ventura Blvd., Suite 203, Encino, CA 91316-3905

All book titles reviewed and/or listed in this journal are available through
Inter-American Development. Send orders to Inter-American Development,
17337 Ventura Blvd., Suite 203, Encino, CA 91316-3905 • (818) 990-1885

LA RED/THE NET, ISSN 1045-1421, is published as two separate publications for the price of one: a journal and a bulletin. La Red/The Net, The Hispanic Journal of Education Commentary and Reviews is published six times a year on general issues affecting the education and particularly the higher education of Hispanos.

Lector

VOLUME 5, NUMBER 2

**SAN FRANCISCO'S
CHICANO MURAL
MOVEMENT**
by
MELISSA PEABODY

**SAN FRANCISCO'S
MEXICAN MUSEUM**
by
ROSAINES AGUIRRE

CALEXICO:
An Essay in Images
*Photography
and Text by*
Harry Polkinhorn

**SELECCIONES
DE LIBROS**
offered by
HISPANEX/I.A.D.

BOOKS REVIEWS

Floricanto Press • 16161 Ventura Blvd., Suite 830 • Encino, CA 91436